BUILDING THE INNOVATIVE ORGANIZATION

Building the Innovative Organization

Management Systems that Encourage Innovation

James A. Christiansen

St. Martin's Press
New York

St. Martin's Press, Scholarly and Reference Division,
175 Fifth Avenue, New York, N.Y. 10010

First published in the United States of America in 2000

Printed in Great Britain

ISBN 0–312–23283–7

Library of Congress Cataloging-in-Publication Data
Christiansen, J. A. (James A.)
Building the innovative organization : management systems that encourge innovation/by James A. Christiansen.
p. cm.
Includes bibliographical references and index.
ISBN 0–312–23283–7
1. Technological innovations—Management. 2. Business enterprises—Technological innovations. 3. Industrial organization. I. Title.
HD45 .C4849 2000
658.5'14—dc21   99–059819

to
Gwen

Contents

List of Figures

List of Tables

Acknowledgements

In the Acknowledgements section of my previous book (Christiansen, 2000), I thanked fifty-one people, twenty-one institutions and companies, and one cat for having helped me produce the book. I also thanked, anonymously, more than three hundred managers from nearly two dozen companies for participating in the research. All of these people (and the cat) deserve to be thanked again.

However, there were others I missed. First of all, I thank Stephen Rutt, my editor at Macmillan, for taking an interest in my work and for managing the process of turning one very long manuscript into two normal-sized books. I also thank his assistant, Gloria Hart, and the rest of the team at Macmillan for doing so many things to help the process along.

I also wish to thank Linda Norris, Maggie Lythgoe, and the rest of the crew at Aardvark Editorial for putting the manuscript into the final, well-edited form that you see it here.

Once again, this book is dedicated to my daughter, Gwen, who maintained remarkably high spirits throughout the project.

Thanks again, Gwen. Thanks again, Marie-Jo. And thanks again, Moustache.

JIM CHRISTIANSEN
Paris

1 Introduction

Under the best circumstances, innovation is an uncertain endeavor. Developing a new product may take months, even years. It can involve many different tasks, different people, and different competences. Many things can go wrong. Ideas may not come when they are needed. It may be difficult to find funds or the people needed to develop the product. Development may be slowed by technical problems or by coordination problems if more than a few people are involved.

The problem is that many companies make innovation more difficult than it needs to be. The kinds of management systems many companies have don't help. They often slow innovation down. Or they block it. Sometimes they kill it entirely. This isn't anyone's fault. It's a result of the fact that many companies are still run with management methods that were developed forty, sixty or one hundred years ago, management methods that were designed to manage routine operations, not innovation and change. Our own management systems and methods slow innovation, block it, or kill it. They often do this even when the managers running the companies sincerely wish that they didn't. They want their companies to innovate. But the methods they use to manage their companies slow innovation down or block it entirely rather than encouraging it.

Many authors have already noted that we need new styles of management and new types of management systems to be able to manage innovation effectively (Ghoshal and Bartlett, 1998; Meyer, 1998). So why aren't companies doing it? Well, it isn't that easy. Too many old practices are involved, too many ingrained habits. Too many things we learned in business school, or during our first months at work, are just wrong for the modern age. Management practice in many companies needs serious rethinking.

It used to be that companies could ignore innovation. Or they could respond only when forced to by their competitor. Competitors used to compete 'nicely'. Many industries were divided up into oligarchies. No one would push too aggressively for fear of upsetting an applecart that was profitable for everyone. While cartels, formal or not, may survive in some industries, such sleepy, innovation-free industries are rarer and rarer. The great wave of innovations that has swept out from electronics, software, telecommunications, chemistry and biology has touched every industry on the planet. The rule used to be, 'Don't innovate unless you have to'. The rule now is, 'Innovate or die!' Companies cannot afford to follow old-style management theories any more. They must develop ways of managing themselves that encourage innovation, or they will see their competitors beat them at every turn.

The purpose of this book

The purpose of this book is to help managers learn how to encourage innovation. Some managers and some companies are good at it already. Some are very good at it. But most are not. Few companies have management systems that consistently encourage innovation. Most have quirks in their management systems that slow innovation projects down, or bring them to a compete halt. Few have gone through the trouble to do a thorough audit of their management practices to see where they cause themselves problems by impeding innovation or stopping it entirely.

Many companies, regrettably, kill ideas that they shouldn't really kill. Or they prevent them from being born. They don't effectively encourage idea generation. Or they put so many roadblocks on the path to funding and development that the ideas they generate never come to fruition. They don't block innovations deliberately. The blockages are often unforeseen side effects of management systems and practices that were put in place for other reasons. But they kill them, nonetheless.

One goal of this book is to reveal how everyday management systems and practices can either encourage or discourage innovation, and to show managers how to run their companies in ways that encourage innovation, not discourage it. Companies that want to innovate more would be well advised to read the book carefully, determine what they are doing that discourages innovation, and correct it.

Other authors have already begun the discussion of how to encourage innovation. But often they have limited their attention to one, two or three management systems. My intention in this book is to analyze as thoroughly as possible how a wide range of management systems and practices impact innovation. Many companies still use management methods that discourage innovation. They can use these same systems to encourage innovation. I intend to show them how.

Links with previous work

This book builds on material I presented in a previous book, entitled *Competitive Innovation Management: Techniques to Improve Innovation Performance*. In that book, I took the reader through the story of an innovation project. Using just one case, I showed how twenty different types of management systems and methods could be used in ways which either slowed innovation projects down, or speeded them up. I built on that discussion to show how managers could identify problems in their innovation systems and plan a change process. I further showed how innovation problems differed by industry, and how these differences impacted the way innovation systems should be designed.

What I did not do in the previous book was take the reader through a comprehensive discussion of how management methods differ across companies. I gave many examples, but the discussion was not comprehensive. In this book I will be as comprehensive as possible, given the limitations of my data. In a longitudinal, cross-industry study of nearly twenty companies, I found that management methods of highly innovative companies differed in many, many ways from those in less innovative companies. The differences were not limited to aspects of project management. Many company-wide general management systems differed as well. Innovative companies had strategies and methods of determining strategy that differed from those of less innovative companies. They managed individual and business unit goals differently as well. Their methods of managing competences and making decisions were different from those of less innovative companies. So were their organization structures and communications systems. The incentives they offered their people were different from those of less innovative companies, as were numerous other aspects of their personnel management systems and culture.

Not surprisingly, innovative companies also managed ideas and projects in ways that were substantially different from less innovative companies. Innovative companies had many more ways of stimulating idea generation. They managed their laboratories differently. They had different types of project funding systems. They organized and managed their projects differently. Finally, their senior managers practiced different ways of relating to innovation projects.

The differences between innovative and less innovative companies were sometimes obvious. But often they were quite subtle. It took months of detailed analysis of case studies and interview notes to tease all the differences out. The results of this study of how management methods in highly innovative companies differ are presented in this book.

Methodology

Virtually all of the material presented in this book comes from a comparative study of innovation management practices in twenty companies. Since I studied eight of these companies in more detail than the others, I often refer to this more limited group as the eight primary sites.

Four of the primary sites were independently managed divisions of a diversified European manufacturing group. The other four were fully independent manufacturers based in Europe or the US. The eight companies compete in five different industries. Three of them are rated as excellent innovators. Four of them are rated as average innovators. The last is somewhat below average. I interviewed approximately ninety managers from these eight companies while I was working at INSEAD, the leading European business school. I charted not only how these companies managed innovation at the time of the interviews. I also charted how their innovation systems had evolved over the ten years prior to the interviews.

Part of the material presented in this book draws on interviews I conducted with managers from twelve additional companies. These companies compete in eight additional industries. Two of them are rated as excellent innovators. Seven of them are average innovators. And three are less than average. I interviewed managers from ten of these companies while working at INSEAD. I interviewed managers from the other two while working as a consultant.

The academic reader will be interested in knowing how I set up and conducted the interviews, what questions I asked, and how I did the analyses. These issues were discussed in the Appendix to my previous book, *Competitive Innovation Management*. Those readers who are interested in these methodological questions should refer to that Appendix. The more general reader will be more interested in knowing who the companies are. Most of them insisted on anonymity as a condition for participating in my research. Nonetheless, I can describe them in general terms here.

Introduction to the companies

Four of the eight primary sites were independently managed divisions of a diversified European corporation called Manufacturing Group Europe, or MGE (a pseudonym). MGE is a diversified manufacturer with interests in a variety of chemical and materials science specialties, as well as in pharmaceutical and consumer products. Each of its divisions is rated as an average innovator (ratings from polls in business magazines). The four MGE divisions discussed in the text include Industrial Chemicals, Advanced Materials, Lawn & Garden, and Northern Pharmaceuticals.

Each division's management team had virtually complete independence in constructing its division's management systems. While each management team was supervised by a member of the Corporate Executive Committee, in practice the Corporate Executive Committee gave the division managers complete freedom to manage their divisions as they saw fit. As a result, the management systems and methods used in the four divisions varied considerably. Brief descriptions of the divisions follow:

■ **Industrial Chemicals** In the 1980s, Industrial Chemicals produced and sold basic chemicals. In the 1990s its management began putting more emphasis on developing and selling applied chemicals, that is, specialized chemical products designed to address specific customer needs. Industrial Chemicals was headquartered in the same city as corporate management. The links between corporate and division management were close.

■ **Advanced Materials** More than Industrial Chemicals, Advanced Materials invested heavily in applied chemical products. Its products were mainly new and specialized materials used in the production of a wide range of industrial and consumer goods.

■ **Lawn & Garden** The Lawn & Garden division produced and distributed a variety of agrochemical products, many designed for the home gardening market.

■ **Northern Pharmaceuticals** A mid-sized pharmaceuticals company, Northern Pharmaceuticals was run more independently than the other divisions. The pharmaceutical business was considered 'different' from the other businesses MGE had invested in. It was also consistently profitable. As a result, corporate supervision of Northern had no visible impact. At times Northern's management acted in advance of the rest of the corporation. For instance, Northern began an innovation improvement program two years before the Corporate Executive Committee began its effort to improve innovation performance in the other divisions.

As I noted above, the four MGE divisions were rated as average innovators. All were involved in chemicals, agrochemicals, or pharmaceuticals. Of the four other primary sites, three were companies with reputations as excellent innovators. In two cases, the reputation was verified via poll results (large panels of managers placed these two companies' innovation performance in the top 10 percent of all companies in their respective home countries). The third was not rated in any available poll, but it had recently won a national award in its home country, an award that cited the high quality of its innovation processes.

One of these three excellent innovators was Eastman Chemical. As a chemical company, it provided a useful comparison for the three MGE divisions involved in chemicals and materials science. The other two were diversified manufacturers. One, ConsumerCo, focused mainly on consumer products. The other, 3M, produced a variety of both consumer and industrial products. These diversified manufacturers provided some variation with respect to industry.

The last of the eight companies was EurAuto, a motor vehicle assembler. I chose it to give industry variation, and, in particular, to obtain a comparison site within the automobile industry. Much research has been done on the management of innovation in the automobile industry (Womack *et al.*, 1990; Clark and Fujimoto, 1991; Wheelwright and Clark, 1992). The presence of EurAuto in the sample helps relate my work to that research.

Brief descriptions of these four companies follow (see Figure 1.1 for a summary of the companies' industries and innovation reputations).

Innovation reputation					
Industry	**Low**	**Med–Low**	**Medium**	**Med–High**	**High**
Chemicals			*Industrial Chemicals* *Advanced Materials*	*Eastman* *Chemical*	
Agrichemicals			*Lawn & Garden*		
Pharmaceuticals			*Northern* *Pharmaceuticals*		
Industrial products					*3M*
Consumer products					*ConsumerCo*
Motor vehicles		*EurAuto*			

Figure 1.1   Companies (primary sites) by innovation reputation and sector

- **Eastman Chemical** A diversified manufacturer with interests in a variety of chemical specialties. An excellent innovator, although not as highly rated as 3M or ConsumerCo. Management very active in trying to improve innovation performance since the mid-1980s.

- **ConsumerCo** A diversified manufacturer focused on consumer products. Rated as an excellent innovator for many years. Management has been concerned with innovation performance for as long as anyone can remember.

- **3M** A diversified manufacturer focused on a variety of industrial and consumer products specialties. Rated as an excellent innovator for many years. Management has been concerned with innovation performance for as long as anyone can remember.

- **EurAuto** A motor vehicle assembler. An average innovation reputation, not rated quite as highly as MGE. Management very active in trying to improve innovation performance since the mid-1980s.

Periodically I cite examples of innovation management practices from thirteen other companies. In all cases I use pseudonyms for these companies. Figure 1.2 shows their names, their industry focus, and their innovation reputations. Brief descriptions of these companies follow.

- **USAuto** A US motor vehicle manufacturer. An average innovator.
- **CementCo** A European cement manufacturer. One of the leaders in its field, but rated as average innovator.
- **USComputers** One of the world's leading computer companies. Rated as an average innovator.
- **EuroChem** A diversified manufacturer with interests in chemicals, pharmaceuticals and consumer products. Rated as an average innovator. Similar to MGE in terms of the nature and breadth of its businesses.
- **MachineCo** An industrial machinery manufacturer. A leader in its niche, with several recent innovative breakthroughs.
- **ConElec** A consumer electronics manufacturer. Rated as an average innovator.
- **OptiCo** A manufacturer of optical equipment. A leader in its niche and an excellent innovator.
- **FinCo** A diversified financial services company. One of several leading players in its industry, but an average innovator.
- **Admin** A public bureaucracy focusing on defense. A mid-range innovator when compared with other defense ministries.
- **AmPro** A large American consumer products company. Rated as an average innovator.
- **USF** A mid-sized American food processor. Rated as a below-average innovator.
- **EurTel** A European telecommunications equipment manufacturer. Rated as an average innovator.
- **FoodCo** A European food processing company. Rated as an average innovator.

Industry	Low	Med–Low	Medium	Med–High	High
Innovation reputation					
Chemicals		*EuroChem*	*Industrial Chemicals* *Advanced Materials*	*Eastman* *Chemical*	
Agrichemicals			*Lawn & Garden*		
Pharmaceuticals			*Northern Pharmaceuticals*		
Industrial products					3M
Consumer products and food	USF		AmPro FoodCo		ConsumerCo
Motor vehicles		*EurAuto*	USAuto		
Electronics and computing		ConElec	USComputers		
Telecoms			EurTel		
Industrial machinery				MachineCo	
Other manufacturing			CementCo	OptiCo	
Services			FinCo Admin		

Note: Primary sites in italics

Figure 1.2 Companies (all sites) by innovation reputation and sector

Outline of the book

Chapter 2 lays out some basic concepts of how to think about innovation. This chapter will largely recap material that was presented in my earlier book, *Competitive Innovation Management*. Readers who have read the earlier book may find this chapter repetitive. If this is the case, they may wish to quickly review the material presented in Chapter 2 by looking at the charts and skimming the text, before moving on to the next chapter. Readers who have not read the first book will want to spend more time on Chapter 2 to ensure that they understand the basic distinctions I am making between different phases of the innovation process, different types of management 'tools'(see below), and different types of outcomes desired by managers.

I will often use the phrase 'management tools' in this book. This phrase is shorthand for the phrase 'management structures, systems and practices'. In *Competitive Innovation Management*, I demonstrated that a wide range of management structures, systems, and practices impacted innovation performance. I also demonstrated that managers could change these structures, systems, and practices in ways that would improve innovation performance. In effect, managers can use them as 'tools', as objects that they can manipulate, to improve their companies' innovation performance.

Chapters 3 to 8 describe how each of the management systems and practices identified in Chapter 2 can be used as a 'tool' to improve innovation performance. These six chapters systematically go through each of the twenty categories of 'tools' identified in Chapter 2, and form the heart of the book. It is here that I present the results of my study of how the management methods of highly innovative companies differ from those of their less innovative cousins.

Chapter 3 looks at how different methods of strategy setting, different goal systems, and different methods of managing competences and components of the company impact innovation performance. Within each of these topics there are as many as fifteen subtopics dealing with different aspects of strategy setting, goal structure and competence management.

Chapter 4 looks at how the structures and processes of corporations and business units impact innovation performance. This chapter focuses particularly on how three categories of tools impact innovation performance. These three categories of tools are organization structure, communications systems and information management, and decision-making methods. Again, within each of these topics there are as many as twenty subtopics which discuss how different aspects of organization structure, of communications systems, and of decision-making methods impact innovation performance

Chapter 5 looks at how personnel management systems and culture impact innovation performance. This chapter focuses on incentives, other aspects of personnel management, and culture. Once again, each topic includes a number of subtopics, ensuring, as far as possible, that all innovation-relevant aspects of the management tool are discussed.

Chapter 6 looks at tools that focus specifically on the management of ideas and projects. This chapter looks at idea management methods, at laboratory management methods, at methods of selecting projects for funding, at different types of project structure, and at different project management methods. I discuss how these project/idea focused tools differ in innovative and less innovative companies. I focus on tools that apply across all the projects in a corporation or a business unit.

Chapter 7 looks at ways managers can influence individual projects. This chapter looks at the impact of setting up a project, the impact of supervision methods, the impact of participation, of coaching, mentoring and consulting to a project team, and of taking control of a project.

Chapter 8 looks briefly at ways managers can invite or encourage others to think about ways to improve the functioning of their innovation system. I refer to this as 'stimulating reflection' on the innovation management system.

Chapter 9 concludes the book. Here, I summarize the results and make suggestions as to how companies can apply them.

How Innovation Works and How Corporate Managers Can Influence the Process

Roadblocks encountered and management tools used during the Chemical Residues project

In my previous book, *Competitive Innovation Management*, I recounted the story of the Chemical Residues project. This project ran into many different kinds of roadblocks during its first four years of existence. Many different management structures, systems, and practices caused delays in the project. Later, division management changed many of these same systems and practices in an effort to improve innovation performance. I will recount the story of the project briefly here.

The story of the Chemical Residues project

In the mid-1980s, Jerry Roth was the head of a business unit in the Industrial Chemicals division of Manufacturing Group Europe (a pseudonym), or MGE. Roth had a problem. His division had a lot of chemical byproducts, or co-products, that he couldn't find markets for. He wanted to build his division's revenue, so he asked two engineers to work part time trying to find uses for the co-products. Over a few months they explored over one hundred potential uses. But, after testing, none of them seemed promising. Roth decided to add a chemist, George Marsh, full time to the project.

After joining the team, Marsh looked over the ideas the engineers had tested and found that one of them looked interesting. It was an idea to use one of the co-products as a catalyst to help remove certain chemical residues from wastewater. The test the engineers had run on this idea had been flawed, and the idea really appeared to have potential. Marsh, who knew both water treatment methods and the chemistry of Roth's co-products could see the flaws in the test and the value of the idea. The engineers, who were not familiar with water treatment technology, had erroneously dismissed the idea.

The irony of the situation was that Marsh recognized the value of the idea only because his career within MGE had been very unusual. He was a chemist by training, but he had also done a second degree in marketing. He had worked in at least four different MGE business units, including a water treatment unit that had been sold. He had picked up the skills needed to recognize the value of the water treatment idea by moving around. But cross-training and moving around were both completely contrary to the normal career patterns at MGE. People normally stayed in the same functions and the same business units for their entire careers. Only Marsh had the precise combination of marketing and technical competences necessary to recognize the value of this idea.

Roth's business unit had a growth *strategy* that incited him to search for new markets for his co-products. The *goals* corporate set for him also incited him to search for new markets. He *set up a project* to manage the search. Unfortunately, the company did not have any systematic methods for *managing idea generation*, and the project team's more or less random search produced little.

Then, by chance, Roth appointed a chemist to the team. The chemist, as it happened, had had a very unusual career. His mixture of chemical and marketing experiences allowed him to recognize the value of an idea that the engineers on the team had dropped. The company's *personnel management methods* produced people with single function and single business unit experience. Marsh was an exception, having crossed both functional and business unit boundaries. Had there been more exceptions like Marsh, perhaps more people would have recognized ideas that fell outside of traditional business unit boundaries.

After seeing the value of the idea, Marsh looked for people who could help him exploit it. Finding them was difficult. Laboratory managers elsewhere in the company were not used to sharing information freely about what their people knew and did. Marsh needed introductions to get information. There was no central competence management system that could tell him what people had worked on. After six months of looking for help, Marsh gave up. There appeared to be no one left in the company with the kind of competences in water treatment chemistry and water treatment equipment that he needed.

The absence of a good *communications system*, and the absence of any kind of *competence management system*, made it difficult for Marsh to find people who could help him.

Marsh then asked Roth for funds so that he could hire help from the outside. Roth refused. While Roth wanted new revenues, he didn't want to have to invest for three years or more to get them. Since business unit managers were the only people authorized to give money to projects, this should have stopped Marsh. Marsh was not authorized to go anywhere else for funds. But Marsh decided to try again. After asking a friend to run an informal survey of demand for new water treatment chemicals, Marsh came back to Roth with the results. Many water pollution agencies were interested in the system Marsh was conceiving. They said they would consider tightening regulations to require its use. With that evidence, and after months of pleading by Marsh, Roth gave in and provided a small budget for the project.

Six months later, Roth's business unit began showing losses. He could no longer afford Marsh's project, so he cut its budget. Marsh began looking elsewhere for money. He found some in a neighboring business unit. But that money didn't last long, either. The neighboring business unit began losing money and cut Marsh's project just like Roth had. Ironically, the second cut came just after a full-scale test in a major European city had proven the feasibility of the project.

Industrial Chemical's *funding system* gave business unit managers monopoly rights to fund project ideas that came up in their business units. Had there been other official sources of funds, Marsh might have been able to find funding sooner.

Roth's *incentives* drove him to look for short-term profits. He was rewarded for short-term profits, not for long-term investments like Marsh's project. Since the division's *decision-making methods* gave him sole control of all decisions in his business unit, no one else looked at the problem. The company's *culture* also discouraged him from taking risks. Corporate *strategy*, which focused on building low cost positions in commodity product areas, also discouraged him from investing in long-term product development. Given all these negative factors, his decision to say 'No' to Marsh was quite logical.

Unnoticed by Roth and other Industrial Chemicals managers at this time was the fact that Marsh was not running the project particularly well. His market survey had been extremely informal. He did not really document how large the market could be now when and how it would development. On the technical side, he was not documenting the results of his tests. Some tests run on the outside were documented more effectively, but they were not documented in sufficient detail to be used as evidence before regulatory bodies. These flaws in project management would later cause the project team to repeat tests Marsh had run, thus losing time.

The absence of systematic, professional *project management methods* would result in delays for the project. No *project supervision* or *mentoring* system existed to ensure that Marsh was running the project well.

At that point, Marsh's luck turned. MGE's executive committee decided to put more emphasis on product innovation. Marsh's project soon had corporate funds and a direct report to senior management. New communications links were set up with potential users of the project and with regulators. One senior manager began participating in project meetings and contributed ideas that helped solve a serious technical problem.

After working with the Chemical Residues project for a few months, Industrial Chemicals managers began analyzing why the project had had such difficulty finding funds. They then reformed the project funding system to assure that projects that fell outside of business unit charters could more easily find funds. They also assured that information on all projects would be reported at least to the division level.

Here senior managers change *strategy* and they begin to *supervise* the project more effectively. One of them even *participates* in the project by contributing key technical ideas. New *communications* links with the outside were set up.

In addition, senior managers began analyzing problems in the project management system. They changed the *project funding system* and the *structure of project teams* (by adding links to senior managers).

At this point, the rigidity of Industrial Chemical's laboratory management systems began slowing the project. Marsh could not get laboratory resources when he needed them, since laboratory work was budgeted and scheduled up to a year in advance. On the positive side, he now had enough resources to hire whatever competences he needed. Senior management involvement, meanwhile, came at an unexpected price. Senior managers insisted on publicizing the project to help build MGE's new image as an innovation-focused company.

Finally discovering that Marsh's project management methods left something to be desired, senior management replaced Marsh as project manager. In addition, they set up formal training programs for project managers to assure that the same mistakes would not be made again.

Here *laboratory management methods* slow the project, while a new policy on hiring *competences* from the outside makes it easier to move forward. Senior managers' willingness to take *control* of certain key decisions for the project turns out to have lasting negative effects. On the positive side, they finally recognize Marsh's limitations and replace him as project manager (*supervision*). Going even further, they set up training programs to ensure that future project managers don't make the same mistakes (*project management methods*).

Several years later, senior Industrial Chemicals managers decided that the division was not producing enough ideas for new products. They decided to reorganize the division to assure that technical people within business units talked to marketing and sales people within the same business units. They thought that this cross-functional contact would help spark ideas for new products they could develop to serve client needs. They also set up permanent contacts between different business units that served the same customers. Four different business units had been serving the paper industry, for instance, without ever talking to each other. Management thought that by putting these business units in contact, they might find synergistic ways to respond to the industry's problems, ways which would never come up if the business units continued working in isolation.

Here management instituted a reform in *organization structure* that was designed to improve *communications* and help the division develop more ideas.

Different types of interventions in the innovation management system

Figure 2.1 is a time line which shows the history of the project over nine years. I have noted, with arrows, each time a management system, practice, or structure worked as a roadblock that slowed the

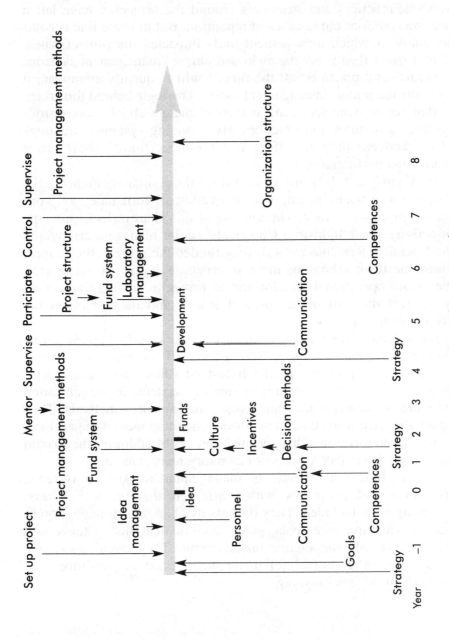

Figure 2.1   Chemical Residues project history

project. Other arrows signal efforts to improve the management systems, practices and structures around the project. I have left a few interventions out in cases of repetition. But the time line is a fair summary of which management tools impacted the project when. (Note: rather than using the awkward phrase 'management systems, structures and practices' all the time, I will frequently abbreviate it by using the phrase 'management tools'. The logic behind this usage is that senior managers can, in theory, change all of a company's systems, structures and practices. By changing systems, structures and practices, they in effect use them as 'tools' to improve innovation performance.)

In Figure 2.2 I begin classifying these management tools. Anyone who wants to improve innovation performance can work on *one project at a time*. The top line of this chart reflects this type of activity. Once Industrial Chemicals' senior managers discovered the Chemical Residues project, they funded the project, they supervised the team (skipping three intervening layers of managers), they made operational decision for the project (deciding to promote it, against the will of the project team), and they changed the project manager.

Later, Industrial Chemicals' senior managers worked on *the whole project management system*. This affects all projects, or, in some cases, all new projects. In the Industrial Chemicals' case, senior managers worked on the project funding system, the organization structure of project teams, and project management methods. They could also have worked on methods of generating ideas within project teams, laboratories or other technical areas. In addition, they could have worked on other aspects of laboratory management.

Finally, Industrial Chemicals' management worked on systems, structures and processes which affected *the entire business*, operating units included. They did this by changing strategy, organization structure, incentives, goals, communications systems, and the methods of competence management. They could also have worked on other personnel management systems, culture, and methods of decision making.

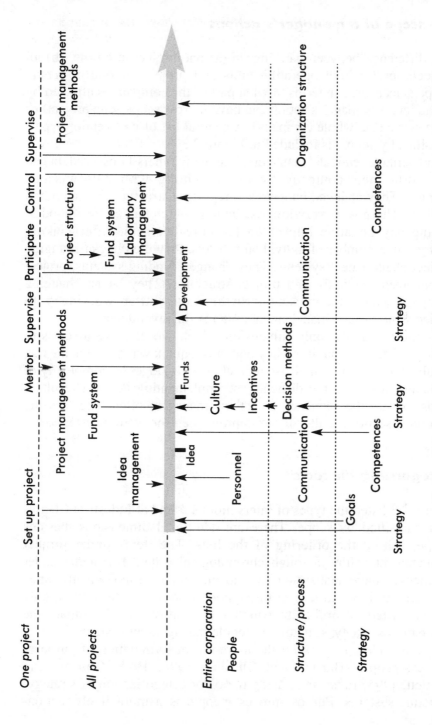

Figure 2.2 Chemical Residues project history: the tools classified

The scope of a manager's actions

The difference between working on (a) one project at a time, (b) all projects, or (c) both operating units and projects is one of *scope*. Scope is measured in terms of what part of the company is affected by the action. A manager's action can have narrow scope (one project) or wide scope (the whole company). A general list of intervention types, classified by scope, is included in Figure 2.3.

Industrial Chemicals' managers, like many others I observed, began to reform their company by experimenting with narrow-scope changes. They changed budgets and reporting structures of individual projects. These were very low-risk actions which had no likelihood of having any negative impact on the core business. After making changes in a number of individual projects, they then began changing project management systems. They changed funding systems, project management methods, and project structures. They began changing company-wide systems and structures only after working with projects and project management systems for several years.

Scope is not the only dimension which we can use to classify managers' actions, but it is a key one. It is a quick way to judge the risk involved in an action. It is also a quick way to judge the complexity of a change, and thus the difficulty of implementing it. As a result, it helps explain the sequence of actions managers often take (see the following section) as they try to improve their innovation systems.

Categorizing the tools

Figure 2.3 listed the types of interventions found at Industrial Chemicals, classified by scope. There are additional dimensions, besides scope, behind the ordering of the lists. The items under project management follow a rough chronological order. The items under business management systems are not classified chronologically, since they tend to have an impact throughout a project's life. Rather, they are classified according to whether they most closely impact the company's strategy, structure or people management systems.

Some readers may prefer the more recent formulation of purpose-process-people (Bartlett and Ghoshal, 1994, 1995; Ghoshal and Bartlett, 1995) rather than using the older categorization of strategy-structure-systems. Purpose-process-people is a more lively, action-

Changing the way business systems are managed			Changing the way projects are managed	Intervening in single projects
Strategy/goals	*Structure/process*	*People*		
Strategy	Organization structure	Incentives	Management of idea generation	Set up
Competences and M&A	Communication and information management	Other personnel management systems	Management of laboratories	Supervision
Goals	Decision-making methods	Culture	Funding system	Participation
			Project structure	Mentoring, consulting
			Project management methods	Operational control
Other: Stimulating reflection				

Figure 2.3   Management tools (intervention types) classified by scope

oriented formulation. And it captures what companies 'do', particularly with reference to process, better than strategy-structure-systems. So I include purpose-process-people along with the more traditional dimension.

Figure 2.4 shows graphically when each management tool has its most important impact on the life of an individual innovation project. Starting from the top, managers can be involved with individual ideas or projects at virtually any time during the course of a project. But at no time is their involvement necessarily crucial. Good *project management methods* are key at the early stages of the project when the most crucial decisions are made. Later on in the project, when most of the key decisions related to the project have already been made, good management methods are somewhat less important.

Project organization structures are key, for different reasons, both at the beginning and the end of the project's life. The strength of the project manager and the project's formal links with the organization can be crucial in giving the project an effective start. But the links, and the project manager's weight, can continue to be crucial if the project team needs the cooperation of other units in the organization during the development process. Finally, at the end, the project's links into the organization can make a crucial difference as the project is launched and integrated into ongoing operations.

The *funding system* is, obviously, crucial during the initial funding stage. It continues to be important later on because most projects are not given all the funds they need at the beginning. Milestones or hurdles are set up and the project must be refunded when it passes the milestones.

Laboratory management is key at the beginning because laboratories and other technical areas are usually involved in the generation of ideas. Specific *methods of idea generation* are also key at this stage. Neither is very important as the project searches for funds. But both become somewhat important during the development process, since ideas for improving the product may come up during the project itself. Ideas for spin-offs (new projects) may come up at this time as well.

Of the business-wide systems, *incentives* and *communication* have a substantial impact on ideas and projects from beginning to end. Academics (for example, Allen, 1977) have been looking at the impact of communications systems on innovation since the mid-1970s. They have found a link between the amount of communication between units and the likelihood that those units will come up with

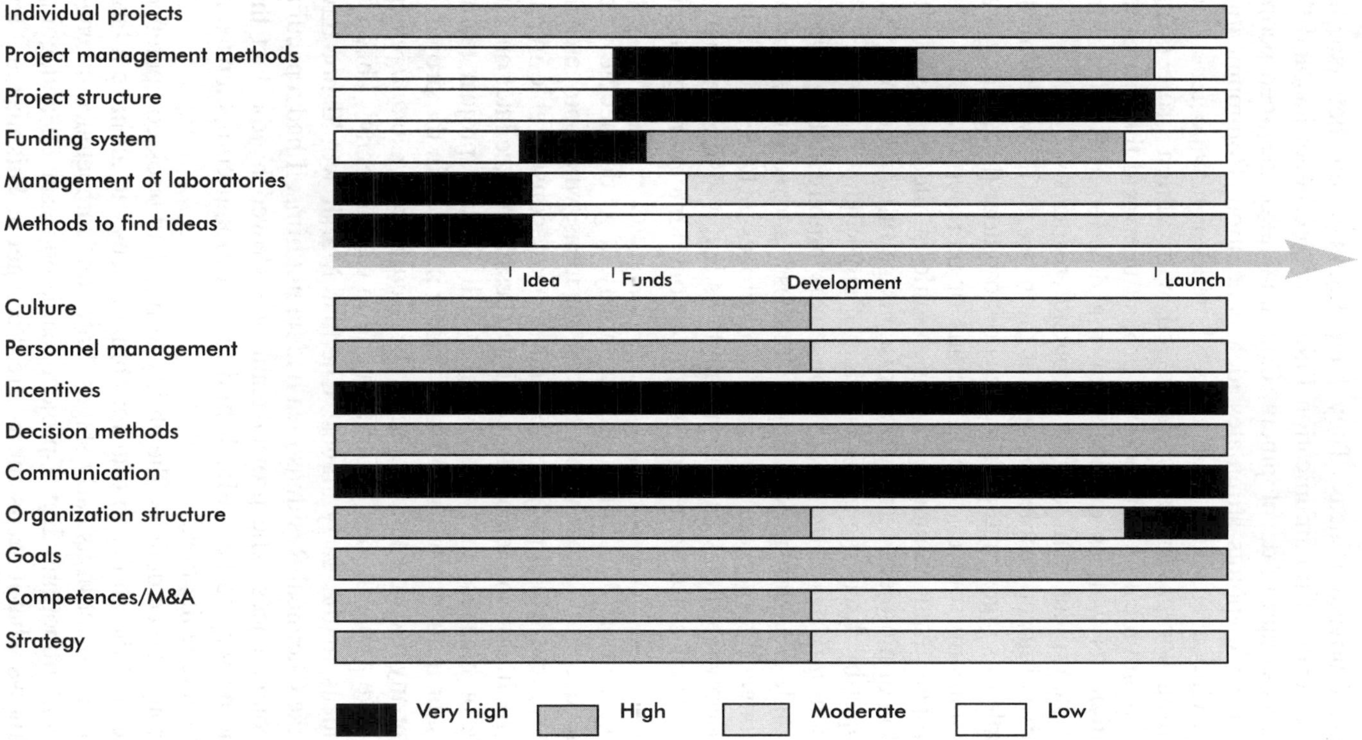

Figure 2.4 Impact of tools/interventions over time

interesting innovation ideas. They have found a link between the extent and types of communication links a project team has and the team's success during development. Communication between people with diverse viewpoints stimulates idea generation. Communication between technical areas (or other areas where ideas may be generated) and funding sources impacts the speed with which projects are funded. Communication between the project team and the rest of the organization, as well as outsiders, during development affects the ability of the project team to draw on outside resources.

Incentives impact people throughout the process. They may motivate people to suggest and pursue ideas or to ignore them. They may motivate funding sources to be generous or ungenerous. They may cause project team members to work single-mindedly toward the completion of a project, or they may discourage full commitment to a risky project by discouraging risk-taking of any kind.

Decision-making methods (by consensus among a large group versus single decision maker, appeal process, and so on) similarly have an impact throughout the innovation process. However, while I found cases where decision-making methods had a visible impact on outcomes, such cases were rarer than for communications or incentive systems.

Strategy sets the direction for the company. It guides people when they make decisions about where to look for ideas, what competences to invest in, and which projects to fund. It has a considerable impact on the early life of an idea or project. It has less influence later on. But corporate or business unit strategy may still guide a project team's decisions, or influence the amount of money invested in the project.

A company's competence base and its *competence management systems* have a role in idea generation and in the company's ability to exploit ideas in the early stages. Chemist Marsh would not have pursued the Chemical Residues idea had he not himself had a peculiar mix of competences. The project team was slowed by the fact that MGE had no way to help Marsh find the additional competences he needed to pursue the idea.

Such competence deficits, the ability to find and track competences with ease, and the ability to transfer competences can all have a large impact on a project in its early stages. Later on, competence management is still important. But a project team, once set up and going, usually knows what it needs and where it can get it. This makes it less dependent on the company's competence management system.

Goals, whether for business units, for project teams, for work teams, or for individuals, can impact the innovation process. In companies where goals are cascaded down to the individual level, the impact is obvious. Individuals may or may not have goals that encourage them to innovate, or to help others who innovate. But even when goals are not cascaded down to the individual level, business unit and team goals can impact individual behavior, either encouraging people to innovate and support those who do, or discouraging them from doing so.

Organization structure has an important effect on communication patterns in a company. As a result, it has an impact throughout the innovation process. But organization structure as it is defined here also involves distributing power. Organizational position determines who is responsible for specific units within the company. It also determines who is responsible for specific activities. As a result, it determines who is responsible for controlling access to the resources an innovation system needs.

Organization structure provides a hierarchical context around individuals and teams. Its effect on innovation, in the early stages, is indirect. It probably has less impact than communications and incentive systems. Later, during development, the project team becomes an independent unit, often separated from the rest of the organization. Here the impact of the organization structure around the project is limited. Later, when the project is launched, the team is integrated into the overall organization. Here the dynamic aspect of the organization structure is key. How easily does the organization accept and integrate new products and business units?

Personnel management systems (other than incentives) involve such things as hiring, career development, and rotation systems. These can have an important impact on idea generation. Marsh acquired the competences which helped him see the Chemical Residues idea by moving around the company. Highly innovative companies like ConsumerCo encourage people to move around.

Personnel management systems also have an impact on a project's ability to bring on new people. A company where people stay within the same business unit and move straight up a functional silo will find it difficult to set up cross-functional project teams. People simply won't have enough familiarity with the vocabularies and work practices of other functions to be able to effectively work with them. In addition, it will be difficult to create project teams outside of an established business area (Chemical Residues was an example of this), since this would involve leaving the traditional, safe career track. A project that is unable to assemble an effective team will find it difficult to make progress.

Organizational *culture* is defined here as 'rules, written or unwritten, which guide people's behavior in ambiguous situations (that is, situations where the best course of action is not clear)'. The dimensions of culture which are most important for innovation include 'willingness to take risks', 'willingness to innovate or change', and 'willingness to support risk-taking or innovation under-taken by others'.

More innovative companies often have explicit rules about risk-taking. People are supposed to take calculated risks. Innovation and experimentation are viewed as good. But less innovative companies often have unwritten rules that discourage risk-taking. Risk-taking is, at best, not rewarded. At worst it is actively discouraged. Such cultural norms can have a large impact on people's willingness to take risks and on their willingness to support others who take risks.

As a result, I have coded culture as has having a large effect during idea generation, initial funding, and the early stages of development. By the time a project is well into development, it will be clearer to fence-sitters whether the project is a winner or not, and the cultural rules will have less impact.

This gives the reader an idea of which management tools are important at different times over the life of a project. In later sections of this chapter, I will present some general theory explaining how the various tools can be used to improve innovation performance. I will discuss each type of tool quite thoroughly in Chapters 3 to 8.

An overview of the innovation process

As I said in the introduction, innovation can be a very complex process. Many steps can be involved in generating an idea and in bringing it to fruition. To be able to think clearly about this process, it is useful to be able to break it into phases, and then to develop a clear theoretical understanding of each phase. That is what I will do in the remainder of this chapter.

In some ways, innovation can be compared to a complex manufac-turing process. The manufacture of a computer memory chip involves several thousand steps. Each of these steps must be performed correctly if the chip is to function. A mistake at any point can ruin the whole chip. Understanding this process involves knowing the tasks that need to be performed and knowing how they are linked to each other (for example, what has to be performed first, and so on). Improving the process can involve improving the performance of each of the individual steps, changing the order of the steps, and/or identifying and eliminating unnecessary steps.

Developing a new product can involve many more steps than the several thousand steps it takes to manufacture a computer chip. To make matters more complicated, innovation projects are not repeated as often as manufacturing processes are. Chip lines run for many months and may manufacture millions of identical chips. The process can be optimized over time. Experiments can be run and improvements put into place because the same process is repeated over and over again.

Innovation systems do not repeat things this often. While a pharmaceutical company may run dozens of compounds through similar regulatory tests, the differences between the compounds and their intended uses will require customization of much of the process. The process of setting up clinical tests may be the same from one compound to the next, but the investigation sites used and the exact data collected may vary, for instance.

In some industries each project may be unique. A diversified manufacturing company may have hundreds of projects running at once in dozens of different business units. Each project may be targeted at a slightly different product-market niche. Nonetheless there will be certain regularities in the innovation process, regardless of how different the projects are.

Some of the regularities in the innovation process may seem simple and obvious, once they are identified. But once identified, they will allow us to think about the process more systematically. For instance, identifying the key phases in the process will allow us to ask questions about the key management problems during each phase.

So what are the key phases of the innovation process? To answer that question, it is useful to identify events that occur in every project.

Each project originates in an *idea*. The idea will have originated at a specific time and in a specific place. The idea for a product innovation will include some kind of *technical solution* to a current or possible future *market need*. The people proposing the idea will have looked for and found *funding* to pursue the idea. Pursuing the idea might involve a few days work (in the case of a very simple idea), or many years (in the case of a very complex and difficult idea). This process of pursuing the idea to fruition is called *development*. When development is finished, a decision is made to *launch* the product. Following this, additional *post-launch development* may occur (see Figure 2.5).

Development is largely an extended exercise in problem solving. Can the vision implied in the idea be made reality? If so, how? What technical problems are involved? What are the solutions to these problems? What kind of marketing and regulatory problems are involved? How can the company solve these? The process of identifying and solving problems is usually the longest and most expensive part of the innovation process. The earlier parts, generating the idea and finding funding, should not be ignored however. Improving these processes can radically shorten the cycle time between the appearance of an opportunity and product launch. It can also result in products that meet market needs more effectively.

In the next part of this chapter, I will give an overview of the innovation process. I will discuss in more detail why it is useful to look at the process as a series of phases. I will discuss how managers try to improve innovation performance during three key phases of the process. Then I will discuss in a general way how each phase works. I will begin with idea generation. Then I will go on to the process of finding funding. Finally I will look at development.

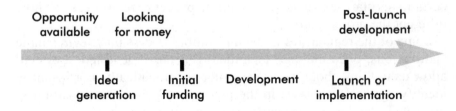

Figure 2.5   Key activities during the project life cycle

A framework for thinking about innovation

In this section I will set up an analytic framework that will give the reader a background for understanding how managers can improve an innovation process. I have already identified the three key phases of the process, idea generation, initial funding, and development (see Christiansen, 2000, for a full discussion). In this section I will look briefly at the goals of the process, and particularly at the question, 'What does it mean to improve innovation performance?' In answering this question, I will identify several components of innovation performance. Then I will discuss how these components apply to each phase.

Components of innovation performance

In my previous book (Christiansen, 2000), I identified four key components of innovation performance. The first two were related to *fit with customer need*. To have any chance of being successful, new products under development have to fit either with *current customer needs* or with *future customer needs*. Sometimes managers try to improve their company's ability to react effectively to current customer needs (in other words, to find ways to fulfil the needs customers are expressing right now). At other times, they try to build a capability to anticipate future consumer needs. The two are conceptually and operationally different, so I treated them as two separate components of innovation performance.

The third and fourth components of innovation performance were *speed* and *cost*. Speed refers to time to market or time to implementation. How quickly can a company get a new product to market? How quickly can a company implement a new process? Cost refers to the cost of the innovation system itself. Is money wasted? Could new products and processes be developed at lower cost?

While managers would at times say that they wanted to 'reduce innovation cycle time,' or 'achieve a better fit with customer needs,' in fact most of their interventions were even more focused than that. Most interventions were designed to impact, not the whole innovation process, but one part of the process.

When they worked on speed, for instance, managers did not try to speed up idea generation, funding decisions, and development all at once. Rather, they would conduct separate interventions for each phase. Some interventions were designed to speed up development. Others were designed to speed up funding decisions. A few were designed to speed up idea generation (that is, to help the company recognize opportunities more quickly).

By analyzing managers' interventions, I identified eight phase-specific goals that they worked on. During the idea generation phase, they tried to :

1. Generate more ideas in relation to current customer needs (following the market).
2. Generate more ideas in relation to future customer needs (leading the market).
3. Speed up the idea generation process overall.

This third goal contributed to the goal of speeding up the overall process. But the interventions needed to speed up idea generation were quite different than those needed to speed up development.

When they worked on the funding phase, managers tried to ensure that the company:

4. Made better funding decisions.

They thought they could accomplish several goals at once by improving their funding processes. The first goal was to fund more ideas fitting either current or future customer needs. This would ensure that more good ideas would get through the system. The second goal the flip-side of this, to fund fewer ideas that didn't fit current and future customer needs. This would help reduce the overall cost of the system. In addition, managers tried to:

5. Reduce the amount of time it took to make funding decisions. This increased overall speed and decreased innovation cycle time.

During development, managers had three phase-related goals. They wanted:

6. Project teams to make better operational decisions while running the project so that the final outputs would better fit current and future customer needs.

	Idea generation	Funding	Development
Fit with current customer need	More ideas: current customer needs	Better funding decisions: a. Fund ideas that fit	Better operational decisions
Fit with future customer need	More ideas: future customer needs	b. Don't fund ideas that don't fit	
Speed	Quicker idea generation	Quicker funding decisions	Quicker development
Cost		Less money wasted (result of better funding decisions)	Reduced development cost

Figure 2.6   Goals by phase

7. Teams to work more quickly, part of the program of decreasing overall cycle time.
8. To reduce the cost of development.

The relationships between these phase-related goals and the overall goals is depicted in Figure 2.6 in the form of a three-by-four matrix. I also include Figure 2.7, which shows the causal links.

On the left side of Figure 2.7, I put 'managers' interventions'. In effect, managers intervened in individual projects, or changed project and business management systems, in an effort to improve innovation performance. They often worked on only one phase or one goal at a time. But a few interventions, such as those related to culture or incentives, had an impact across all the phases.

I identified and listed the general categories of interventions in my previous book (Christiansen, 2000) and in the analysis of the Chemical Residues case at the beginning of this chapter. In Chapters 3 to 8, I will explore each of the categories of interventions in detail. But first, in the remainder of this chapter, I will look at ways of diagnosing problems in an innovation system.

Diagnosing problems in an innovation system

The advantage of having a theoretical understanding of the innovation system is that it gives us tools that will help us to diagnose problems

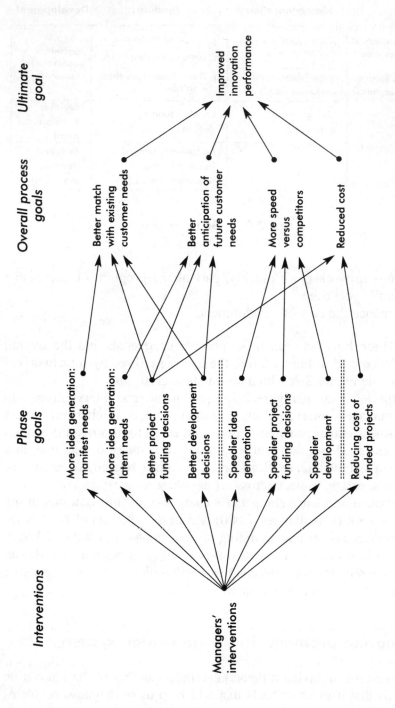

Figure 2.7 Managers' goals as they intervened in the innovation system

in an innovation system, and to identify means of fixing problems. Even if no problems are manifest, it will allow us to identify both opportunities for improvement and means of making the improvement. The best way to demonstrate this is to illustrate how the theoretical structure just presented can be used to find problems, to diagnose their source, and to design a solution. This is what I will do in this section.

A systematic method of diagnosing problems

If your innovation system is not performing up to your expectations, the best way to figure out what to do about it is to ask lots of questions. The general sequence of questions that is most likely to lead you to a solution is the following (see Figure 2.8 for a summary):

1. What is the problem? On which performance dimension is the innovation system failing to meet management's expectations? In other words, which of the typical innovation system goals is the system not reaching? Is the innovation system (a) producing products that don't *fit customer needs*? Is it (b) too *slow*? Or is it (c) too *costly*?

2. What part of the innovation system is the source of the problem? During which phase does the problem arise? If the problem is *lack of fit with customer needs*, then where in the system does this problem arise? Do our people (a) come up with *ideas* that don't have much relevance to customer needs, present or future? Do we (b) have some good, customer-relevant ideas that we fail to *fund*, while funding others that aren't so customer-relevant? Or (c) do we fund customer-relevant ideas, but somehow lose the customer focus and customer relevance somewhere in the *development* process?

    If the problem is *speed*, then where does this problem arise? Is it that we (a) don't recognize opportunities (that is, generate *ideas*) until long after competitors do? Is it that (b) our *funding* system takes a long time to allocate funds to new ideas, or that it underfunds good ideas? Or is it that (c) our *development* process is slower than that of competitors?

    If the problem is *cost*, then why does the overspending occur? Is it that we (a) *fund* too many projects that bring nothing to the company? Or is it that we (b) spend more than necessary on projects during the *development* process?

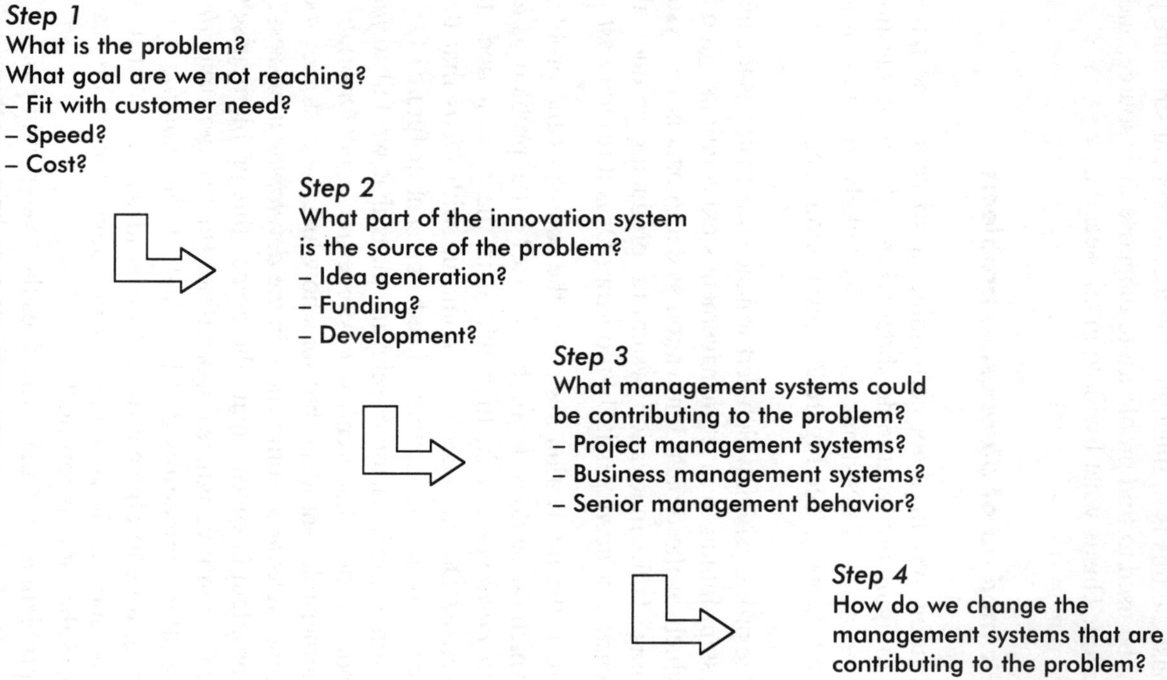

Step 1
What is the problem?
What goal are we not reaching?
– Fit with customer need?
– Speed?
– Cost?

Step 2
What part of the innovation system
is the source of the problem?
– Idea generation?
– Funding?
– Development?

Step 3
What management systems could
be contributing to the problem?
– Project management systems?
– Business management systems?
– Senior management behavior?

Step 4
How do we change the
management systems that are
contributing to the problem?

Figure 2.8   How to find and analyze problems in an innovation system

Answering the questions under numbers 1 (what goal is not being reached) and 2 (what phase does the problem arise in) will go a long ways to help a management team specify the problem and identify where it arises. But once the location of a problem is identified, it is still necessary to determine its cause. To determine the cause it is useful to ask more questions. Assuming the management team has succeeded in defining the problem in more detail and in identifying what phases of the process it arises in, then the following questions are in order.

3. What aspects of the company's *project management systems* could be contributing to the problem? What aspects of the company's *business management systems* could be contributing the problem? What aspects of *senior management behavior* could be contributing to the problem? Many additional diagnostic questions could be asked to identify what precise aspect of a company's management systems (or of top managers' behavior) could be causing the problem.

    If a management team wants to be thorough, it can look systematically at how each category of management system and management behavior could be contributing to problems in its innovation system. The management team can use the discussions in Chapters 3 to 8 as guides to determining what parts of their management systems are innovation friendly and what parts are not.

    Once the management team has identified what systems or behaviors could be causing problems, the following question is appropriate.

4. How do we fix the problem? The discussions in Chapters 3 to 8 give examples and ideas which managers can use to guide their efforts to improve their company's management systems. In the case of each management structure, system, or practice, I give examples of how highly innovative companies use the tool in ways which encourage innovation rather than discouraging it.

Executing solutions and evaluating results

Once managers have got this far, the next step is to execute the solution. In my previous book (Christiansen, 2000), I gave some general guidelines on how to plan and execute an innovation system improvement program. Once a management team executes its chosen solution, its members should look back to see if the solution has worked. Are the ideas and the products coming out of the system achieving better fit with customer need? Is the process speeding up? Is it costing less?

Once they have the answers to these questions, they may find that the problem hasn't been fixed, or that there are still problems in the system. If so, the best thing for them to do is to go back to the beginning of this list of questions and go through the diagnostic sequence again, focusing on what they may have missed the first time.

It often occurs that serious problems in one area mask less serious problems in another area. For instance, problems in a project funding system can have such serious effects on innovation outcomes that they completely mask problems in idea generation or even in development. The latter problems may not be seen until after management has fixed the problems in the funding system.

Identifying opportunities for improvement

Managers often believe that there is room to improve an innovation system, even when no particular problems are evident. When this is the case, they can systematically go through a similar series of diagnostic questions as a means of finding ways to improve the system. Here a typical sequence of questions would be the following (see Figure 2.9 for a summary):

1. Which dimension of innovation system performance could be improved? Which dimension of innovation system performance does management want to improve? Does it want to improve the resulting products' *fit with customer need*? Does it want to *speed* up the system? Or does it want to reduce the system's *cost*?

2. In what part (phase) of the system is there the most room for improvement? If the management team wants to improve *fit with customer need*, could this most easily be done by improving the quality of *ideas* generated? Or by making more customer-focused choices in the *funding* process? Or by assuring that decisions made during *development* take better account of customer need?

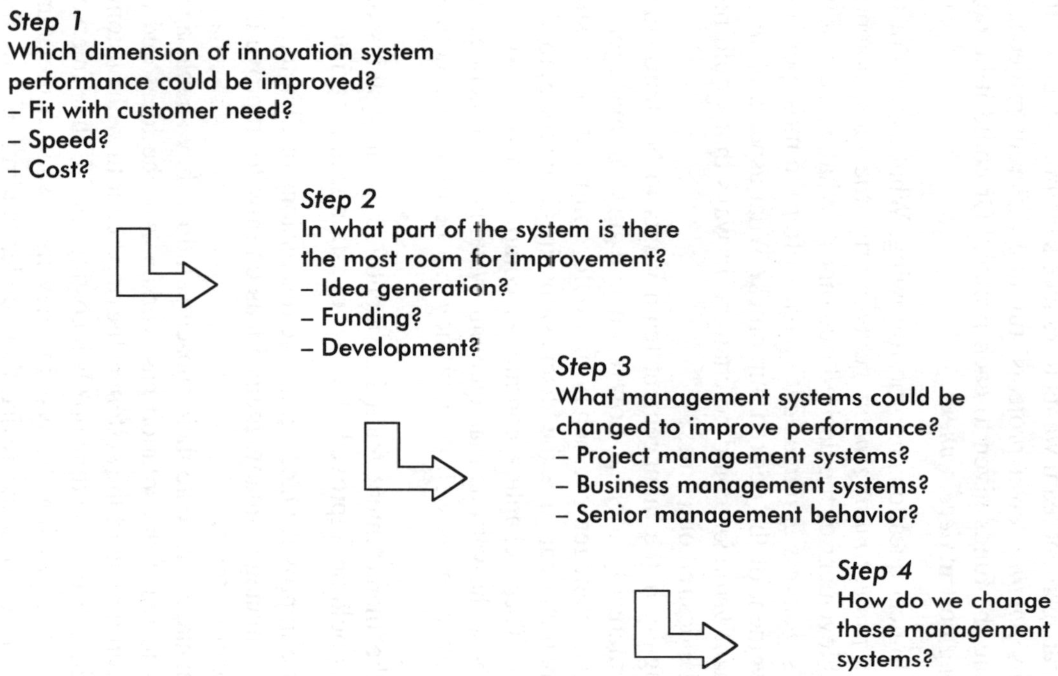

Step 1
Which dimension of innovation system
performance could be improved?
– Fit with customer need?
– Speed?
– Cost?

Step 2
In what part of the system is there
the most room for improvement?
– Idea generation?
– Funding?
– Development?

Step 3
What management systems could be
changed to improve performance?
– Project management systems?
– Business management systems?
– Senior management behavior?

Step 4
How do we change
these management
systems?

Figure 2.9 How to find opportunities for improvement in an innovation system

If the management team wants to *speed* up the system, could this be done by recognizing opportunities and developing *ideas* more quickly? Or by making *funding* decisions more quickly or funding good ideas more generously? Or by speeding up *development*?

If the management team wants to reduce system *cost*, could this be done by *funding* fewer projects, funding different projects, or by reducing the funds given to each project? Or could it be done by reducing cost in *development*?

3. The next logical questions are the following. What aspects of the company's *project management systems* offer the most potential for the achievement of the desired outcomes? What aspects of the company's *business management systems* offer the most potential for achievement of the desired outcomes? What aspects of *senior management behavior* could be changed in ways that would help achieve the desired outcomes?

   Once again, if the management team wants to be thorough, it can systematically look at how each category of management system and management behavior could contribute to system improvement. It can use the discussions in Chapters 3 to 8 as guidelines. These chapters contain as complete a discussion as exists of how the various management systems and practices can inhibit innovation, as well as how they can be used to encourage innovation.

   Once the management team has identified what systems and behaviors could be improved, the next question is appropriate.

4. How do we improve? Once again, the discussions in Chapters 3 to 8 will give managers many, many ideas on how to improve their management systems.

   Once managers execute their chosen solution, they should again look back to see if the solution has worked. Are the ideas and the products coming out of the system achieving better fit with customer need? Is the process speeding up? Is it costing less? If their interventions are not improving the system, they may want to reevaluate what they have done and revise their understanding of how their management systems and behaviors are affecting the innovation process. They may want to go back to the sequence of questions, beginning with Question 2, to see whether they really understood correctly what was affecting the dimension of innovation system behavior that they wanted to influence.

On the other hand, if their interventions are actually improving the system, they may not want to rest on their laurels. They may want to continue going forward and find more ways to improve their system. In that case, they should go back to Question 1, decide what dimension of innovation performance they want to work on, and proceed with a new diagnostic of how to do it.

The procedures described in this section follow fairly standard procedures of general problem solving. For more detailed discussions of the process of problem solving itself, the reader may wish to refer to Ackoff (1978), Hayes (1989), or Arnold (1992).

This concludes my discussion of how to think about innovation. In the next six chapters, I will look in detail at each of the management structures, systems and practices and how they affect innovation performance.

3 Corporate and Business Unit Management Tools 1: Strategy and Goals

As I noted in Chapter 2, the nine types of business management tool can be divided into three groups. In this chapter I will deal with the first group, which includes tools related to *strategy* and *goals*, or *purpose*. Three types of tools appeared under this entry in Figure 2.3:

- Strategy
- Components of the company (competences and mergers and acquisitions)
- Goals.

I will discuss each of these areas in turn.

Strategy

Three different types of tool fall under the heading of strategy. Corporate leaders often set strategy for an entire corporation, including a number of business units. This *corporate strategy* normally goes well beyond giving directions for any particular business unit. Rather, it involves giving guidance for the overall development of the corporation. Business unit leaders, meanwhile, are concerned with the development of products within their business unit and the positioning of these products within the marketplace. This *business unit strategy* is the second category of strategy. The third category is *responsibility for strategy*. In some companies the corporate center may keep tight control of strategy making. In others, business unit heads or individuals even lower down may

Table 3.1   Questions to ask about your strategy

Corporate and business unit strategy

- What direction are we going in:
  - In terms of developing our product-markets?
  - In terms of developing our competences?

- Does everyone in the company know what direction we are going in, and what they need to do to help?

- How much emphasis should we put on innovation within each product line?

- Do we have a clear view of the future of our company and of our industry?
  - Does everyone know what that view of the future is?

- Do we know who our potential partners are?

- Do we know who our potential competitors are?

Business unit strategy

- How much resources should we invest in innovation?

- What types of innovation do we want to focus on:
  - Product innovation? Which products? What types of new features?
  - Process innovation? Which processes?

- How will planned innovation fit with our product-market strategy?

Responsibility for determining strategy

- Who is responsible for determining strategy:
  - Corporate?
  - Division/group heads?
  - Business unit heads?
  - Product managers?

- Is strategy determined at the appropriate level? Is more centralization or decentralization needed?

- Do the people responsible for strategy actually do what they need to do to set and implement the strategy?

have effective responsibility for strategy. The location of strategy-making responsibility can have implications for a company's innovation performance. (See Table 3.1 for a list of key questions to ask in the area of strategy.)

Corporate strategy

Level of emphasis given to innovation At least three aspects of corporate strategy have an impact on innovation performance. The first is the general level of emphasis given to innovation. Innovation may be high on a corporation's list of priorities, as at 3M, or it may be quite low, as at Industrial Chemicals in the mid-1980s. This will impact the amount of resources and management attention given to idea generation and innovation projects. It will also, in the longer term, impact people's interest in pursuing innovative ideas.

Managers of a company which puts a high emphasis on innovation will generally find ways to get the other dimensions of management right. Innovation will prevail over other potential priorities, such as managing short-term profits. Managers at companies which do not emphasize innovation will often tolerate roadblocks and systems which limit the company's innovation performance. Other priorities, like short-term profits, will win when in conflict with innovation. In addition, a high emphasis on innovation implies internal growth. A company which puts a low emphasis on innovation may rely on acquisitions for growth.

Vision of how the industry and the company will develop Corporate strategies sometimes include a vision of how the industry, or industries, in which the company competes will develop and how the company itself will develop. Such a vision can be a great aid to fostering innovation. A detailed vision of future market trends, future technological developments and the role the company can play in them can serve as an inspiration for much innovation activity. It can also provide guidance for investment and research activities.

In addition, the existence of an explicit vision gives the company a reason to check constantly the reality around it. Are things going as the vision suggests? Are unexpected things happening? Must we update the vision? What are the implications for our operations? These are some of the reality-checking questions that a vision can inspire.

In the absence of a vision, a company may drift from opportunity to opportunity, not knowing which to invest in and which to ignore. It will not know what aspects of reality are important to its future, so it won't know what to monitor and what to keep careful track of. Innovation investments, if they occur at all, will tend to be haphazard and opportunistic, and thus less likely to bear useful fruit.

Whom to compete with, whom to cooperate with The third aspect of corporate strategy is the decision of whom to compete with and whom to cooperate with. Some companies cooperate with no one. In a sense, they even compete with their suppliers (and/or their customers). They view their suppliers as adversaries and they fight them to obtain the largest possible portion of the common pie, revealing no information beyond the minimum necessary.

Such an attitude may sound barbarically unenlightened, but that is not necessarily the case. Everyone has heard about the advantages Japanese automobile companies gain by cooperating with their suppliers. But not all suppliers are willing to limit themselves to working with one customer, as the Japanese automobile suppliers usually are. Suppliers can convey information from one competitor to another. For that reason some companies quite logically exclude them from their information flow and treat them as potential adversaries.

The key issue for innovation is whom one can cooperate with. Bringing a supplier or customer into a development process widens the scope of available information, while also providing more heads to work on any given problem. It can also bring more accurate information. By excluding suppliers and customers, a company limits both the information and the skills it can bring to bear on an innovation problem.

I have focused on cooperation with suppliers and customers. But in many areas, such as telecoms, cooperation with competitors or with companies in related industries is common. Again, the issue is with whom can we cooperate. Some large innovation problems, such as delivering multimedia entertainment through a telecoms-based infrastructure, require such large cooperative efforts that no one company can do it alone. By creating joint ventures or other cross-company links, managers create the context for innovation efforts that could not otherwise occur. (See discussions of strategic alliances, such as Doz and Hamel, 1998, for useful elaborations of the advantages and problems of cooperation.)

Business unit strategy

Level of emphasis given to innovation In many corporations, business unit heads are able to determine themselves what level of emphasis to give to innovation. Those who think there is an advantage, personal or otherwise, to be gained in investing in innovation may invest heavily in it. Others may invest little. Either strategy may be found in the same industry, as some players stand pat or pursue follower strategies while others make speculative investments that they hope will pay off at some time in the future.

What type of innovation to focus on Business unit heads are usually able to determine what type of innovation to emphasize. Some will choose to invest in radical product innovation. Others will invest in product line extensions or other less radical product variations. Yet others will focus on service innovations. Finally, those pursuing low cost strategies may focus on process innovations. They may further decide what types of new competitive advantages they wish to develop. These decisions will all have an impact on the level and type of investments made in innovation.

Product or service strategy Finally, other aspects of a business unit's product or service strategy may have an impact on its investments in innovation. A business unit head may give specific directions on how a product should evolve, thus legitimizing some innovation investments and excluding others. Such decisions do not necessarily inhibit innovation, but they do slow the progress of innovation projects which are not compatible with the directions chosen by business unit management.

Who has responsibility for strategy?

At what level is strategy determined? At different companies, different levels of managers may have responsibility for setting strategy. In some, business unit heads have a wide degree of latitude as to whether they emphasize innovation or not, and what kind of innovation they emphasize. In other companies, corporate heads control this. Business unit heads either invest in innovation or they don't, depending on what their corporate superiors tell them to do. In the former case, the company's innovativeness depends on corporate's level of interest in innovation. In the latter case, innovation performance depends on the level of interest in innovation among its business unit managers.

At some companies, like Eastman Chemical, corporate level managers negotiate with business unit managers about how much emphasis each business unit will put on innovation. Some invest little in product innovation. Others will follow innovations pioneered by competitors. Others attempt to stay at the leading edge. Some will invest in process innovation. Others will not.

Another variation on this theme can be found at 3M. There, all business units are required to invest in innovation. But what types of innovation they invest in is up to them. Each business unit is free to set up whatever innovation programs it pleases. Some business units set up very specific programs with clear goals. Others may not have a 'business unit program', but rather will encourage their people to come up with lots of interesting ideas during the course of a year, with the expectation that many of these ideas will bear fruit in the form of new products.

The only thing business units at 3M can't do is stand still. The 3M system gives much more flexibility to people lower down in the organization to decide how to innovate. The center gives the order to innovate, letting those lower down choose how to do it.

All this would not matter to us, except that in some cases pushing responsibility downward increases innovation performance. In some companies, the reins of financial control from the center are quite tight. When these reins are loosened and business unit heads are given the freedom to invest as they please, some will invest in innovation, thus increasing the company's innovation performance.

MGE's Lawn & Garden division followed this pattern. For many years, division headquarters controlled nearly all investment in new product development. As a result, most investment went to products intended for the three large markets where the headquarters and laboratories were located. When regional business units were given the freedom to make investments themselves, they invested in many region-specific products. This resulted in an increase in the number of new products the division produced.

Centralization, or keeping decisions at the corporate level, usually limits local initiative. But centralization of innovation decisions is necessary when the bets to be made are very large. If a bet is large enough to make or break the company, then corporate management would be irresponsible not to get involved. If bets are not so big, then corporate may only delay and bias investment decisions by getting involved. When bets are not big, it is better to push these decisions down to where the best information to make them is available. This is usually at a level well below that of corporate management. Decentralization, or pushing decisions down, usually encourages initiative and allows people who are closer to the technology and markets involved to make the decisions. (This point was made already in the late 1960s by Lawrence and Lorsch, 1969.)

Taking (or failing to take) responsibility for strategy 'Having' responsibility for strategy is not the same thing as 'taking' responsibility for strategy. Some managers and management teams do not do what they are supposed to do. There may be quite logical reasons for not deciding on a strategy. But failing to give direction to a company often results in drift and lost opportunities.

FinCo (a pseudonym), a large American financial service organization, experienced a logjam in its strategic decision processes because of the risk involved in charting a new course. For years, the company had relied on independent sales people to sell its insurance products. By the early 1990s, several members of the senior management team were convinced that the company could increase sales by selling its products through other channels. But if FinCo used new channels, there was a risk of a backlash from the traditional channel, the independent sales people. If they saw FinCo's investment in new channels as a threat to them, they could stop selling FinCo's products and replace them with those of another insurer. This could kill or seriously damage FinCo's core business.

Supporters of change within FinCo argued that the company could develop the new channels using different products. This would not threaten the independent insurance agents. They argued that the company could not afford to continue selling only through independent agents. Too many other channels were available, and they risked eclipsing the company's independent agents.

Their arguments did not carry the day. The head of the core business blocked all experiments with new channels because of the risk of damaging his business. Since the company practiced consensus management at the most senior level, no change could be made without his approval. As a result, for five years, the company suffered from a strategic logjam at the top. A majority of the management board believed that the current strategy was not viable. But innovation, even experimentation with new channels, was blocked.

Failure to make or execute a strategy, whether because of conflicts within the senior group (such as at FinCo), or because of simple failure to take initiative, can limit or suppress innovation activity. If a logjam at the top prevents movement, innovative initiatives may be blocked. Failure to take responsibility for strategy may leave room for initiative lower down. But it may also create a context which discour-

Table 3.2   Strategy tools and their impacts

Aspect of strategy	Tool or variable . . . . Impact	
Corporate strategy	■ Level of emphasis given to innovation overall	■ Overall level of support, tight or loose budget, little experimentation or lots of it
	■ Vision of how the industry and company will develop	■ Detailed guide of how and where to develop business
	■ Whom to cooperate with, whom to compete with	■ Who to share development tasks with, if anyone
Business unit strategy	■ Level of emphasis given to innovation	■ Overall level of support, tight or loose budget, little experimentation or lots of it
	■ Which types of innovation to emphasize (product, process, service)	■ Guidance on investment decisions
	■ Details of product/service strategy	■ Detailed guide on directions to pursue
Responsibility for strategy	■ Level where responsibility for strategy is held:	■ Level of flexibility/ diversity in approaches to market:
	– Corporate responsible	– Centralized control, focused strategy
	– Business unit head responsible	– Dispersed control, diversity, reactivity, but less coordination, focus
	– Product teams, other low level groups responsible	– Even more dispersed control, more diversity, more reactivity, less coordination
	– No one takes responsibility	– Drift, inertia

ages initiative by failing to provide resources and failing to follow up on successes. (See Table 3.2 for a summary of the dimensions of strategy that impact the innovation system.)

Components of the company

This heading includes two things which are normally considered quite different: merger and acquisition (M&A) activity and competence management. What they have in common is that they both involve the questions of:

- Which competences will be contained within the company
- How the desired competences will be developed and managed.

If a company needs to obtain a set of competences that are far from its current domain, or if it needs new competences quite quickly, it may decide to obtain them through acquisition. If on the other hand, it wants to invest in a few competences that are closely related to those it already has, it may decide to develop the competences internally, filling gaps through hiring or training. Thus new competences may be built either by acquisition or by internal development. In either case, the need for new competences and the development of existing competences may be tracked and managed through a competence management system. (See Table 3.3 for a list of key questions in the area of components of the company.)

Mergers and acquisitions

Companies acquire other companies for a lot of reasons, some of which are related to innovation. I will briefly discuss the three most common patterns related to innovation.

Acquiring competences In the first pattern, the company makes an acquisition in order to acquire competences needed to develop a new product. If a company has some, but not all, of the competences needed, it may acquire a company with the missing competences in order to be able to develop the product. In some cases it may be possible to set up a joint venture. This works best when the contributions needed from each company are clear and the companies can agree on how to share ownership. Alternatively, if the competences

Table 3.3   Questions to ask about competences and other components of the company

Components of the company, or determining what competences to have and how to get them
■ Do we have the right mix of competences in the company?
■ Can we innovate more by enriching our mix of competences?
■ When we expand competences, should we do so by bringing in competences from the outside (buying them, or hiring people), or through internal development? Do we have effective means to determine this in each case?
■ Should we allow people to take more initiative in developing their own competences, without demanding that senior management approve each decision to expand competences?
■ Are there activities (or competences) that are not linked to the rest of the company, and might be better disposed of?
Managing competences effectively
■ Do we know what competences we have?
■ Do we know what competences we are developing? What competences we are investing in?
■ Do we manage our competences effectively?
■ Do we distract our people from innovation and competence building by doing to much merger and acquisition activity?
■ Can we transfer competences effectively when we need to?

needed can be added piecemeal, it may be possible to hire individuals to fill the gap rather than buying a whole company.

Acquiring a distribution system In the second pattern, a company may acquire a distribution system or other assets which will help it exploit an innovation more effectively. If, for instance, a North American company develops a product which it can exploit worldwide, it may acquire overseas competitors to be able to push its product through their distribution systems.

Acquiring small companies and helping them innovate The third pattern is, in effect, a reverse of the second. A company with distribution, marketing skill, or other broadly useful assets may acquire smaller companies with innovative products. After acquiring them, it gives their products wider or more effective distribution. ConsumerCo has done this frequently, buying smaller, innovative companies who could benefit by having their product put through ConsumerCo's highly effective worldwide distribution system.

Divestiture inhibiting innovation In the cases discussed above, M&A activity works to the benefit of innovation. Companies willing to acquire to support innovation may, as a result, be more innovative. But M&A activity can also work to inhibit innovation.

I spoke with managers of a business which had been sold three times in the course of five years. While they said that their final 'home,' the company that owned them when I talked to them, was reasonably supportive of innovation, several of the companies which had held them briefly were not so supportive. In particular, once they had been put up for sale, they had been told in clear terms that they were not to invest in any new product development. They were to think only about short-term profits. They were not to do anything which would not pay off within six months.

More interested in the future of their business than their (temporary) owners, they ignored this directive to the extent they could. They hid promising projects from their superiors. But they were not able to hide everything. They had to cut some investments that were too large to be hidden. This shows that pressure to focus on short-term results in order to 'pretty up a unit' for divestiture can seriously inhibit innovation.

M&A activity as a distraction from innovation M&A activity can slow innovation in another way. Making and digesting an acquisition is a process which can take considerable management time and effort (Haspeslagh and Jemison, 1991). Managers who are absorbed by the problem of integrating an acquisition may not be able to pay much attention to their 'day jobs.' Their day jobs may involve running or supervising innovation projects. Managers at Pharma, a pharmaceutical company which resulted from a merger, reported that all projects were delayed by six months while managers figured out how to organize the new company's R&D system.

Competence management

Since Prahalad and Hamel's well-known *Harvard Business Review* article (1990), 'competence', or 'core competence', has become a new word in the manager's vocabulary. While the concept is much talked about, some companies have gone beyond talk to develop formal competence management systems. Key issues for innovation are:

1. Whether such a system exists and what it consists of
2. Whether it is used to support innovation
3. Whether the company's competences are closely enough related to form a useful product development network
4. Whether the company has the means to transfer complex competences when the competences needed on a specific project are separated by wide geographic distances.

The competence management system A competence management system can involve any or all of the following features. First and most fundamental is to understand what competences the company has. You may recall that when Marsh thought of the Chemical Residues idea, he tried to find people who could help him within MGE (Chapter 2). But no one in MGE could tell him what competences people in the company had. There was no place he could go to find out who could help him, or whether anyone could help him at all. As a result, he spent six months in a fruitless search for help. If MGE had had an effective competence management system, he could have saved that six months of effort and moved the project forward faster.

The second role a competence management system can play is to make sensible decisions about what competences the company should invest in. Once competences have been identified, the competence management team can determine where each competence is used, where it could be used, and how crucial it is to the company's present and future operations. The competence management team can also determine where gaps exist in the company's competence profile. On the basis of this information, the company can make sensible decisions about which competences to invest in, which to retain as is, and which (potentially) to divest.

Inspired in part by Hamel and Prahalad's (1990) article, Eastman Chemical built a competence management system which does all of these things and more. Eastman early on identified the competences it considers key to each of its businesses. Investments in these competences are routinely tracked. When a new product or process development project involves investing in a competence, these investments are coded. The investments made by all projects are summed at budget time, and management then determines whether the investments being made in each competence are sufficient to maintain or increase the competence to an adequate level. R&D budgets may be adjusted to increase investment in neglected areas, or to reduce investments in less needed areas.

Using a competence management system to support innovation Such a system can be used to support innovation in several ways. The first is to support information search. When someone, like George Marsh, has an idea, a competence tracking system can quickly tell him whether the competence he needs is available within the company and where it is available. Second, managers like those at Eastman can determine what kinds of competences might be needed to support innovation activity and invest in them.

Who makes decisions to develop new competences is an important question. Most companies make such decisions centrally. Senior management will decide whether or not to invest in major new technical (or marketing) competences. But some companies allow people well down in the hierarchy to make such decisions as well.

At 3M and similar companies, technical people are free to spend 15 percent of their time working on the project of their choice, as long as the project offers some potential benefit to the company. This rule gives technical people the freedom to proactively develop the competences necessary for their '15 percent' projects. Companies that give this kind of flexibility can develop the competences needed to address emerging opportunities far more quickly than companies which control people's time more rigidly.

A scientist at an agrochemical company saw an opportunity to develop a new type of fungicide in the mid-1980s. The catch was that he needed to learn a lot about new methods of applying fungicides to be able to pursue the opportunity. No knowledge of this type was available within his company. So he developed it on his own, against the wishes of his superiors. His superiors ordered him not to invest his time in learning new fungicide application methods, but he did so anyway, in his own time, when he had the time.

A few years later his idea bore fruit and he developed a fungicide which became a profitable niche product. But he had developed the skills needed to develop the product on his own initiative, contrary to his management's wishes. Had the company supported his efforts to broaden his skill set, the product might have been ready a year sooner. Had the company succeeded in its efforts to stop him, it would never have had the new product at all.

Through its management of competences, a company may either encourage or discourage innovation. The company may systematically explore new ways to use its existing competences. It may look at competences it can add which would allow it to develop new activities. Or it may allow individuals within the company to explore such issues on its own. All these activities would encourage innovation. Alternatively, it may suppress such explorations and thus discourage innovation.

Related or unrelated competences Companies with linked sets of competences may have more opportunities than other companies to develop new products and new businesses. A company like 3M has a multitude of technical competences, most of them related to adhesives, coatings and surfaces. New developments and recombinations of these competences have led to an unending stream of new products.

Companies with only a few competences, or with competences which are not linked (for example, a conglomerate), have fewer opportunities to develop and recombine their competences. As a result, they are likely to be less innovative.

Transferring complex competences When a company's competences are geographically dispersed or separated by rigid business unit boundaries, transfer of competences may become an issue. An innovation team may need competences housed in a different unit to pursue its idea. The team will be able to finish its work more quickly if the company has established methods of transferring competences across these barriers.

Once again, 3M provides an example of good practice. Suppose an innovation team at 3M needs a competence which is housed within the company but at a distant location. A member of the team will be designated to go to the laboratory which houses the competences and learn it. The learning period may be as long as six months. But after six months of working alongside the people who hold the competence, the team member will have absorbed much explicit and tacit knowledge about the competence. He will then return to his original team, bringing the competence with him. (See Table 3.4 for a summary of tools related to components of the company.)

Table 3.4   Tools related to components of
the company and their impacts

Type of component management	Tool or variable . . . . . . Impact	
Merger and aquisition activity	■ Acquire competences needed to develop a product	■ Enables development of a new product
	■ Acquire distribution	■ Allows wider distribution of new products
	■ Acquire products to put through distribution	■ Allows more sales of new products through existing distribution
	■ Prepare a unit for sale	■ May inhibit or suppress innovation in unit
	■ Any M&A activity	■ May distract management, personnel from innovation
Competence management	■ Understand what competences a company has	■ Helps people find needed competences, which supports innovation activity
	■ Make decisions about investing in competences	■ Identifies key competences needed to support innovation
	■ Determine who makes decision to develop new competences:	■ Determines who can expand company's competence base:
	– Corporate or business units	– Centralized control of expansion, diversification
	– Individual	– Entrepreneurial expansion, diversification (from grass roots)
	■ Develop means of transferring complex competences	■ Facilitates innovation in geographically dispersed organization

Goals

The last area in the strategy and goals section is goals. Goals are related to strategy but typically are more specific. They identify the milestones that a business unit, team or individual must meet if the company as a whole is to achieve its overall strategy.

I will divide my discussion of goals into three parts. I will first look at the overall structure of goal systems. Then I will look at financial goals. Then I will discuss how goals can be set for specific phases of the innovation process. (See Table 3.5 for a list of key questions in the area of goals.)

Goal structure

A number of issues are involved in the structure of a company's goal system. I will first look at the complexity of the goal structure and then

Table 3.5   Questions to ask about goals

Goal setting
■ What are the company's goals?
■ Are individuals' goals linked to the company's goals?
■ Who sets the company's goals?
■ How are they set?
■ How are the company's goals linked to customer preferences?
■ Do we have appropriate goals for the innovation process itself:
– For idea generation?
– For the funding process?
– For development?
– For product launch and market entry?

Goal management
■ What happens when different people or groups inside the company have goals that conflict?
■ Do we effectively manage the trade-offs between financial goals, operational goals, and long-term goals and investments?

at the nature of the company's goals. After that, I will briefly discuss how goals are set, the impact of customers' preferences, how conflicts among goals are resolved, and how a goal system as a whole evolves.

Complexity of a company's goal structure Goal structures can be simple or complex. In the extreme case a company could have one goal, perhaps a specific level of profit, with no other goals being explicitly set. Such a company would have an extremely simple goal structure.

At the other extreme we might find a motor vehicle company, where in one motor vehicle project team alone we might find hundreds or even thousands of specific goals. There might be a goal indicating when the design for each vehicle part should be finished. Other goals would relate to subassembly design. Other goals would relate to overall vehicle design and evaluation. Still others would relate to the timing of development of the manufacturing process or the marketing plan. Still others would relate to the professional development of people on the project team. Other units within the motor vehicle company would have other goals, some related to marketing and sales, others related to finance, technological research, or other activities. The result would be an extremely complex goal structure.

At the other extreme we might find a motor vehicle company, where in one motor vehicle project team alone we might find hundreds or even thousands of specific goals. There might be a goal indicating when the design for each vehicle part should be finished. Other goals would relate to subassembly design. Other goals would relate to overall vehicle design and evaluation. Still others would relate to the timing of development of the manufacturing process or the marketing plan. Still others would relate to the professional development of people on the project team. Other units within the motor vehicle company would have other goals, some related to marketing and sales, others related to finance, technological research, or other activities. The result would be an extremely complex goal structure.

One feature of a complex goal structure is that goals are related to each other. They are often 'nested,' that is, the accomplishment of some large goals involves the prior accomplishment of numerous subgoals. The final design for a subassembly cannot be completed until the designs for the individual parts are completed. The design for the car cannot be completed until the subassembly designs are completed. The achievement of goals at one level depends on the achievement of goals at lower levels.

One factor driving the complexity of a goal structure is the technical complexity of the product being designed. This is clear in the case of the motor vehicle. There are many parts and many subassemblies. There are goals related to each part and to each subassembly, in addition to the goals related to the product as a whole.

Another factor leading to complexity is horizontal or sequential linkage among goals. If two laboratories are dependent on each other for the completion of a cooperative project, their goals may link in a temporal sequence which may become quite complex. For instance, a motor vehicle's engine and power train are intimately linked. But an engine and its accompanying transmission may be designed by two different teams. In such a case, the teams' goals and workplans are likely to be linked at a multitude of points.

A simpler case of horizontal linkage occurs when one team's work occurs prior to another's. In a pharmaceutical company, the toxicity laboratory will test a new compound's toxicity in animals before the clinical laboratory begins clinical trials in humans. While the clinical team may begin work before the toxicity team is finished (for example, they may begin developing their plan for testing the product), the bulk of clinical's work (the tests themselves) occurs after animal toxicity tests are finished. In this case, one team cannot do much work on its goals until after another team has accomplished its goals.

The nature of a company's goals In general terms, the goals of an innovation project may relate to the technical performance of a product, process or service, to the aesthetic characteristics of a product (people's subjective reactions to it) or to market acceptance of a product. There may be one technical goal related to overall performance (a simple case), or there may be many technical goals related to numerous features of the product's technical performance (for example, an automobile's technical performance has many, many dimensions).

Many technical characteristics can be measured objectively, but in some cases, subjective perceptions are key. There may be little or no technical difference between, in the first instance, a car whose noise level increases smoothly as the car speeds up, and in the second instance, a car whose noise level stays the same over the lower half of the range and then quickly increases to a much higher plateau. The latter pattern may not indicate any kind of technical problem, but will disturb people nonetheless. Such subjective perceptions can only be detected by having people drive the cars and report on what they experience (in other words, we must ask people to report on their subjective impressions).

The aesthetic characteristics of a product are generally considered to be subjective, but companies measure them nonetheless, sometimes extensively. Examples of aesthetic characteristics include the following: the appearance of the product, its fit with current fashion trends, its lifestyle image (affected by packaging and advertising, as well as by the product itself), and the appearance of its packaging. Products which come into contact with the human body (clothes, cosmetics, other personal care products) may also be evaluated on such things as their odor and 'feel'.

Companies vary to the extent that they identify and measure the aesthetic characteristics of their products. In consumer product areas, it is probably safe to assume that companies which identify and measure how consumers evaluate their products' aesthetics (that is, their customers' subjective impressions) will be more innovative. Why? Because these companies will have identified more dimensions of the product which can be improved and/or altered.

How goals are set Companies have a variety of means of setting goals related to product characteristics. One automobile manufacturer I visited looked at three types of inputs before setting any goals. First, the design team for a new car would look at the performance of similar cars built by the company in the past. Second, it would test competing products to set benchmarks. Third, the team would look at what customers wanted in their ideal 'dream car' in the product class. With all this data in hand, the team would begin the task of setting goals.

The team's overarching goal, imposed on the them by the company, would be to design a car which would be best in its class on all important dimensions at the time of launch. The team would try to estimate how much competing products would improve by the time their car was launched (typically four to six years later). They would then construct a preliminary set of goals which would involve a substantial improvement over where they expected competing cars to be. In addition, this would normally involve a substantial improvement over the company's own past performance. In some cases, the team might adjust goals either up or down, depending on how good their company's previous cars had been. Finally, they might add or delete features, depending on their customers' view of the ideal dream car. In general, they would add any features of the dream car that they thought feasible.

In the case of such a complex product, trade-offs between goals are inevitable. For most classes of cars, price, and thus cost, matters. But raising performance characteristics, or adding features, will add cost. So the team typically adds what it can within a cost limit. The final goal set for a motor vehicle is likely to include, in addition to cost, a variety of technical and aesthetic characteristics, sales volumes by geography, and such after sales measures as number of breakdowns and number of customer complaints.

Goal setting for less complicated products is simpler. Goal setting for an entirely new product may be very simple at first: 'give me one that works!'

Who sets goals Goals are not always set by the product team. They may be set by senior management, by business unit management, by functional management, by the inventor himself, or by anyone in between. In the famous case of the Sony Walkman, the chairman of Sony himself, Akio Morita, set the goal of making a cassette player which he could carry in his pocket and listen to while golfing.

Customers' preferences and their impact on innovation goals Two dimensions of customers' preferences have a large impact on innovation projects. The first is whether customers' preferences are unitary or diverse. The second is whether customers' preferences are predictable or unpredictable.

Similarity of customer preferences If all customers have the same preferences (for example, all buyers of computer memory chips want more memory at a lower cost), then differentiating the market may be impossible. The market may become a commodity with all players in the market chasing after the same goals. In such a situation, an innovation project team may have no flexibility whatsoever in setting its goals. It will simply have to join the race to be first with a new improvement in the commodity.

If customer preferences differ from one customer to another, then an innovation team may have far more flexibility to experiment with various product configurations. For when customer preferences differ, there may be room to develop a variety of niches in the market, any one of which the team could address.

Predictability of customer preferences When customer preferences are predictable, the innovation team can target a stable set of product characteristics. It can set goals in relation to desired product characteristics with some confidence in how customers will react to the product if they succeed in achieving the goals they set. But if customer preferences are unstable, unknown, or otherwise unpredictable, then their planning task is much more speculative. They may set goals and develop the product without having any real clue as to whether customers will ultimately like it.

This is the situation teams developing entirely new products often find themselves in. They must design a product which they think will have maximum appeal to customers, without any certainty that they are making the right product design decisions.

Teams working in fashion driven businesses face this problem in a particularly acute form. Consumer reaction to product appearance may change within a few weeks. In such businesses, teams which devise ways to postpone decisions about fashion-related characteristics will succeed better than teams which make such decisions early. Benetton, for example, succeeded in the clothing businesses in part because it found ways to postpone decisions about product color until only a few weeks before products appeared on store shelves.

This being said, customers' reactions to cost variations are almost always predictable. Their reactions to variations in technical characteristics are usually predictable, except in the case of entirely new products. It is their reaction to aesthetic characteristics which is the most difficult to predict.

Methods of forecasting customer preferences The more a company knows about what a customer wants, the more easily it can plan its innovation program. As a result, many companies interview their customers extensively to be able to predict, as accurately as possible, what their customers will want in the future. Some companies search actively for 'leading customers'(Von Hippel, 1986). Leading customers are those which are furthest ahead in their own fields, those which are exploring and creating the future themselves.

Some industrial products companies go further down the value chain to interview their customers' customers in an attempt to understand what final consumers want and what they are likely to pay for. By interviewing their customers' customers, they increase their understanding of their customers, of the pressures their customers are under, and what motivates them when they make buying decisions.

Goal conflicts Innovation teams frequently need cooperation from other units within their own company. One team I visited needed cooperation from a manufacturing plant which made a key raw material for the team's product. Initially they did not get any cooperation, since the plant manager preferred loading his plant with high volume orders. Such orders were far more profitable. Since his plant's primary goal (virtually its only goal) was to make the maximum profit, he saw no reason to take low volume orders from the innovation team.

It took the intervention of the business unit head who supervised the project to break this logjam. He went to the division manager who supervised both units and explained the situation. The division manager altered the factory's incentive plan so that the factory and its managers would not suffer in any way by working with the innovation team. He then instructed the factory to fill the team's orders.

Companies which want to innovate need to have means of resolving or preventing such goal conflicts. In this example, the goal conflict only cost the team a few weeks. It could have been worse. But it would have been better to prevent the conflict in the first place.

Some more innovative companies have a general rule to 'support innovation.' Supporting innovation is considered more important than, or at least as important as, maintaining short-term profit. Incentive systems and other management tools at these companies are set up in such as way as to encourage, not discourage, support of innovation projects.

Evolution of goal systems Through much of this discussion, I have focused on the goals of innovation project teams. But other parts of the corporation, such as business units, divisions, and the corporation as a whole, have goals as well. I will not discuss these larger goal sets in any detail. But I will note that specific goals to encourage innovation can be set at all of these levels.

3M is famous for its goal to produce at least 30 percent of sales in each business unit from products/processes which are four years old or less. 3M's way of framing this goal is not shared by all innovative companies. But all innovative companies I visited had corporate, team and business unit goals which encouraged innovation. Less innovative companies didn't.

When overall goals for supporting innovation are in place, subordinate goals, which involve completing individual projects or reaching specific milestones, tend to evolve over time. When one goal is reached, it is, more or less automatically, replaced by another, more difficult goal. In this way, the company is continuously stretching itself to reach ever higher goals. No one can rest. Perhaps no one ever wants to rest, since they want to keep innovating.

Impact of the nature of goals on the organization I've discussed above how the complexity of a project team's goal structure will be driven by the technical complexity of the product it is designing. But the nature of the product and customer goals have other impacts as well. A key issue is whether product quality and consumer choice are primarily driven by purely technical issues or whether it is driven by more subjective issues related to consumer taste. This drives some differences in the way a company is organized.

When consumer choice is driven by subjective criteria (for example, consumer markets driven by product look, feel and image), there is a strong likelihood that there will be many possible dimensions of variation in the product. It will very likely be possible to establish many viable niches in the product's market. People trained in marketing are likely to have a lead role in finding and exploiting these niches. It may be possible and desirable to make many frequent, inexpensive changes in products. If so, there will be a premium on flexibility and speed of response. Successful organizations are likely to have flat hierarchies and a large number of small units.

By contrast, when objective, technical performance criteria drive customer choice (for example, typical industrial markets), only a few niches may be possible, depending on the number of technical variables which matter. And people trained in engineering and other technical subjects are likely to take lead roles in company leadership and project management. Marketing may be handled by people whose first training was in technical subjects, and who have learned marketing on the job.

Financial Goals

Relative importance of financial goals The most overarching goals a company has are often its financial goals. These goals may relate to company-wide profits or revenue. Financial goals may be cascaded down into goals for business units and individuals. They may be the only overall goals the company has and be viewed as more important than any other goals. Or the company may have product-related goals, quality goals or other nonfinancial goals which are considered to be of equal importance.

Some corporations have quantitative, company-wide goals which are not financial. Examples include innovation goals, such as 3M's percent of revenues from new products and processes, quality goals such as zero defects goals, and process efficiency goals like reducing throughput time or product design time.

Companies can have trouble innovating when they make short-term profits their most important goal. This can lead to under-investment in products which will take more than a few months to develop. Since most really new products take several years to develop, a focus on short-term profits can shut off investments in new products entirely.

In the last few years, many companies have become more conscious of the negative long-term effects of a short-term profit focus. Some have developed methods of combating the problem, putting growth or quality goals on an equal footing with financial goals. The Balanced Scorecard, a tool invented by Kaplan and Norton (1996), has proved to be a very popular management innovation. It allows, even forces management teams to set up customer-related and internal process-related goals which have equal weight with the company's financial goals.

Time spent negotiating financial goals When financial goals are primary (also sometimes when they are not), managers within a company may waste a tremendous amount of time haggling over who is to get credit for what and how to keep score. This can be a particularly serious problem when personal compensation is linked to business unit profit, to the achievement of a unit's budget, or to other local financial targets. In such cases, many days may be wasted in arguing over what level a budget should be set at, what transfer prices should be, and how budgets or other compensation formulas should be adjusted to take account of special cases.

Managers in MGE's Lawn & Garden unit grew tired of such haggling and established two rules which cut haggling time in the unit by 90+ percent. The first rule was, 'last year's results are this year's budget'. The second was, 'predicted costs (for a new product) equal the transfer price'. At a stroke, all haggling over budgets was eliminated, and transfer prices for new products were set equal to whatever manufacturing predicted they could produce them for. Manufacturing had an incentive not to price things too high, since then no one would try to sell them. But once it estimated its cost, it could keep (by the formula) any gains it made.

ConsumerCo deals with this problem differently. It has never computed compensation by formula. Rather it evaluates managers on the basis of a wide variety of criteria, including not only financial performance, but also how the performance was achieved. Managers who exploit a product or a brand without investing in it are penalized, since this is viewed as stealing from the future. And supervisors know whether a manager has been investing or not, since ConsumerCo has a consensus decision-making system which involves them in many decisions made by junior level managers.

Goals for phases of the innovation process

Some companies set goals for the overall outcomes of the innovation process. Goals about revenue generated from new products are an example. But other companies find it useful to break the innovation process down and to set goals for each phase. Pharmaceutical companies have done this more than companies in other industries, but the practice is not unknown elsewhere. Typical goals relate to idea generation, the funding process, development and entry. When these goals affect only projects in the innovation system, they would be classified as project management interventions. But at times business units will be expected to generate ideas, fund projects, or develop projects on their own. As a result, I list them with other business management interventions.

Idea generation In industries where there is a long history of innovation, such as pharmaceuticals, some companies set goals (quotas) for the number of new ideas to be generated over a given time. At Northern Pharmaceuticals, the new head of R&D appointed in 1992 decided that the company's discovery unit should produce X (a specific number) new ideas per year, X new chemical entities which were sufficiently interesting to be investigated as potential pharmaceutical products. He based this quota on the experience of discovery laboratories in other, more innovative companies. He was confident it was achievable, given his own past experience at these companies.

To set a quota like this, a company's managers must have a clear idea of what counts as a new idea. There must be a quality or feasibility hurdle by which new ideas can be measured before they count against the quota. Otherwise, it will be too easy to fudge the quota. In addition, it is useful to have quantitative records of the number and types of ideas produced in the past. Such records can be used to demonstrate the feasibility of the quota or the level of stretch needed to reach it.

Not all idea generation goals are quotas. Other idea generation goals may relate to the types of new product or process ideas to be developed, or to the estimated value of these ideas.

Eastman Chemical sets goals for the value of ideas produced. The company has developed a sophisticated method of estimating the value of an innovation idea. In the case of a new product idea, estimates of the potential size of the market are made by the person who has the idea and validated by other, more objective people who are knowledgeable in the area. Estimates are then made of price and market share achievable, variable and fixed costs, and time to market based on the company's past experience in similar areas. With this information in place, cash flows can be projected and net present value (NPV) computed. The estimates are refined as the company learns more about the product and its potential market.

Such valuation methods do not come up with 100 percent accurate results, but Eastman Chemical finds it to be a useful tool nonetheless. In their experience most new products do not reach their estimated revenues. But a minority do and a smaller minority go so far beyond the estimates that they make up the shortfalls on all those products which don't make their estimates. So, in the aggregate, Eastman's estimates of value are accurate, although the estimates for individual ideas are often not accurate.

At some companies, scientific personnel have goals for the number of patents or scientific papers they produce. Such goals do not necessarily help innovation. The work done to produce a scientific paper may have little to do with the company's ongoing business. Patents are typically more useful, they indicate that a new product idea has been developed. But they may not be any more fruitful than papers in producing revenues. Northern Pharmaceuticals allows its scientists to write academic papers, but in the early 1990s it set up quotas for new product ideas in an effort to direct its scientists' attention away from writing academic papers and toward developing new products.

Funding process Relatively few companies set explicit goals related to the funding process itself. But in companies that do set such goals, they played an important role. There are typically two types of goals: goals related to the quality of the process, and goals related to its speed.

In the mid-1980s, the funding process at Northern Pharmaceuticals was highly politicized. There were six semi-independent laboratories, and each laboratory manager had his own pet projects. How much money each project got depended on how well the manager of its laboratory liked it, how well he liked the people running it, and how much influence he had at corporate. There was a tendency to give some money to all projects, and corporate particularly spread its money around evenly to avoid arousing political conflicts.

In the late 1980s, Northern Pharmaceuticals' management decided that the funding process should be run differently. They decided that each project should be evaluated on the basis of objective criteria, criteria related to the likelihood of technical success and the size of the potential market. To avoid any appearance of conflict of interest, they brought in a reputable consultant to do an initial evaluation of each project. The consultant estimated the potential market size and the probability of success of each project in house and recommended elimination of the bottom half of the projects.

A new R&D head, appointed in 1992, carried this movement further. He set up clear objective milestones for each project to meet. The goal was to make the funding process objective and to base project funding decisions on criteria of potential market size, competitors, and likelihood of technical success.

3M and ConsumerCo have a different type of qualitative goal. These highly innovative companies believe that no worthy idea should go without funding. As a result, both companies have relatively generous innovation budgets and a variety of means of funding projects. The many methods used, and the logic behind them, will be discussed further in the section on funding systems.

More common are the time-related goals I found at several companies. At the National Products Company described by Bower (1970) in the late 1960s, the funding process for new investments took months. Funding requests had to make their way up from functional specialists to business unit heads to division heads and finally to corporate management. Then the decision had to be communicated back down the chain and implemented. The whole process took months. Other companies had similarly laborious process, leading to great delays in getting projects funded. By the mid-1980s, consultants like Stalk and Hout (1990) began telling companies to reduce turnaround time for funding requests. Some companies set goals in this area, and achieved reductions in average turn around times of 80 percent or more.

Development Many companies have set goals for the development phase. The most common goals relate to the time invested in development. Many companies, particularly those in pharmaceuticals, automobiles, and electronics, have discovered that getting a new product out one year earlier means one year of additional profits as well as a shorter reaction time to changes in consumer preferences.

Time is not the only area where companies set development goals. Other areas include the levels of success needed or milestones to be met to continue support for a project, technical areas to be researched during a project, the resource levels to be maintained for each project, and/or the cost to be incurred.

Entry A few companies set hurdles that a project must meet before any investment can be made in product launch. These goals typically relate to market viability as demonstrated in market tests, or to product quality. Companies with brands or reputations to protect may be particularly concerned with achieving a high level of product quality and reliability before allowing entry into the market.

Other measures of innovation performance

Goals can be set using a number of different types of measures of innovation performance. The overall goals discussed earlier in this section (for example, revenue generated from new products) relate to the final outcomes of the innovation process. By contrast, the phase-goals just discussed involve measurement of interim results of the process. Goals can be set for levels of inputs as well. These would typically take the form of a goal to re-invest X percent of revenues in R&D, or to employ X number of people in innovation projects.

Outcomes that can be measured go beyond levels of revenue or profits generated. Companies may measure customer satisfaction, customer complaints, expressions of concern, or other comments. Such qualitative, after sale measures of success can be used to detect areas where further innovation is needed and would be rewarded by the customer, thus providing a nice feedback loop which leads into the next innovation cycle. (See Table 3.6 for a summary of key issues related to goals.)

Table 3.6   Goals and their impact

Aspect of goals	Tool or variable . . . . Impact	
Goal structure	■ Complexity of the goal structure (linked to complexity of the product)	■ Number of levels of nested goals (superior and subordinate goals), links between goals of different units
	■ Nature of the goals: – Technical – Aesthetic – Market acceptance	■ Type of measurement: – Objective, directly measured – Opinion, taste important – Objectively measured, but acceptance may be based on taste
	■ How goals are set: – Benchmark previous performance – Benchmark competitors – Compare with customer desire – Internal vision	■ What is the inspiration? – Do better than last time – Do better than competitors – Please/thrill customers – Achieve stretch vision
	■ Who sets goals: – CEO, senior manager – Project team	■ Acceptance, stretch: – Stretch possible – Buy in certain
	■ Identify structure of customers' preferences – All the same or diverse – Predictable or not	■ Ensure the right type of bets are being made: – One product versus multiple niches – Known target versus speculative bets
	■ Methods of forecasting customer preferences: – Interviews – Lead customers	■ Improves product targeting: – Identify current preferences – May lead market
	■ Manage goal conflicts	■ Facilitate innovation and change
	■ Manage evolution of goal systems	■ Goals renewed, replaced as they are achieved
	■ Organization (impact of nature of goals): – Engineering led – Marketing led	■ Management competent to deal with key issues: – Good with technical goals and products – Good when consumer choice based on subjective criteria

(cont'd)

Table 3.6 (cont'd)

Aspect of goals	Tool or variable . . . . . Impact	
Financial goals	■ Relative importance of financial goals ■ Time spent negotiating financial goals	■ Short-term profit focus can kill innovation ■ Negotiations over budget, transfer pricing can waste lots of time
Goals for phases of the innovation process	■ Idea generation goals: – Quotas for number of ideas – Value of ideas – Patents ■ Funding system goals: – Objective (versus political) criteria – Goal to fund all worthy projects – Quick decisions ■ Development goals: – Time to completion – Level of success/ progress for continuation – Outcomes: new knowledge – Outcomes: customer acceptance ■ Entry goals, like market viability or product quality ■ Inputs	■ Can impact laboratories and business units: – Can increase discipline among scientists – Adds market focus – More fundamental research, less business focus ■ Can impact idea generation as well as funding process: – Improves outcomes, better projects and products Encourages idea generation, diversification – Speeds innovation process ■ Guide development team: – Speedier development – Closer attention to milestones – Closer attention to knowledge gained – Closer attention to customer need/preference ■ Ensures quality level at entry, protects brand ■ Can limit investment, or insure a minimum level of investment
Other measures of innovation performance	■ Outcomes	■ Can identify areas of weakness, needs for further investment

4 Corporate and Business Unit Management Tools 2: Structure and Process

I will discuss three types of management tools in this chapter: those related to organization structure and the allocation of power, those related to communications systems and information management, and those related to decision making methods. The first of these is at the core of traditional discussions of structure. Communication is so closely linked with organization structure that I discuss it immediately after. The third, decision-making methods, is so closely related to both communication and to the application of power within an organization that I discuss it in the same chapter.

This chapter is labeled 'structure and process' since structures frame processes. As Ghoshal and Bartlett (1995) have noted, managers manage processes as well as structures. What the company does is a process, and performance oriented managers are well advised to pay close attention to a company's processes, not just to its structures. But processes are still, to a great extent, framed by structures. Thus the chapter title includes both words, rather than one or the other.

Organization structure

This section will be one of the more complicated ones in this book. Organization structure can have so many different impacts on a company's ability to innovate that it will take time to lay them all out. Its primary impacts involve the organization of work, focusing attention, and focusing communication.

The chapter will be organized as follows. I will look first at hierarchy and its traditional dimensions. This section will give an overview of the organization of work and of the impact of organization on communication. Then I will look at methods of using

Table 4.1   Questions to ask about organization structure

Managing performance

- How does our organization structure impact our performance, particularly our innovation performance?

- Does the organization put people in stimulating situations that help them see new opportunities and develop ideas?

- Do we communicate effectively about the opportunities?

- Do we effectively match the structure of units within the company with the tasks that have to be performed?

- Do we have effective cross-functional and other cross-department links?

- Do we give enough visibility to innovation within the organization?

Questions individuals may be asking

- Who is my boss? Or who are my bosses?

- Who, and what should I be paying attention to?

Managing people's attention

- Do we effectively use the hierarchy and supervision to focus people's attention on the most important issues?

- Do we use hierarchy and supervision to focus their attention on innovation?

- Do we effectively use our organization to manage what people pay attention to?

Special structures

- Do we effectively manage key competences? Do we make such competences available to everyone who needs them?

- Do we provide appropriate growth paths for new businesses?

Distributing power

- How do we distribute power over key decisions?

- How does the distribution of power impact communication and innovation?

organization structure to manage performance. This has a major impact on focusing people's attention. Then I will discuss other ways to use organization structure to manage attention. I will then look at other special structures used for special purposes. In the last part of this section, I will look at the problem of changing an organization. (See Table 4.1 for a list of key questions on organization structure.)

Hierarchy

The core principles of hierarchy have been explored in depth by several generations of organization theorists (see Daft, 1989; Hall, 1996; Hatch, 1997, for a summary of work in this area). To avoid any possible confusion, let me specify how I am using the word 'hierarchy'. In this book, hierarchy refers to the network of boss–subordinate relationships existing within the company. A boss can have a number of different responsibilities towards a subordinate, the primary ones being to give direction to the subordinate, to organize the subordinate's work, and to be primarily responsible for the subordinate's evaluation and career development.

A superior–subordinate relationship normally involves power. The boss has obvious power over the subordinate's daily life and career development. The subordinate has less obvious power. The subordinate's power comes from the fact that by playing his role well or badly he can make the boss look good or bad, thus having a considerable impact on the boss's performance, reputation and career prospects.

Hierarchies vary along a number of dimensions. The most commonly discussed include the basic form of the hierarchy (that is, is it based on functional links, business unit or task links, or is it a matrix?), the number of levels in the hierarchy, and the span of control (number of subordinates per boss). The location of certain types of power (centralization–decentralization) is also a key variable. It is so key, in fact, that I will discuss it in a separate section. (See the later section on Decision territories.)

Hierarchical forms In principle, hierarchies do not randomly assign people to bosses. Rather all people doing similar tasks or related tasks are assigned to the same boss. In large companies, many different tasks are done and the people performing these tasks are grouped into ever larger units, with several layers of bosses coming between the lowest level workers and the head of the whole organization.

Workers were traditionally grouped on the basis of function, product line, geography or some combination of the above. There has been a tendency in the past decade to group workers less by function or even product line and more on the basis of shared responsibility for a common task. This has resulted in a decline in the importance of functional groupings and a great proliferation of cross-functional teaming even at quite low levels in the hierarchy.

To understand the impact of this trend, it is useful to discuss the history of business organizations, as recounted by Chandler (1962) and many others. Early business organizations were organized on a functional basis. Sales people reported to a head of sales. Production people reported to the head of production. Accountants to the head of accounting. And so on. Each of the functional heads reported to a general manager who headed the company. In such a functionally organized company, the general manager was the only person who had cross-functional responsibility.

Functional organizations still exist. Many small companies are functionally organized. But some large companies are as well, with the Chrysler Corporation until recently being a famous example.

A more complex form began to emerge in the 1920s. DuPont is a classic case, described by Chandler (1962). As DuPont grew and diversified into new businesses after the First World War, the functionally organized management team found that it could no longer manage the company effectively. It had grown too complex. The head of production, for example, could no longer effectively supervise production in a wide variety of different plants. The solution DuPont's management team found was to divide the company into separate business units, each with its own set of related products. Each business unit had its own functionally organized management team. The former senior management group evolved into a corporate management team with responsibility for integrating the whole. The result was a multidivisional organization, or 'M-form'.

Some large European companies adopted similar organizations at about the same time. But companies such as Unilever did not divide along product boundaries, but rather along geographic boundaries. A British company would set up subsidiaries in France, Germany, Italy and elsewhere. A German company would do the same. All the functions and products of the head office would be duplicated in each foreign subsidiary. While in part a response to management complexity, as in the DuPont case, this was more a response to geographic distance and to trade barriers erected along international borders. Rather than setting up business units which manufactured and sold different products, the European companies divided into series of nationally focused business units.

These stories illustrate *the main dimensions of a traditional organization*:

- Function
- Product line
- Geography.

Until the 1960s, most business organizations took one of these dimensions as its primary principle of organization, with the company being divided primarily on functional, product line, or geographic dimensions. People at lower levels within these traditional companies typically had one boss, a functional, product line, or geographic specialist.

The next step came in the 1960s when a number of multidivisional companies found that it was no longer enough to focus on one dimension of the hierarchy. Some management teams decided that product and function (or geography and product) were equally important. So the company, at all levels, was divided on two dimensions, with each person reporting both to a functional boss and to a product-line boss. This multiple reporting system quickly acquired the name of 'matrix system.' A few ambitious companies developed three-dimensional hierarchies, giving equal weight to function, product line and geography.

The logic behind these matrix systems was simple. People in these companies needed to pay attention to functional excellence, product line technology, and local market issues (geography), all at the same time. What better way to get them to pay attention to all these issues than to give them two (or three) different bosses who would each make sure that they paid attention to their own area.

More recently, companies have begun to fragment further. Task forces, development teams, customer focus teams, and other specialized bodies proliferate until the organization begins to look like a loose coalition of semi-independent groups, organized around a set of loosely related products, customers or technologies.

There is no widely accepted name for this project-based organization, but it has been widely described as a successor to the M-form. Labels which have been applied to it include 'heterarchy' (Hedlund and Rolander, 1990), 'N-form' (since N comes after M in the alphabet), and 'the Transnational' (Bartlett and Ghoshal, 1989). Project-based organizations are widely seen as more sensitive (to technological and market trends), more flexible, and more innovative than comparably sized functional or M-form organizations.

Number of levels and span of control Hierarchies have levels, or 'ranks' of people with roughly similar titles and similar levels or organizational status. It is common to count how many levels of hierarchy exist in an organization, from the CEO down to the lowest management levels (or even below). 'Flatter' organizations are thought to be more flexible, innovative and responsive than 'taller' organizations with many levels.

Managers in flat organizations tend to have wide spans of control. That is, they supervise a large number of people. This suggests that subordinates will have more freedom, since their superior will not have much time to look over their shoulder. But, at the same time, the superior will have little time to engage in extensive training or coaching. Nor will he have time to become intimately familiar with the subordinate's work. Thus, the impact on innovation of flattening a hierarchy may be ambiguous. More innovation may happen early on as the loosely controlled subordinates experiment more. But as the organization ages, innovation may decline as reduced middle-management resources make it difficult to invest in training and other forms of personnel development.

Managing performance

Communications paths: speed and effectiveness of response to new opportunities Besides the traditional dimensions of organization discussed above, there are a variety of more micro-level dimensions which managers can manipulate to improve innovation performance. One is the network of communications paths. I define a one-step communication path as an established and regularly used link for spoken, two-way communication between two people. A multistep communications path is an indirect link for spoken communication, that is, a link which passes through one or more intervening people (A communicates with C, whom he doesn't know, by talking to B, who passes the message on to C).

All organizations will have communications paths which run up and down the hierarchy and horizontally within work teams. Subordinates and bosses speak to each other now and then, as do team-mates. Thus, the network of communications paths is closely linked with the hierarchy and with the structure of day-to-day workgroups. But most organizations also have horizontal communications paths that cross subunit boundaries. These horizontal paths may be linked to special structures which have been set up to overlay the hierarchy, such as inter-unit coordinating committees. Or they may result from informal attempts to coordinate across units, affinity, or accident. The density of these inter-unit horizontal paths can vary enormously from one company to the next.

Why are communications paths important when one is trying to improve innovation performance? Two things matter about communications paths. One is their presence or absence. The other is their length (that is, how many steps it takes to get from A to B, and how long the process takes). Both of these factors impact the speed with which communication passes between two people, as well as the amount of distortion the message will incur in the process.

There are a number of key communications links for any innovation project. When an idea is new, the links between the person(s) generating the idea and funding sources will be key. When adapting a technology to a particular customer's need is important, then links between customers and technical functions will be key. When a new product is under development, links between technical functions, marketing and sales, and all the support functions will be key, since all these functions must work together to make an effective product design. Similarly, when several different units in a company serve the same customers, the links between them will be important to uncover any synergies.

Since innovation activities often involve communicating across these dimensions and others, the presence or absence of communications paths matters. If there is no way to communicate, the information won't be found, or the work won't get done. The length of the paths matters as well, since quick, distortion-free communication is far better than slow, distorted communication. Improving communication by shortening existing communications paths or developing new ones can speed up innovation processes and improve innovation performance.

The link between communication and organization has been studied extensively since the 1970s (see Allen, 1977). I will discuss it at much greater length in the section on communication and information management.

The point here is that changes in organization structure can affect patterns of communication in an organization, thus speeding up (or slowing down) communication and reducing (or increasing) distortion of the information and knowledge communicated. The link with innovation comes from the fact that an organization which communicates faster will respond to changes in technology and markets more quickly. Similarly, an organization which communicates with less distortion will respond to changes more effectively.

Matching units with tasks: efficiency, effectiveness and account-ability In an old-style functional organization, each organizational subunit was made up exclusively of people trained in the same function. Despite this, the organization would still have to perform some tasks which involved multiple functions. Developing a business plan is a task which crosses functional boundaries, as is developing a new product or service.

To get such tasks done, the traditional functional organization had to coordinate people who were housed in quite separate (and often distant) organizational units. These organizations often did not perform these tasks well, as stories from the automobile and pharmaceutical industries amply illustrate (Clark and Fujimoto, 1991).

Part of the problem was an absence of effective horizontal communication across the subunit boundaries. Clark and Fujimoto (1991) famously report how the traditional development system would involve development 'tossing the project over the wall' to manufacturing only when development had completely finished its work. Marketing might not hear about the new product until manufacturing had finished figuring out how to build it. The result was a very slow (and inefficient) product development process. Companies fixed this by gathering all design tasks into a new specialized structure, the high powered project team, where downstream functions could be involved much earlier, and communication could flow much more quickly.

But slowness was not the only problem of the traditional system. As Clark and Fujimoto (1991) pointed out, designing a car optimally involves making trade-offs between what is technically feasible, what is manufacturable, and what the customer will buy. When the functions did not work *together*, there was no means of making these trade-offs.

It was 'every function for itself', as each function designed the car (or the marketing program) which was optimal from its own parochial perspective. Companies improved the trade-off process greatly by setting up high powered project teams which put all the design tasks into the same organizational unit. This led to a far more explicit discussion of trade-offs, and to a far more effective design process.

Even this was not all. Under the old system, no one had overall responsibility for the project. There was no one who could be held accountable if the product failed. Marketing and manufacturing could say that the designs they were given were defective. Development could say that the design they sent on was hopelessly messed up by those working downstream. Each could point the finger at someone else, meaning that no one would learn or change their ways. A better match between task (designing the car) and organization was established by moving from functional silos to an integrated cross-functional team.

The point is that efficiency, effectiveness and accountability can all be improved by improving the fit between task and organization. This is easy when each person in the organization is involved in only one task. But it can be difficult to do when people are involved in multiple tasks or when they are involved in optimizing several things at the same time.

In the former case, people may simply become members of several project teams, reporting to several different project managers. In the latter case, matrix organizations may result. For example, in the automobile industry example, the members of a project team may be obligated not only to design the best car, but also to maintain a certain level of functional excellence. Their first boss, the project manager, will assure that they design the best car. Their second boss, the functional boss, will assure that they maintain functional excellence.

Cross-functional and cross-unit contact: stimulating ideas It is believed that bringing people who have different experiences and different types of training together will stimulate the generation of new ideas (Dougherty, 1992). The logic behind this idea is that talking with people who look at the world differently will force people to get out of their own frameworks and perhaps see the world in a new way. Seeing the world in a new way may give them new ideas.

I will discuss this principle in much greater detail in later sections on idea generation. Here I simply wish to make the point that organization structure can be used as a way of bringing people with different training/experience together. The functional organization segregated people by training. Cross-functional contact was, in effect, minimized. Dividing into business units sometimes improved things. In principle there was cross-functional contact at the top of each business unit. But the business units could, and often did, establish functional silos themselves.

Companies with matrices put each person in touch with several bosses, each with a different specialty. This increased the amount of contact with unfamiliar frameworks and ideas. But organizing large numbers of people into cross-functional teams went much farther, as each individual was forced to work with people from three or four different functions.

High placement of innovation specialists: increasing the power of those with innovation tasks Another organizational tool for managing innovation performance is to give people concerned with innovation a high rank. In the past ten years, some companies have established chief innovation officers. Putting someone whose title and job are innovation on the highest executive team does two things. It gives a signal to the entire organization that innovation is important. And it gives those concerned with innovation a powerful and high-placed advocate who can argue the case for changes that are needed to improve innovation performance.

Another, similar, tool is to manage where innovation projects themselves are placed in the hierarchy. A project manager who reports to the CEO will have far more power than a project manager who reports to a functional chief six levels down from the CEO. He is also likely to get a much quicker response to requests for funds or other resources. Not all project managers can report to CEOs, nor should the CEO be the only supervisor of a project, since he or she will have many other things to think about as well. But companies such as Eastman Chemical identify a few projects as being key to the entire future of the company.

These key projects may report to a business unit head or to an R&D chief. But, in addition, they have a dotted line report to the CEO. The CEO does two things for the projects. He makes sure both that they have access to all resources they need, and that the project team knows the whole company is behind them and wants them to succeed.

Special techniques for managing attention

Organizational tools may be used to manage performance directly, as in the examples cited above. But management tools can be used in a more subtle way, to direct people's attention to particular problems. Presumably, once they are aware of the problems and of their importance, they will then work to find innovative ways to solve these problems. Three examples follow.

Dedicated client/industry teams: focus on clients At the beginning of this book, I told the story of how the Industrial Chemicals division created industry teams to focus the attention of its sales and technical people on the problems of a few key industries. In an organization that wants its people to pay more attention to the needs of specific clients, this is a useful tool.

Dedicated teams can be set up to identify and deal with the problems of specific clients. The team may not have all the resources necessary to solve the problems identified. But it will be able to act as an advocate for the client within the organization. By acting as an advocate it can borrow resources from elsewhere in the organization and apply them to solve a client problem. Without the dedicated team as a 'detector' and 'amplifier,' the client's needs, and the means to solve them, might go unnoticed.

Cross-functional teams: paying attention to multiple needs I have discussed above the effect cross-functional contact has on generating ideas. In part this occurs because cross-functional teams force people to pay attention to multiple aspects of a client's operations and needs. They also force team members to pay attention to multiple aspects of their own company's operations. They cannot design a product without paying attention to its manufacturability, because there is a manufacturing representative on the team. They will find it difficult to design a product without talking with the customer about what he or she wants, since there is a marketing representative on the team.

Multiple bosses: paying attention to multiple needs Another, similar way to force people to pay attention to multiple needs is to give them multiple bosses, each concerned with one aspect of a multifaceted problem. The traditional organization practiced 'unity of command,' with each person having one boss. Matrix management led to people having two or three bosses. In one innovative company, ConsumerCo, this trend goes much further. People in marketing, manufacturing or product management commonly have three or more bosses. Organization charts are so complicated that people rarely bother to draw them.

ConsumerCo takes the logic of the matrix, that people will pay attention to things their bosses are concerned with, to an extreme. People in complex roles, like product management, have many bosses. Some of these bosses supervise them on different projects. Some have functional concerns. Others are specialists in different customer groups. Some people at ConsumerCo say they have as many as six bosses. Together, an individual's many bosses make sure that they pay attention to all the important facets of their work.

Special structures for special needs

Not all organizational change methods involve changing the overall characteristics of the organization. Some innovation problems can best be solved by setting up special structures, or by developing special methods of changing structures. I will give two examples.

Structures for managing centralized competences In some organizations, a handful of people hold a competence which is needed in a number of different places within the organization. The people holding the competence may not be numerous enough to assign one to each group that needs the competence. As a result, an individual's competence may need to be shared across a large number of units.

Companies use several different methods to share competences. First of all, such widely useful competences are usually held in a central laboratory or some other centrally-controlled organization. The point of holding them centrally is so that they will be accessible to all the units that need them. They should not be 'captured' and 'monopolized' by any one unit. Several means of allocating them out can be used.

First, they may be asked, simply, to respond to any request for help which comes their way. This works as long as the number of requests does not exceed their capacity to deal with them. When they become capacity constrained, some means of allocating their time will be needed. At that point, some companies begin to price their time. This is the second solution: time allocation through a market mechanism. This works when the project teams and others who need their time have budgets that they can spend, when needed, on special resources.

Providing growth paths for new businesses Another problem which demands special treatment is that of developing a growth path for project teams which become new businesses. The transition from project to business can be a difficult one (Dunn, 1977; Argyris and Schon, 1978; Leonard-Barton, 1988). Project teams typically lack at least some of the resources needed by a business unit. It may be a long time before they develop sufficient revenues to be recognized formally as business units within a company's governance system (Burgelman, 1983). But, if a company is to innovate successfully, some means must be found for project teams to evolve into business units.

As in so many other areas, 3M has found a solution to this problem. Most 3M divisions are mixtures of new business units and older business units which are exploiting existing products. When a project team is close to putting its product on the market, it will be set up as a shadow business unit. It will normally be part of an existing business unit, and will share some of the resources (finance, accounting, and so on) of the parent business unit. As it begins to build revenues, it will gradually separate itself from its parent, eventually becoming a full-fledged business unit on its own. It may retain a link to the parent. It may, in fact, be a formal subsidiary of the parent. But it will have all the necessary personnel and resources to conduct business on its own.

ConsumerCo similarly has developed means of handling this transition. At ConsumerCo it is common for a new product to be handled entirely by an existing business unit. Radical new technologies may also be handled by an existing business unit. I asked a laboratory worker at ConsumerCo if this caused any special problems. Didn't people resist the introduction of new technologies or new products into an older business unit? Didn't people prefer to protect their own, older products, rather than working to build new ones?

His answer was revealing. There were so many innovations in existing products at ConsumerCo that running a new product through the system hardly made any difference. People were so habituated to dealing with change and newness that the whole idea of resisting change was utterly foreign. When people dealt with changes in existing products every day, introducing an entirely new product or technology was viewed as an interesting variation on the daily routine. In such a situation, anyone who resisted change would find their status in the organization falling precipitously.

With people adapting so easily to change, a new product typically begins its life as part of an existing business unit. When the product's sales became significant, it may be moved into a new business unit, taking some people with it from the business unit which gave it birth.

Changing an organization

As the examples discussed here reveal, many means of improving innovation performance involve changing organization structure. But the process of changing an organization has short-term costs. People will be distracted from innovation-related tasks for a period of time while they learn their new jobs and new relationships. The problem is obvious to anyone who has been part of a reorganization. What I am concerned with here is not the problem, which is obvious, but the solution, which is not.

Part of the genius behind what happens at 3M and ConsumerCo is that organizational change is gradual. At 3M, the project team gradually becomes a business unit. None of the change is precipitous. People's jobs change slowly as they are gradually released from their jobs in the old business unit and they gradually spend more time with the new product.

Organizational development at ConsumerCo is similar. When the new product is introduced, there is no organizational change. The product is simply inserted into an existing business unit. Only when the product is established will a new business unit be built around it. And then, when that business unit is established, it will consist largely of people who have already been working with the new product. They will continue doing their old job, but within a new organizational unit. So, none of the individuals involved have to deal with very much change.

Decision territories: distributing power to make key decisions

Up to this point, I have talked about only one type of power, the power embedded in hierarchy, that is, the power bosses have over subordinates. But power is evident in many other aspects of organization. Who has responsibility to make decisions about specific clients? Who has power over making decisions about specific products? Who has power over the design of the organization structure itself? In more colloquial words, in whose 'territory' does each of these decisions lie?

The issue of territories is more complicated than it looks. Power over a territory can exist at several hierarchical levels. And organizations do not necessarily give clear responsibility for territories. If fact, I will discuss five different aspects of decision territories in this section: hierarchical location of power, exclusive versus overlapping areas of power, use of multiple teams to solve a single problem, fixed responsibilities versus vague boundaries, responsibility for outcomes versus power over inputs, and control of critical resources.

Hierarchical location of power Decentralization is a word that has appeared quite often in the business press in the last decade. In its colloquial use, it means 'pushing decision-making power down into smaller units of a large company'.

The theory behind decentralization is that people in the smaller units will be more up to date on the key technical and market issues in their business areas. They are 'closer to the action'. Therefore they will be better informed on the key issues, and better able to make key decisions.

Put so baldly, the logic of decentralization is so compelling that we may wonder why any senior management team would retain power centrally. There are, in fact, good reasons why a senior management team would retain some control over operational decisions. For instance, in some companies, key investment decisions involve betting the company's entire capital, or at least a large fraction of it. Developing a new motor vehicle, a new pharmaceutical product, a new computer chip: these are all very expensive propositions. It is reasonable that a company's senior management would be involved in these decisions.

In single business companies it is equally logical to retain power centrally. Only the senior management team will be in a position to obtain all the information necessary to make key decisions. All the people below them are likely to be functional specialists with fragmented views of the business.

It is in multi-business companies that the logic of decentralization is most compelling. In most multi-business companies, many investment decisions are made which do not involve betting the company.

Many small product development decisions will be made. Many product adaptations may occur which do not involve significant investments of corporate capital. In these cases, the logic of decentralization becomes compelling.

If the logic is so compelling, why, then, do corporate management teams sometimes retain power over decisions they don't really need to control? There are several answers. One is inertia. Some multi-business companies are former one-business companies that grew up quickly. In cases like this, the senior management team may be the same team that once controlled a single business. The team may never have lost the habit of controlling the details.

A second reason may be lack of trust. Some company cultures are control-based. The assumption behind the management system is that people cannot be trusted. If they are given too much freedom, they will feather their own nests or do other things that do not benefit the company. A senior management team that does not trust its subordinates will monitor all the decisions they make, no matter how much this slows up or distorts the decision-making process (Ghoshal and Bartlett, 1998, give some examples of this).

A third reason may be desire for power. Some people like to have power over others. Such people will maintain power over key decisions, even if others could make them better. A variation of this (the fourth reason) is the desire to stay involved. Most senior managers were once operating managers themselves. They may have enjoyed making operating decisions. So they keep on making them. They stay involved in operations whether their involvement is useful or not.

For all these reasons, corporate managers in a diversified company may retain more power over operating decisions than they really should, given their role. In such companies, innovation decision-making may be improved if the decisions are pushed down to a lower level. But decentralization is tricky. The central management team may announce a decentralization without actually withdrawing from the decisions. They may 'investigate and intervene' so often that the formal decentralization may, in fact, be a fiction. The desire to decentralize must be followed by a change in behavior (or a change in personnel at the top) which allows junior level managers to take effective control of the decisions which are being delegated to them.

This implies, of course, that junior level managers are ready to take more responsibility. This is not always the case. Some people don't like having responsibility. They are quite happy if their superiors make decisions for them. They wouldn't have it any other way. Others are more willing to take responsibility, but they adapt to a situation where their superiors don't want them to. They become habituated to letting their superiors make decisions for them. In centralized companies, many junior managers may fit one of these two profiles. They may adapt with difficulty to a decentralization imposed from the top. In such cases, decentralization may have to be accompanied by retraining and/or replacement of numerous junior managers.

In the ideal case, both junior and senior management may decide at roughly the same time that decentralization is necessary. This happened at Lawn & Garden, an agrochemical company which was one of the primary sites. Lawn & Garden had suffered a severe blow to its pride. A new product that management had thought would be a best seller had failed, by an unprecedented margin, to meet sales projections. The reason for the failure was a series of bad decisions by top management. The company's executive committee had, in effect, taken control of the project, making decisions on price, distribution channels, and product configuration. These decisions had turned out badly and the product launch failed to meet expectations.

The lesson the whole company drew from this experience was the value of decentralization. Top management readily admitted that it should not have taken control of the project. They resolved to not let such a thing happen again. The entire management team took a look at its procedures, structures and practices and redesigned the system. The result was a new system which devolved much more power to junior levels. No one resisted implementation, since everyone could see that it was necessary, and all management levels had been involved in planning the new system.

Exclusive versus overlapping areas of power Everyone has heard about decentralization. But few people have heard of other dimensions of variation in the ways companies allocate power. One is the extent to which people's areas of responsibility overlap.

Americans and others sometimes make the assumption that the best system involves 'unitary command' or, in my terminology, exclusive decision territories. According to this logic, to avoid conflicts and encourage efficiency, each decision should be clearly the responsibility of one and only one person.

The problem with this logic is that it ignores factors like the value of bringing multiple viewpoints to bear on a decision. A person who is solely responsible for a decision may, of course, ask other people for information and advice. But nothing obliges him to. Nothing forces him to communicate with anyone about the decision at all. In such a situation, some managers will make decisions without consulting anyone at all, or only by consulting those who will agree with their own viewpoints.

Contrast that with a situation where two people are jointly responsible for a decision. Their decision territories overlap, and for some decisions they must agree. These people will be forced to communicate, for the decision will not be made if they don't. If they have different viewpoints, so much the better. They will have to discuss their different viewpoints and come up with a way of making a decision that satisfies them both.

The reader may object. But won't they just avoid making a decision? Or won't they find some way of avoiding their underlying differences and making a decision that just smooths them over? Indeed this could happen. But in ConsumerCo and FinCo (an American financial services company), both of which practiced overlapping territories, decisions were made anyway. Both companies had mechanisms that encouraged people to surface differences rather than hiding them. At ConsumerCo there was a rule that no one could ever agree 100 percent with anyone. 100 percent agreement was not considered to be credible. ConsumerCo valued differences of opinion and senior managers were not shy about saying so. At FinCo, managers welcomed multiple propositions for solving any problem. At both companies, people were told to find ways to work out their differences. They were not allowed to avoid problems or to pass them up the hierarchy for resolution elsewhere.

Multiple teams to solve the same problem While most companies and most managers believe that work shouldn't be duplicated, some good companies disagree. ConsumerCo frequently gives the same problem to two different teams. The teams will be urged to try somewhat different solutions to the problem, but otherwise their assignments will be the same. They are free to explore any solutions they want, and ConsumerCo is willing to accept that some work will be duplicated.

What ConsumerCo gets out of this duplication of effort is more variation. Pairs of teams rarely come up with the same solution. In addition, the knowledge that another team is working on the same problem spurs each team on to greater effort. Neither team wants to be embarrassed by the other, so each will work as hard as they can to find the best solution.

Fixed responsibilities versus vague boundaries Whether people's responsibilities are exclusive or overlap is one issue. Another issue is whether the boundaries of a manager's territory are fixed or whether the manager can attempt to move them at will.

In many companies, such boundaries are, in principle, fixed. The CEO allocates areas of responsibility to subordinates, who in turn allocate areas of responsibility to their subordinates, and so on down to the lowest levels of the organization. An individual's allocations of power and responsibility are presumed to be fixed until they are changed by a superior officer. In such an organization, attempts to enlarge one's area of responsibility by any means other than the official route are often considered to be inappropriate 'political' activity.

This type of organization is relatively easy to live in. One knows what one is responsible for and who else is involved in a decision, if anyone. But, if someone is not doing their job effectively, the process of giving the responsibility to someone else can be a cumbersome one. First, the person observing the problem will have to discuss the situation with the individual's boss. If the boss agrees that there is a problem, he will then have to devise a way of reallocating power. Or he will have to find someone else who can do the job. Similarly, if a new opportunity comes up, delays in addressing it may occur as people discuss whose responsibility it should be.

ConsumerCo is quite different. At ConsumerCo, no one's job has fixed boundaries. People are free to try to expand their responsibilities if they wish. They can also shed responsibilities, as long as someone else is there to pick up what they no longer want to do. This leads in some cases to open competition for responsibilities. A manager can challenge another manager's right to do something if he thinks he can do it better.

While this more fluid and unstable system is harder for some people to live with, it has some clear positive aspects. If someone is not performing a key responsibility, someone who notices this can simply take over, rather than waiting for approval from above. Delays in correcting the problem are likely to be less. And, if someone notices a new opportunity opening up, he can simply address it, without waiting to be given official responsibility.

Responsibility for outcomes versus power over inputs There is an important difference between being responsible for an outcome and having power over inputs. The two do not always go together. A project manager may have responsibility for the success (outcome) of his project without having power over all the inputs.

At Industrial Chemicals, George Marsh had, at best, minimal power to obtain resources (inputs) during the first four years of his project. He could ask for resources and negotiate with those who held resources without having any means of assuring that he would get the resources he needed. Even when he received a large and stable budget, he was not able to obtain all the resources he needed in house, since some key resources were already committed elsewhere.

By contrast, a function head in a matrix-managed company, such as an automobile company, has power over inputs without having direct responsibility for outcomes. Project managers, who have responsibility for results, must negotiate with him for resources. Even when the project managers have budgets, and are, in theory, able to command resources, the function head may still choose to cooperate or not. He or she may allocate resources when they are needed, or allocate them late. He or she may have enough resources for some projects while being short on others. He or she may pick the best people, or the worst, in grade for any given project.

The better innovators try to match power over inputs with responsibility for results. They try to assure that project managers obtain the resources they need when they need them. They do this through a number of means, including:

- Giving project managers budgets
- Making functional areas (the sources of resources) dependent on projects for their budgets
- Allowing project managers to hire help from the outside
- Making sure abundant resources are available.

Control of critical resources In many innovation projects, a few resources, often technical resources, are key to the outcome of the project. In companies with many innovation projects, there may be a few key resources, often technical resources, which are key to many projects. For instance, at a pharmaceutical company, certain key skills in biology, biochemistry and chemistry are key in all projects. But even at a more diversified company like 3M, a few technologies, like adhesive technology, are key to many projects.

When key resources are shared by many projects, who controls them can become an issue. The resource may be plentiful. Many people understand adhesive technology at 3M, for instance. In this case, the resource may be distributed out into business unit laboratories, as needed, rather than being kept in central laboratories. In that situation, any innovation project will have easy access to the resource, even if it is located in a business unit far removed from any central lab. The business unit will be able to respond quickly to customer requests for change, since it controls the resource locally. When the resource is less plentiful, then it may have to be controlled from the center, and the company will have to find some way of allocating it out to those who need it. I have discussed a variety of methods for doing this above, in the section on *Structures for managing centralized competences*.

Whether a laboratory and the competences in it should be controlled by corporate headquarters or by business units depends on the time horizon of the work done by the lab. If they are doing long-term fundamental research which has no impact on the company's current activities, it is better to hold the competence centrally, where the laboratory can be protected from the fluctuations of individual businesses. But if one business unit uses the laboratory for its current innovation work, it may be better for that business unit to control the lab. If several business units use the lab, the company may divide the lab's resources between them. Or it may ensure via budgets or other means that both have easy access to it. (See Table 4.2 for a summary of key issues related to organization structure.)

Communications systems and information management

The second set of tools which affect structure and/or process relate to the communications system and to the related issue of how information is managed within the organization. In this section I will first look at the general issue of the structure of internal communications systems. Then I will look at other aspects of internal communications, in particular common language (since communication is impossible without it), search for information and knowledge, the communication of complex technical information, and the management of internal publicity in relation to innovation. Then I will turn to communication with the external world to discuss how this important aspect of communication can be managed to improve innovation performance.

Table 4.2   Organization structure and its impact

Aspect of organization structure	Tool or variable . . . . . Impact	

Hierarchy	■ Hierarchical forms:
	  – Functional
	  – Product focused
	  – Geography focused
	  – Matrix
	■ Number of levels and span of control:
	  – Many levels, narrow span of control
	  – Few levels, wide span of control
		■ Focuses attention on:
		  – Functional excellence
		  – Product/market concerns
		  – Geography concerns
		  – Multiple concerns
		■ Amount of control, also amount of coaching possible:
		  – Tighter control, more time for coaching
		  – Less control, more flexibility, but less time for coaching

Managing performance	■ Density, length of communications paths ■ Good matching between unit boundaries and tasks ■ Cross-functional and cross-unit contact ■ High placement of innovation specialists	■ Speed and effectiveness of response to new opportunities ■ Efficiency, effectiveness, accountability ■ Stimulates idea generation and more effective development ■ Gives greater prominence, priority to innovation
Managing attention	■ Dedicated client/industry teams ■ Cross-functional teams ■ Multiple bosses	■ Focus on clients ■ Pay attention to multiple needs and perspectives ■ Pay attention to multiple needs and perspectives
Special structures for special needs	■ Structures for managing centralized competences ■ Providing growth paths within the organization for new businesses	■ Rare but key competences used by all that need them ■ Facilitates transition from project to business unit
Changing an organization	■ Provide means of gradual change, transition (people's jobs and status change slowly)	■ Facilitates change

(cont'd)

Table 4.2 (cont'd)

Aspect of organization structure	Tool or variable . . . . . Impact	
Decision territories: distributing power	■ Hierarchical location of power:	■ Affects flexibility, focus:
	– Centralized at top	– High focus, less flexibility, reactivity
	– Decentralized, dispersed to bottom	– Easier to diversify, try new things, more reactive, but less focused
	■ Exclusive versus overlapping areas of power	■ Overlap assures multiple viewpoints will be considered, reduced chance that something will be missed
	■ Multiple teams to solve the same problem	■ Increases variation, chance of finding good solution
	■ Fixed responsibilities versus vague boundaries	■ Vague boundaries allow for quick adjustment in case of change in responsibilities or failure to take responsibility
	■ Responsibility for outcomes matched with power over inputs	■ Assures that innovators will have the power to advance their projects
	■ Critical resources controlled in a way to allow sharing	■ Facilitates use by many projects

After discussing communication at some length, I will then turn to the related subject of information management. Here I will focus first on the types of information which flow through a communication system and how they can be formatted. I will then discuss the types of information which can usefully be gathered from outside the organization, and particularly from customers. (See Table 4.3 for a list of key questions on communications systems.)

Table 4.3   Questions to ask about communications systems

Internal communication
■ Is there rich communication across internal boundaries, such as functional, product line, and geographic boundaries?
■ Do we have effective internal networks in areas where communication needs to occur frequently?
■ Is it easy to create new communications links when they are needed?
■ Are people encouraged/required to communicate when others need their information or knowledge?
■ Can we effectively transfer information and technical knowledge when we need to?
External communication
■ Is there in depth communication with customers and other key outsiders?
■ Do we collect all the information we need from the outside?
Encouraging communication
■ Do we use all the appropriate tools to encourage the communication we need?

Internal communications structure

Vertical links to innovation projects The questions here are: how far down in the organization do you have to go to find someone who is knowledgeable about the organization's innovation programs? Is the top team aware of the company's innovation initiatives? Are they knowledgeable about them, or involved in them? The more tightly linked they are to the process, the more people will believe that innovation is a high corporate priority. And the more readily problems can be fixed and new opportunities addressed.

Senior managers can link themselves into the innovation process by setting up a reporting system which reaches their level. They can make vertical communication, about specific projects or about the progress of the system as a whole, obligatory. But vertical links are not just about senior management. The life of any project can be significantly affected by who it reports to. A project that uses a business unit's resources will often report to the head of that business unit. But a project team may use resources from several business units, marketing competences from one and technical competences from another, for instance. In such situations, the question of who the project should report to can become deeply political, with both business unit heads wanting to claim the project, if it is successful, and both wanting to disclaim it if it is not successful. The best thing for the project would be for both business unit heads to be informed about the project and to give whatever help and insight they could, regardless of who formally supervised the project. In most such situations, supervision can be shared.

Horizontal links Members of a department or team who are in daily contact with each other will normally communicate quite a lot. But not everyone who contributes to an innovation idea will be on the same team. Communication across team boundaries may be key to the generation of the idea, to its funding, and to its development. As a result, companies with dense networks of horizontal communications tend to be better innovators than companies which communicate less (Allen, 1977; Nohria and Ghoshal, 1997, Chapter 4).

Horizontal links may cut across functional boundaries, business unit or product line boundaries, geographic boundaries, or any other boundaries within the organization. Even within a single lab, there may be boundaries between different technical specialties within the lab. Entire books have been written about the importance of communicating across these boundaries (Allen, 1977; Ashkenas *et al.*, 1995).

As the point has been covered in detail elsewhere, I will not belabor it here. I will only note some of the reasons why horizontal communication is key. At the idea generation stage, a high level of horizontal communication is likely to stimulate more idea generation. For the more horizontal communication there is, the more often people with different bodies of knowledge and different ways of thinking will talk with each other. At 3M, Spence Silver invented a weak adhesive. Years later Art Fry wanted a sticky-but-removable bookmark. The two men were not in the same department. Had 3M not had a rich network of horizontal communication, they might never have talked to each other and the Post-It® Note might never have been invented.

At the next stage, initial funding, horizontal communication can be key as well. Some funding requests go straight up, to the boss of whoever generated the idea. But the boss may not be able or willing to give funding. In that case, the idea's champion may have to look for funding elsewhere. How quickly he finds funding will be determined, in part, by how quick and how direct the communications paths to other funding sources are. Does he have to make a formal request for funds, a request which is then passed through several hands and ultimately reviewed by a faceless committee? Or can he simply walk up to someone who has funds and ask if he can use some?

During development, a project team may frequently need information or knowledge from other people within the company. In such cases, the length of communications paths between the project and the information/knowledge source can make a difference to the speed of the transaction and the ultimate success of the team. Teams with close links to sources of all the information and knowledge they need are likely to succeed more quickly and more often than teams without such links (Allen, 1977).

Length of key links: speed and distortion When an innovation process involves communication, and all do, the length of key communications paths can have an important impact on the project's outcome. The key communications paths include those frequently used by the team, plus those which play a role at crucial moments in the project's history.

The length of these paths can have an important impact on the project's outcome for two reasons. First, the longer the communications paths, the slower communication will flow, and the slower the project will proceed. If a regularly used communication path works slowly, the whole project will move slowly. If a little used, but crucial communications path (for example, the path to a funding source) works slowly, then the project may find that its progress is blocked at crucial moments, while the team waits for an answer to a key request.

Second, a message which passes through a longer path, which by definition involves more intervening people, is likely to suffer from more distortion. The more distortion of key messages which occurs, the more likely the product will not fit the market it is designed to serve.

Key links which matter all the time include links between customers and the technical people who design the product, or links between the project team and key technical resources which are housed at some distance from the team. Key links which function at crucial points only, but which may cause considerable delays, include links to funding sources or, in some organizations, links between design and manufacturing.

Means of facilitating direct contacts between functions

In many organizations, contacts between functions are among the most difficult to forge. In part this is because functions in many companies are organizationally and physically separated. But there are also more fundamental reasons. Product managers share a common vocabulary and common values, even if they manage different products and different businesses. But technical managers and marketing managers often have quite different vocabularies and, worse, quite different values. Even if they work on the same product, they may not be able to communicate with each other without a translator (that is, someone who understands the language and values of both functions).

Since it is particularly difficult to establish communication across functional boundaries, companies have developed a variety of means of encouraging this kind of communication. I will discuss six here: liaison functions, key customer account teams, other cross-functional teams, co-location, other mandated contact, and building a common language.

Establishing a liaison function ConsumerCo long ago recognized the difficulty of maintaining communication between technical and marketing people. One of ConsumerCo's solutions to the problem is to find technically trained people who are willing and able to learn marketers' language (or, less commonly, the reverse), and to use these multifunctional people as liaison people between technical and marketing teams.

These liaison people talk extensively with marketers about their ideas for a product. When the marketers' ideas are only half-formed, as they often are, the liaison person may talk with them at length to get an idea of what the key features of the new idea are. The liaison people may sometimes reject ideas as technically unfeasible or undesirable. But mostly they organize them and translate them into technical language. They then discuss them with the relevant technical functions.

The value of their work comes not only from the translation, but also from the fact that they are able to take a long, unorganized wish list from marketing and turn it into an organized, prioritized agenda. It is ConsumerCo's view that its laboratory people would often have difficulty understanding marketing's requests without a translator.

They would certainly have difficulty organizing and prioritizing marketing's requests without the help of a translator. As a result, the translator/liaison function saves laboratory people (and sometimes marketing) considerable time.

Key customer account teams Many companies, including 3M, Industrial Chemicals, and others, have established key customer account teams. Part of the reason for establishing such teams is to force people from different functions to talk to each other so they can more effectively and quickly solve the needs of a specific client. This also serves to focus the attention of representatives from each key function on the client's needs.

Co-location People who sit next to each other communicate much more often than people who sit on different floors of a large building. The latter, in turn, communicate much more than people in different buildings (Allen, 1977). The managerial implications of this are as the follows: if you want to increase communication, have people sit together.

Many companies require project teams to sit together. They do this to encourage people on the team to talk to each other more. At 3M, co-location is a deliberate policy for team building. Young people are, early in their careers, assigned to work on a cross-functional team. They learn to communicate and work with members of other functions by sitting with them and working with them for months at a time. They work more closely with their peers on the team than they do with their functional colleagues. The team has a clear and often client-focused purpose. There is a clear cause and effect relationship between the outcome of the team's work, the individuals' personal success, and the company's financial health. People find this a sufficient motivation to learn to work with their peers.

At Eastman Chemical, people often have several bosses and several sets of responsibilities. One way Eastman encourages people to pay attention to several sets of responsibilities is to use both hierarchical links and co-location. A person's primary boss is usually his functional boss. The company assumes that the person will always pay attention to functional concerns, since it is his functional boss who will follow him through large parts of his career. Since that link is presumed secure, co-location is used to secure other links. If a person must work with people from another function routinely, he will be co-located with those people, not with his boss. The company believes that co-location will assure that he will pay attention to the needs of people from outside his function.

Other mandated contact ConsumerCo does not have cross-functional teams in its core businesses. Nor does it practice co-location. Nonetheless it has very effective cross-functional coordination, as evidenced by its enviable innovation record. One key way it achieves this is by mandatory contact. Mandatory contact is of two types. One involves bi-weekly, or sometimes monthly, meetings between all parties involved in managing a particular product. At these meetings all opportunities and threats are discussed. Each function can discuss its concerns and its ideas at length. All functions are expected to understand the concerns and ideas of each of the other functions. The meetings occur as often as necessary to obtain and preserve this level of understanding.

The second type of mandatory contact is with customers. Any person in a management position, and anyone in marketing, must spend a minimum of one day per month on a sales route, talking to customers. This gives managers and marketers at all levels a common base of experience in talking about what customers want. It also limits the risk that managers will lose touch with the marketplace.

Cross-functional work teams I have talked about cross-functional teams in the context of innovation projects. But these are not the only situations in which cross-functional teams can be used. Many tasks, from order handling to the design of marketing materials, can be handled by cross-functional teams. By creating such teams, managers force people to communicate and work together across functional boundaries, increasing the number of people within the company who will be skilled at cross-functional work.

Specialized innovation networks

Another approach to facilitating communication across a large company is to set up a network dedicated to communication about innovation. Specific people can be designated 'innovation contacts', 'innovation officers', or whatever. These people will be expected to act as key nodes in a network of communication about innovation.

In companies that have this kind of network, people at the nodes have two roles. First, they publicize the fact that the company needs to innovate, and that management is interested in hearing about innovation ideas. Second, they act as receptors, or listeners, to people with innovative ideas. People with ideas are encouraged to talk to their bosses first.

But if they aren't satisfied with the response, they can come to the innovation officers, who will give their idea a second hearing. The innovation officers often have special funds which they can allocate to projects which haven't found funds through normal channels.

I found two examples of this type of dedicated network in organizations which had been run as tight patriarchies. One was a military organization, the Ministry of Defense of a large European state. The traditional rule in most military organizations is that a person's immediate superior has the last word on any decision. This was the case in the Ministry of Defense. But several key senior officers in the ministry became convinced that more innovation was needed in their military than could be provided by a rigid hierarchical system.

They did not want to give up the hierarchy, so they set up a special 'innovation bureau' which was charged with two jobs. It was given a budget to publicize the need for innovation. Everyone in the ministry and in the armed services of the country was to hear, each year, that innovation and new ideas were needed. At the same time, the innovation bureau served as an alternative to the normal hierarchy. If someone in the military had an idea that their hierarchical superior refused, they could bring it to the innovation office. The innovation office had a small budget to fund ideas that it found worthy.

A large chemical company in the same country set up a similar innovation office. This company, while not a military organization, was very hierarchical, nonetheless. The traditional rule in this organization, like in the military, was that the boss had the last word. If someone brought an idea to their boss, and the boss refused it, that was the end in most cases. Senior managers told me that few people had the courage to go around their boss. This was viewed as a serious breach of the hierarchy. As a result, they believed, many good ideas simply got 'put in a drawer' because the boss was unsympathetic at the first hearing.

This company built an innovation network much like that in the Ministry of Defense. Senior management created an 'innovation office,' which reported directly to corporate headquarters. 'Innovation officers' were appointed throughout the company. The rule was that there should be one full time innovation officer for each 1000 people in the company. These innovation officers publicized the need for new ideas, and they asked people to come to them with new ideas when their bosses refused them. Every attempt was made to eliminate any penalties for 'going around the boss' with an innovative idea.

Summary of methods of altering internal communications structure

Communication structure can be improved in several ways. Communications paths can be shortened to increase speed and reduce distortion. This will help assure that products arrive on the market quickly and that they fit real customer needs when they arrive. Direct horizontal links can be set up between functions or other groups by a variety of means. Such links improve the organization's ability to coordinate innovation activity across functions or other groups. Finally, some organizations set up dedicated networks to facilitate communication about innovation. These networks assure that all people within the company hear that innovation is important. They also can act as 'eyes and ears' for new innovation ideas. Often they have the resources to fund innovation ideas that have not found funding through normal channels.

Other aspects of internal communication

Up to this point, I have focused on tools that affect the overall structure of communication within the company. Now I will look at tools that serve a more specialized purpose. Inter-functional communication cannot occur without a common language, so building a common language is often a high priority. Similarly, people with ideas often need help. They sometimes have to find others within their company who have technical knowledge that they need. Companies that facilitate this search for help tend to be more innovative.

Such searches can reach dead ends if people refuse to communicate. Communication between units can be blocked if there are incentives to hoard information. Managers at the most innovative companies are careful to ensure that there are incentives to communicate, not to hoard information. Finally, many companies use their internal communications system to publicize their commitment to innovation. Such communications serve as a lesson to employees on how they should act. I will deal with each of these five specialized topics in turn.

Common language In the section on cross-functional communication, I alluded to the fact that people need a common language to communicate across functional boundaries. The languages and values of people in production and people in marketing are different enough that communication does not flow easily between these two functions. To innovate effectively, organizations need to have some people who are willing and able to communicate across functional boundaries. To do this, they need people who speak the languages of several functions.

Companies can encourage such multilingualism. The way to do it is to encourage people to learn a common, multifunctional language. There are several ways to do this. 3M places people, early in their careers, on cross-functional teams. They are forced, by the conditions of their job, to speak regularly with peers from other functions. ConsumerCo puts its promising junior managers through a ten-week, multidisciplinary management training school. At the school, they learn the languages and principles of any functions they weren't already familiar with. They also work closely with people from other functions for the entire ten weeks. By the end of the ten weeks, they have learned a common, multifunctional language.

Other ways to encourage the development of a common language include the following. Many technology based companies hire large numbers of people with a common base of technical training. Marketing and other nontechnical functions in such companies are often populated with people whose original training was technical. With this common base of training, communication flows relatively easily. Another method is to rotate people through functions over the course of a career. A person may start his career in a technical function, but after a three-year rotation in marketing, he will know marketing as well as his original home function. In addition to its ten-week training program, ConsumerCo rotates people through functions, meaning that any middle- or senior-level manager will have worked in at least two (or even three) functions in the course of his career.

In the absence of a common language, there are other ways to encourage communication. I've already mentioned that ConsumerCo uses liaison people to help facilitate communication between marketing, sales, and technical functions. These liaison people speak the languages of several functions. They are, among other things, translators who convert the esoteric language of each discipline into something understandable to the other discipline.

Searching for information and knowledge An important function of a communications system is to facilitate the search for new information and knowledge. I am not here referring to knowledge that is entirely new to the company. Rather, I am referring to the fact that people in large companies often have to search for information and knowledge which is, or might be, held by someone else in the same company. How, when there are 5000 technical people, do you find the technical knowledge you want? How, when there are 5000 marketers, do you find the information you need about a specific market? Companies such as 3M have developed methods of dealing with this problem.

At 3M, a dense network of communications pathways and personal links exists across the company's many laboratories. Senior technical managers try to keep track of the work junior people in their laboratories are doing. At the same time, they know other senior technical managers. They take an interest in what is going on in each other's laboratories. As a result, they are quite knowledgeable about technical activity throughout the company.

In addition, there are many horizontal technical networks at lower levels in 3M. People in a technical specialty meet with each other several times each year. One of these meetings is likely to be a 'science fair' at which people will show off their work.

As a result, when someone at 3M needs information on some technology, he can go to any senior technical manager and ask for ideas about who he could talk to. If the technology is studied anywhere within 3M, the senior manager will be very likely to have heard about it. He won't necessarily know who exactly is doing it, but he can probably direct the inquirer to another laboratory manager who will know more. By following this chain of references, the inquirer will soon find the experts he needs.

Sometimes it isn't necessary to go to a senior manager. Sometimes people at lower levels have enough horizontal contacts to help the inquirer as well.

What happens during a search process is that a new communications link is formed. Some companies, like 3M, encourage and facilitate the formation of new communications links. Others, like Industrial Chemicals in the 1980s, discourage communication outside the hierarchy and thus block the formation of new communications links. Since innovation often involves forming new links, companies that facilitate this will be more innovative than companies that don't.

Incentives to communicate For communication between different units to be successful, people have to be willing to communicate. In some companies, like Industrial Chemicals, this is not the case. People are discouraged from communicating outside their workgroup by bosses who view knowledge as power. In such a culture, no information or knowledge is to be given up unless clear and equivalent compensation is received. Since this is rarely possible, inter-unit communication never gets a chance to start. The only exceptions are in the case of personal relationships. One might share information with a friend, because a friend will reciprocate. But strangers are not to be trusted, even when they work at the same company you do. Since most people from other units are strangers, little inter-unit communication occurs.

ConsumerCo and 3M present an opposite culture. In both companies the rule is that technical information is to be shared with anyone within the company who needs it. This is a rule. It is a rule that is frequently repeated in both companies. Anyone breaking this rule would be breaking a fundamental rule of the culture. The rule of communication is so fundamental that anyone breaking it would be warned not to continue this behavior. One ConsumerCo manager told me that if someone persistently refused to communicate with others who needed his help, he would risk being thrown out of the company.

ConsumerCo and 3M have strong cultural norms to communicate. In effect, these companies have incentives in place which support communication. Industrial Chemicals had the opposite incentives. Communicating with strangers was viewed as dangerous and anyone who shared technical information without authorization risked punishment by bosses who did not want to share information without compensation.

For an effective inter-unit communications system to exist, incentives must be in place to support it. These incentives are not necessarily monetary. They involve rules of behavior which may be explicit or implicit. If the rules are broken, the person will be warned. Their status in the eyes of their boss, will diminish. As long as the person changes behavior, there will be no further penalty.

Communicating complex technical knowledge Suppose you are employed by one of the more innovative companies. Suppose further that you have a problem. Your team needs technical knowledge that someone else in your company has. The problem is that the person who has the knowledge is on the other side of the world. There is no conceivable way that you can learn everything you need to learn from them over the phone. Trying to do it by e-mail would be even worse. What do you do?

Companies like 3M use the obvious solution. They move you to the laboratory that has the information. You will be able to stay there for six months or more, as long as is needed for you to absorb the information and knowledge your team needs. In some cases, the person who has the information may come to you. But normally the best place for the learning to occur is in the home laboratory of the person who has the knowledge. There she has all her equipment, her colleagues, and the records of her past work. There you can absorb much tacit, as well as explicit, information about how the technology works. So you will stay there for a few months and learn.

When you come back to your home labaoratory, you will be a living encyclopedia of the new technology. It is very likely that you will be able to carry on pioneering work of your own in the new technology. You will certainly be able to help your colleagues when they need the new technology in their work.

ConsumerCo has a similar system. When a team in a development laboratory develops a new product, someone from the team will follow the product into the factory where it is produced. For a few months before product launch, this person will work with technical people at the factory to assure that any problems that come up are solved. He will normally stay in the factory until several months after launch. He will stay to help solve any problems that come up as the factory gears up for volume production. Then, when high volume production is working smoothly, he will return to his home laboratory to work on another product.

In short, these companies transfer technical knowledge by transferring people. The transfer is usually temporary, but it can easily last for six months or more. When people need to learn complex bodies of technical knowledge and information, no better way has been found than to put the learner and the teacher into direct contact for a long period of time. This is, in effect, a short-term apprenticeship system that is applied as needed. Other methods do not seem to work nearly as well.

Internal publicity Up to this point, I have talked about communicating technical and market information across a company. But the internal communications system has another use as well. It can serve as a publicity vehicle for messages which senior managers want to send to the rest of the company. This is 'internal communication' in a much narrower sense than I have been using the phrase. To avoid confusion, I will use the phrase 'internal publicity' to refer to this kind of top-down communication by senior managers.

Managers in the most innovative companies often publicize their company's commitment to innovation. This is not just for external consumption. They do this to tell people inside the company that part of their job is to innovate: that they should follow up on their 'crazy ideas', that they should persist when they think they have ideas that will work, and that they should support innovative activity by other people. Eastman Chemical publicizes successful innovations widely within the company. Managers cite them as examples of behavior others in the company should follow. Managers at 3M do the same thing.

Managers can publicize their commitment to innovation through many media. Written publicity and speeches are probably the most common. Some companies, like Eastman Chemical, hold formal seminars on innovation. At these seminars, managers discuss the company's past innovation successes. They talk about current innovation programs. The whole seminar is conceived of as a cultural intervention. People should view innovation as very natural activity within the company. In addition, they use the seminars to explain how the process of innovation works within the company. They sensitize people to the problems that can come up and how to deal with them.

3M and ConsumerCo do not have such formal programs. But managers at these companies talk about innovation constantly. Anyone who talks to a manager from one of these companies is likely to hear a story about innovation. Their speeches are peppered with them. And each story is not just publicity for the outside, it is a moral lesson for those within the company as well.

At EuroChem, senior managers are not in the habit of talking about innovation. But EuroChem has a network of innovation officers (discussed above), part of whose mission is to publicize the company's commitment to innovation. The message may not be as powerful as one coming from the CEO. But it has an effect, nonetheless.

External communication

While I have focused all my attention up to this point at communication which occurs within the company, this is far from the whole story. People inside innovative companies don't just talk with each other. They talk with people outside their companies as well. Sometimes they talk with outsiders extensively. Communication with the outside is important because information about customers, markets and competitors has to come from the outside. In many industries, much useful information about technological developments comes from the outside as well.

There are two main categories of contact with outsiders. These are contact with customers and contact with technical resources outside the company.

Contacts with customers Contact with customers can occur at many levels within the company. In nearly all companies, sales people have direct contact with customers. Who beyond the sales department has direct contact with customers can vary considerably from company to company.

Among the companies I have worked with, the most innovative companies have the most extensive contact with customers. At 3M and ConsumerCo, many, many people have contact with customers. ConsumerCo expects managers, all the way up to the CEO, to spend at least one day each month on a sales route, talking to customers. Marketers at all levels in ConsumerCo follow the same rule.

At 3M, contact with customers is even more widespread. Technical people, other than those in fundamental research laboratories, talk to customers regularly. Many technical people have jobs as technical service people which put them into contact with customers for two or three days per week. 3M's marketers and managers have regular contacts with customers as well.

Another way to bring technical people into contact with customers is to put laboratory resources in a location close to customers. Several years ago I visited a 3M business unit located in Europe. For many years laboratories located in North American had taken care of the business unit's product development needs. But then the needs of European customers began to diverge from those of North American customers. As a result, the business unit set up its own laboratories, so that it would have technical people who would be geographically close enough to European customers to communicate with them directly and easily.

Many companies conduct customer surveys regularly. A few industrial products companies, including 3M, survey their customers' customers. By surveying far down the value chain, they get a better idea of the demands their customers are facing. They use a formal survey to look for gaps between customers' desires and the performance of products currently in the market. A large gap indicates potential for a breakthrough. Anyone filling the gap with a new product has the potential of taking over the market.

Another way to learn about an industrial customer is to attend conferences and seminars in the customer's industry. Attending a conference in a customer's industry shows people what the customer is thinking about. The topics at the conference are likely to be key issues in the customer's industry. This will give people insight into how the customer thinks. It will also give them things to talk about and inquire about the next time they see the customer.

Companies can improve communication with customers by learning the customer's language. One 3M technical representative learned the vocabulary of his principal customer. The customer put all of its internal communications into a particular format. The tech rep found that he could communicate far more easily with his customer if he put his communications into their vocabulary and their format. Then the things he said and wrote did not have to be altered before being distributed within the customer organization. The recipient could copy them and send them throughout his company without alteration. He found that his messages achieved far wider circulation within the customer organization after he adopted their vocabulary and format.

Contacts with technical resources outside the company Many companies compete in industries where at least some technical information is shared publicly. University researchers may do work in areas that are important to the industry. Independent laboratories may do research in the area. In either case, the company would be well advised to set up regular personal contacts with these outside laboratories.

When scientists in universities or independent laboratories are doing work that is important to the company, they can be hired as outside consultants. Companies can, in effect, turn them into part time employees, or consultants on call, so that they can draw on their expertise whenever it is needed. Other ways of using outside scientists are to give them specialized research contracts (in other words, to pay them to work on problems which are important to the company), to visit them and communicate with them regularly, to make donations to their schools or laboratories, or to hire their students.

In some industries, competitors share technical information freely. Technical people at the best companies may talk to each other regularly. They discuss common technical problems with the expectation that any sharing will be reciprocated. I help you with your problem today, and you will help me with my problem tomorrow. The best companies will not necessarily share with competitors who are technically behind. But companies lower down the learning curve may share with each other, just as the top-level companies do. Such sharing, when it occurs, can be used as an important source of technical learning (Von Hippel, 1987).

Information management

I have written about managing the structure of a communications system at some length. I have also discussed the problem of transferring knowledge. But now I will discuss not knowledge, but information.

The difference between knowledge and information is the difference between 'what' and 'how'. Information is descriptive. It describes the state of some phenomenon. It is often easy to transmit. Knowledge involves understanding links between different bits of information. The links may be simple or complex. They may involve juxtapositions, sequences, correlations or cause and effect relationships. They may involve understanding of how to manipulate a phenomenon to achieve a desired effect. Knowledge, particularly deep knowledge of a subject, can be very difficult to transmit.

I have discussed the transfer of knowledge in an earlier section. Here I will discuss the collection, transformation and transfer of information.

Information type and format

Information can be hard (quantitative, verifiable by others) or soft (descriptive, often related to personal perceptions or feelings). It can relate to financial matters, to aspects of the market (customers, competitors), to technical issues, or to organizational phenomena. While all organizations use all types of information, some favor different types.

Consumer products companies are famous for collecting huge quantities of information about consumers. Technology companies are active collectors of information about various technologies. American managers are said to favor quantified information, while Asian managers are said to be more sensitive to qualitative or soft information.

The most innovative companies collect and share a balanced mixture of all types of information. ConsumerCo is a consumer products company. Like other companies in its field, it collects large amounts of information about customers. But it also invests heavily in its research laboratories, which are at the top of their field. ConsumerCo's investment in R&D is comparable to that of a technology company.

3M is a technology company at heart, as evidenced by its huge investment in laboratories and research. But few companies collect more information about customers. 3M was not always that way, until the 1970s one could say it was a technology led company. But the 3M we know today surveys its customers and its customers' customers extensively. It forms links with its industrial product customers at many different levels. Its technical service people are as knowledgeable about customers as are the marketers in many consumer products companies.

Many less innovative companies seem to focus on technical information while drawing little information from their customers. In the 1970s and 80s EurAuto invested heavily in new technologies, both for automobile components and for manufacturing processes. Some of its technology was excellent, but it built cars people didn't particularly want. Its engineers consistently over-designed some parts of the car, in an urge to build the best possible car. But they missed some aspects of car design which were very important to the consumer, like ease and frequency of repair. In the 1990s EurAuto's management began redressing this balance and investing more in determining what the consumer wanted.

Companies that build complex technology products like automobiles must deal with large quantities of hard technical information. But when these products are sold directly to consumers, they are well advised to look at soft or subjective information as well. Consumers evaluate complex technical products like automobiles on many different dimensions. Many of these dimensions involve subjective evaluations. The company that can deal with consumers' subjective judgements as easily as it deals with hard technical information will be more effective in the long run.

When it began to pay more attention to consumers, EurAuto did two things. First it had panels of consumers drive its prototypes. These consumers were asked to make comments on the cars, but they were also asked to rate the cars on dozens of different dimensions, including noise, comfort, handling, appearance inside and out, and so on. By using a questionnaire with formal numeric scales, EurAuto was able to turn the subjective impressions of its customers into quantitative data, data that it could transmit and deal with as easily as quantitative technical data.

EurAuto also began coding customer complaints. Looking at thousands of customer complaints collected over several years, a team of analysts determined that they all could be classified into about 200 categories and subcategories. Each of these categories was then analyzed to determine what part of the car could cause it. The classification system developed was then used to classify new complaints coming in so that they could serve as an early warning system of after-sale technical problems in a car.

Using these techniques, EurAuto demonstrated that soft information could be turned into hard information. This was a useful thing to do at EurAuto for two reasons. The company had an enormous quantity of information to deal with. It had information about technologies, about cars, and about the way consumers reacted to their cars. With so much information to analyze, the company found it easier to quantify all of it rather than dealing with a mixture of numbers and customer comments. In addition, in a company full of technically trained people, management found that people would pay more attention to quantified information than they would to simple lists of customer comments.

The EurAuto example shows that soft information can often be turned, at least partially, into hard information to facilitate transmission and analysis. This does not mean that this is always a good thing to do. ConsumerCo, like any consumer products company, collects much quantitative information about customers and their buying habits. No one collects more information about sales and market share than ConsumerCo. But when the company's managers try to understand why consumers are acting as they do, they tend to look toward customer comments, not quantitative analyses.

One ConsumerCo manager explained to me the way she determines how a new product is doing. She could, obviously, wait for the initial sales results, which would come in several weeks after launch. But she finds it more interesting to listen to the first fifty customer comments. She gets on the phone and listens to the first thirty or forty customers who call in to talk about the product. She reads any written comments that come in, as well as any comments from sales people.

She told me that the first comments almost always give a clear indication of whether the product is going to be a success or not. In addition, they give a clear indication of why the product will be successful, or why it will fail. If customers don't like the product, they say why, and sometimes they say things the development team didn't foresee at all. If they like it, they also say why. In effect, for ConsumerCo customer comments are both a predictor of quantitative results (which tend to come later) and a source of richer understanding of what customers like and don't like about the product.

Information from the customer

Three dimensions of customer information gathering are important. There are different types of information to be gathered, to be sure. In addition, in the case of an industrial customer, there are different places within the customer where information can be gathered. These dimensions are well known. The third dimension that the most innovative companies pay attention to is the dimension of who within the company collects information from the customer. In the most innovative companies, the answer is 'everybody.' This may seem to be a trite observation, but it may also be a key to how these companies maintain a focus on the customer's need.

Before discussing the third dimension, I will briefly discuss the first two. Many different types of information can be collected from customers. Good marketing texts (for example, Kotler, 1997; Kotler and Armstrong, 1999) discuss this in far more detail than I will. What I will discuss is the types of information managers collect which are most useful for new product development.

Types of information collected from customers Not surprisingly, the information managers collect relates to customers' needs, their reactions to existing products and to possible future products, and their ways of using products. They measure response to products by looking at buying behavior, returns, complaints, expressions of concern and other customer comments. Some of them also measure customer reactions by direct observation of how customers use products. This can be particularly important when customers react in ways that are different than those imagined by the product designers.

Observational data can be very useful for alerting people to unnoticed reactions and new uses of products. Comments give evidence not only of customers' reactions, but also of what they value and how they reason about the product. Observations and comments are often collected in the field after the customer has purchased or used the product. But they can also be collected in a proactive way by inviting consumers to join focus groups.

The focus group, like a test market, gives companies a way to gather observations and customer comments prior to product launch. Many companies, from consumer product companies to automobile manufacturers, use focus groups as a way to get consumer reactions to products before they have gone into volume production. In the case of large, expensive products like automobiles, managers use focus groups to limit the risk of a full product launch. Designs are tested in focus groups to gauge consumer reaction. They are tested before launch when the company can still change the design without spending large amounts of money for retooling.

Where information is gathered within an industrial customer Consumer products companies have it easy in some ways. Their customers are individuals. To get one sale, they only have to sell to one person. (I am deliberately ignoring the problem of getting distribution to make a point. Industrial companies often have to get distribution as well.) Industrial products companies can have a much more complex sale. They may have to convince several entire departments of people, as well as senior management, before they are able to make a sale.

Since their customers are complex organizations, rather than individuals, they have many more choices of where to gather information from any given 'customer'. Some try to simplify this problem by talking only to buyers, the people who formally do the buying. From the point of view of innovation, this is a mistake. While it is necessary to talk to buyers, it is better to also seek contact with those who use the product within the customer organization, with those who test it, and with those who supervise both operations. It is also useful to have contact with others, like marketers and sales people, who sell the products the customer makes. They will be able to tell you about how your product helps or hinders them as they do their job.

Your customers' development engineers can be a valuable source of information. They will have a good idea of what the customer's products will look like in the future. So they will be a good source of information on how your products will need to change to fit the customers' future needs.

Who gathers customer information In the introduction to this section I said, a bit flippantly, that in the best companies 'everybody' gathered customer information. But from my observations of 3M, that seemed to be very nearly true. There may have been some people lost in the finance and accounting departments who never spoke directly with customers, but other than that everyone seemed to have weekly or monthly contact. Fundamental researchers did not have systematic contacts with customers. But they were working on things that management believed would be important to customers in the future.

Other technical people at 3M seem to routinely have contact with customers. Production people, who may never have contact with customers at other companies, visit customer plants regularly at 3M. They, like everyone else, learn how customers use their product. They also learn something which is key to their work, how their product fits into the customer's production system. With this knowledge they are better equipped to adapt their products so that they fit most effectively into the customer's production system.

Development people at ConsumerCo do not have direct links with customers. But they are directed by marketers who themselves have direct contact with customers. Apart from that, marketing, sales and general management personnel are all expected to have regular contact with customers. People in finance and other disciplines are likely at some point in their career to rotate into other functions where they will have direct contact.

Other information from outside the company

Customers are not the only source of information outside the company. Information can also be gathered from others in the market such as suppliers, competitors, and potential customers. People in neighboring markets (upstream and downstream markets, as well as markets using similar technologies) can be useful sources of information. In addition, commercial market research organizations, technical research institutes, universities, trade associations, and conference organizers can often be useful sources of information.

You can collect many types of useful information from noncustomers. Some of the most useful include information about technology, manufacturing processes, and competing or complementary products. In addition, one should obtain information from a variety of sources to get a general picture of a market. Finally, ideas about potential future markets can come up almost anywhere. The richer one's information sources about current events and ideas, the more likely one will see a potential future market before anyone else.

One final source of information must be mentioned. Information doesn't only come from people. One ConsumerCo manager told me how she insisted that all her subordinates spend a lot of time with ConsumerCo products and with competitors' products. She set a good example. She literally had dozens of ConsumerCo and competing products sitting around her office. She expected her subordinates to do the same. She expected them to look at the products, to feel them, to smell them, to see how they worked, on a daily basis, just as she did. She believed that there were things she could learn by touching, holding and smelling the products that she would not learn any other way. It appeared to be a good way to gather tacit information about the products, and to put one's self in the place of a customer, who can test and use a wide variety of products.

Some people in other companies were similarly obsessed with products. It is well know that automobile companies buy and dismantle competing products. They 'reverse engineer' these products to see how they are made. Japanese automobile companies give their employees several different cars each year so that the see how well different cars in their product range work. (See Table 4.4 for an outline of key issues in communications systems and information management.)

This ends my discussion of communication and information management. Two key issues are to maintain a high level of communication across internal boundaries, and to maintain extensive contacts with customers and others outside the company with important information and knowledge. I discussed many detailed aspects of internal communication that have not been discussed elsewhere. In the next section, I will turn to the issue of decision-making methods.

Decision-making methods

All companies have ways of making decisions. The issue here is who is involved in making operational decisions for a company and how do the different actors in any particular decision interact with each other. In most companies, particularly in the United States, one person is responsible for each decision. But in a few companies, including some of the most innovative, several people are involved in each decision and the rule is decision by consensus.

Table 4.4   Communications systems and their impact

Aspect of communications systems	Tool or variable . . . Impact	
Internal communications structure	■ Vertical links to innovation projects	■ High level report helps access to resources
	■ Horizontal links	■ More idea generation; better funding contacts; more effective, quicker development
	■ Length of key links	■ Shorter links increase speed, reduce distortion
Ways to facilitate direct contact between functions	■ Establish a liaison function	■ Facilitates communication between groups that don't know each other's vocabulary well
	■ Key customer account teams	■ Focuses attention of all functions on the real problems of a real customer
	■ Co-location	■ Facilitates communication, development of a common perspective
	■ Other mandatory cross-functional contact	■ Weekly/monthly meetings oblige functions to communicate
	■ Cross-functional work teams	■ Focuses attention of all functions on a common problem
Specialized innovation networks	■ Innovation office can publicize need for innovation, serve as 'back channel' for publicizing, funding ideas	■ Helps facilitate idea sharing and funding in companies where line bosses are not focused on innovation

(cont'd)

Table 4.4 (cont'd)

Aspect of communications systems	Tool or variable . . . . Impact	
Other aspects of internal communications	■ Develop common language	■ Greatly facilitates cross-functional, cross-unit communication
	■ Established methods of searching for needed information, knowledge	■ Having methods in place makes it easier for people to find help when they're exploring on a new idea
	■ Incentives to communicate	■ Essential for formation of new links (essential for exploiting new ideas)
	■ Methods of communicating complex technical knowledge	■ May be essential for exploiting new ideas in geographically dispersed company
	■ Publicizing importance of innovation	■ Helps people become more motivated to innovate
External communications	■ Multiple contacts with customers, contacts with customers' customers	■ Multiple contacts, contacts across all functions, speed identification of customer need
	■ Contacts with technical resources outside company	■ Speeds identification, learning of new technical knowledge
Type and format of information collected	■ Many types of customer and market information can be collected: – Objective and subjective (for example, customer opinion) – Technical and market	■ Broader range of information improves judgement: – Broader understanding of customer need – Broader understanding of market trends and how to deal with them

(cont'd)

Table 4.4 (cont'd)

Aspect of communications systems	Tool or variable . . . . . Impact	
Information from customers	■ Many types can be collected (observational, conversation, opinion survey, sales data)	■ Collecting a broad range gives a better, more intuitive understanding of customer behavior
	■ Where information collected (within industrial customer)	■ Collecting from a variety of places/functions gives better understanding of customer thinking
	■ Who gathers customer information	■ Having different functions collect information spreads understanding of customer throughout company
Other sources of information	■ Non-customers, independent research organizations, independent laboratories, universities, trade associations, and so on	■ Using wide variety of sources broadens understanding of market

Another difference involves the role of top management. In some companies, top management functions as a court of appeals. In others, top management rejects this role and pushes disputes down for resolution at lower levels. I will discuss these two dimensions of difference, and their effect on innovation performance, in this section. (See Table 4.5 for a list of key questions on decision-making methods.)

Unity of command versus consensus

The traditional organization practices 'unity of command.' Each decision is the responsibility of one and only one person. This makes for

Table 4.5   Questions to ask about decision-making methods

How do we make decisions?
■ Do people make decisions by themselves (sole responsibility), or in collaboration with others (consensus or consultation)?
■ Do we have enough communication about the decision that are made?
■ Are the right people involved in the decisions?
■ Do people hide their opinions for fear of rocking the boat, or offending the boss?
■ How can we encourage people to communicate more effectively about pending decisions?

Appealing decisions
■ Can people appeal decisions?
■ Does the appeal system make people less responsible?
■ How can we help people be more responsible?

clear lines of responsibility and accountability, but there is a cost to this system. The decision-maker has his or her own viewpoint on each problem. This may be a wide or narrow viewpoint, but it is only one viewpoint. It is the decision-maker's option whether to bring any other viewpoints into the discussion.

As a result of this fact, the unity of command system can become a 'single viewpoint system' of decision making. It can lead to narrow-minded decisions which fail to take account of the obvious concerns of significant actors in a system, such as customers, suppliers, or unrepresented functions within the company.

To fight the risk of overly narrow focus, ConsumerCo practices consensus decision-making. All significant decisions are the responsibility of several managers, often coming from different levels or different functions. Multiple viewpoints must be considered, since representatives from several functions or levels are represented on the decision-making body.

One reason why this has an impact on innovation is that making decisions together forces people to communicate. It is one method, in addition to those presented earlier, to ensure that cross-functional communication occurs. It also forces functional or other specialists to begin to look at the problems presented from the viewpoint of the company as a whole. As they listen to the concerns of others involved in the decision, they learn their perspectives and enrich their own understanding of how the company, its technology, and its market work.

There are obvious dangers to the consensus system which lead many companies to stick with unity of command. It is worthwhile to look at these dangers and to discuss how companies like ConsumerCo deal with them. The chief dangers are:

- Failure to reach decisions
- Delays in making decisions
- Vague responsibility and lack of accountability
- People not voicing opinions (too easy agreement)
- Dominance of a group by one function or a few influential people.

ConsumerCo is a competitive organization and everyone in the company knows that. As one of their personnel managers explained to me, one core requirement for being hired and becoming successful at ConsumerCo is to understand and accept what it means to be in a competitive organization. At ConsumerCo, it means to recognize that decisions (choices) have to be made and that the organization must act. People know they have to reach decision and act on them, so they manage their consensus decision-making accordingly. Viewpoints are expressed, differences are noted, and the people involved look for some reasonable way to resolve the differences. Sometimes evidence can be brought to bear. Sometimes an experiment can be set up. Sometimes it is not possible to know which option is best, and the company must simply choose one option and act on it. Everyone knows these things, so they learn to participate in consensus decision-making in an effective way.

There are five clear rules of participation. The *first* is, *express your viewpoint*. Each individual in a decision-making body is there because he or she has a unique viewpoint. All are considered important to the outcome of the decision, so all are expected to express their viewpoints. Silence is discouraged by asking people what they think. People are discouraged from agreeing with each other too easily by the *second* rule, which is, *never agree 100 percent with anyone*. This is viewed as abandoning one's responsibility to point out potential flaws and omissions in someone else's position.

A junior marketing manager recounted to me one conversation she had with ConsumerCo's CEO. At some point, she said that she agreed 100 percent with him on a certain point. He immediately told her never to say that, not even to him. She should always pay attention to what she sees that is different. She should always look for ways she could improve the company's collective understanding of things. 'This is how we keep our edge', the CEO said to her. 'If we start agreeing with each other too easily, we will lose our edge.'

The *third* rule is, *listen to the viewpoints of others*. It is widely recognized that the system won't work if people don't listen to each other. Managers are expected to examine their own position (and behavior) for flaws. The ability to do this is viewed as one of the key requirements for advancement at ConsumerCo. Rigidity in sticking to a flawed position is not viewed favorably. In short, pushing one's own viewpoint without taking account of others is out. Enough humility to recognize and correct errors and omissions is in.

The *fourth* rule is, *find reasonable and intelligent ways to resolve differences*. Differences are viewed as inevitable. In fact they are viewed as essential to the company's success, since they alert people to different interpretations of phenomena and to different ways of reacting to things. But, nonetheless, consensus must be reached and actions taken. So at some point the differences must be resolved enough for the company to take action.

The first step in resolving differences is to listen (rule three). After that, once the differences have been recognized, people are expected to find a way to bring evidence to bear on them. A corollary rule at ConsumerCo is that the hierarchical position of the protagonists should not have a role in the outcome of the decision. The decision is to be based on evidence, not on past accomplishments or influence.

Evidence may be at hand in the form of market studies or the results of previous tests. If not, groups are expected to construct a test to determine which of the alternatives is best. If no test can be constructed, then it may be necessary to take a calculated risk, based on one of the options. But my informants at ConsumerCo told me that this occurs only rarely. Normally it is possible to obtain evidence which supports one option or another.

Finally, the *fifth* rule is, *remember that the goal is the long-term health of the company, not the health of any particular function or individual*. All are expected to have this goal uppermost in their minds. It is obvious to everyone in the company that individuals will have particular interests. But they are expected to put those interests aside and to look at what is good for the company when they make decisions. This may seem idealistic, or unrealistic to some readers. But several managers at ConsumerCo told me that consistently self-centered behavior would be punished in the long run. The person would acquire a reputation for lack of cooperation or lack of ability to work in a group. Such a reputation would be a death sentence at ConsumerCo.

Returning to the list of dangers cited earlier, let us look at how ConsumerCo deals with them. The *first danger* of a consensus system is the *risk of not reaching decisions at all*. ConsumerCo deals with this by hiring and promoting people who recognize the need to make decisions and who are willing and able to reach decisions by consensus with other people, following the rules outlined above. The process can take time. The *second danger* is the *risk of delays*. But efforts are made to minimize delays through co-location. All the people who run any given business unit will have offices together in the same building. When quick turn-around is needed, a decision can be made, by consensus, at an *ad hoc* meeting, or through informal discussions in the halls.

The *third danger* is *lack of responsibility and accountability*. At ConsumerCo these are team-based. Management believes that no lone individual should have responsibility for decisions that affect the health of the company or major pieces of it. Responsibility should be shared and the team as a whole should be accountable. Managers reported to me that by and large this worked. Teams took responsibility and made decisions. The results came back quickly enough that they could be held accountable. People stayed in the same positions long enough that they had to live with and learn from the results of their decisions. They could not simply move on without looking back. At times, it was said, the company got stuck because no one would take responsibility for a risky new initiative. But this was said to be rare.

The *fourth danger* is that *people will not voice their opinions*. Two things minimize this danger: the expectation that all will participate in meetings, and the rule that prohibits 100 percent agreement with anyone. The *fifth* danger is that *one unit or individual will dominate decisions*. Two things mitigate this: the requirement to focus on the long-term health of the company, and sanctions for those who focus on their own or their unit's interests.

Monitoring and appeals

In some companies, senior management sits as a court of appeals. Disputes not resolved at lower levels are pushed up to senior management for resolution. In a functional organization this can result in situations which border on the absurd. Lower-level people from different functions may have to work together on a routine basis. But they may not agree on how to structure their relationship or how to plan their work. So they refer their dispute to their respective supervisors. But their supervisors don't agree either, so the dispute is resolved further up.

A EurAuto manager described one such dispute which involved the use of new materials in new car models. The laboratory that tested new materials had developed one set of criteria for including new materials in new cars. But the design area had different criteria. The dispute had to be referred up three levels up for resolution. Not having time for such disputes, EurAuto's senior managers fixed the problem by making the new materials laboratory report to the design area.

Blockages in a consensus system and appeals When decision-making in a consensus system breaks down, how senior management reacts is important. If they want to make the point that the group responsible should reach a decision, they can push the decision back down with the message, 'Resolve your differences intelligently, and do it yourself'. Any other reaction will tend to undermine the consensus system.

If, for example, senior management hears the appeal and makes the decision, they disempower the team below them by doing so. At the same time, they allow the team to abandon its responsibility to make the decision. ConsumerCo's senior managers routinely reject appeals for adjudication, telling teams to reach decisions themselves. Repeated requests for help from a team are viewed as a sign that the team, and its members, are not functioning properly. With their reputations at stake, teams learn to make decisions themselves without resorting to appeals to higher levels.

Senior management monitoring of operational decisions While it is not wise for senior managers to 'let teams off the hook' when they fail to make decisions, there are other situations in which senior management involvement can have a positive impact. In particular, there are situations where senior managers should monitor decisions to prevent serious mistakes. There are other situations where input from senior management can have a useful impact.

At ConsumerCo monitoring occurs for both reasons. Senior management reviews decisions in core businesses to prevent mistakes. It also reviews decisions throughout ConsumerCo so that it can offer suggestions for doing things better. Monitoring does not involve taking control. But in the core businesses, senior managers' objections have to be met before a team can proceed.

The frequency and impact of monitoring varies in different ConsumerCo business units. In the core businesses, the 'cash cows', it is frequent and constraining. In smaller, more peripheral business it is very light. The logic for this difference is the different level of risk the company is exposed to in each case.

In the core businesses, the company has a very high market share (50+ percent) in key markets. It also has a long-standing and carefully built reputation to protect. As a result, senior management is very concerned to avoid mistakes. Mid-level managers run the business, but they are obliged to discuss any product changes or new marketing plans with a board of senior managers prior to launch. Any of a dozen senior managers may raise objections which have to be answered, with evidence, before a new product or marketing program can be launched.

This heavy monitoring slows the process of launching a new product, as ConsumerCo management recognizes. One laboratory manager in this business told me that at times competitors come out with products in six months, while ConsumerCo takes 18 months or even two years to develop a similar product. What led to the difference? ConsumerCo went through much more extensive tests, safety tests, effectiveness tests, and market tests, before launching the product. ConsumerCo had a reputation and a position to protect, which was not the case with its smaller rivals.

In several of its core businesses, ConsumerCo is conservative about change. It shows no such conservatism in its many smaller businesses. Here the hand of senior management monitoring is very light. Business unit managers must bring each new product launch and each new marketing program before a board of senior managers before launch. But the board is much smaller. It may be the CEO by himself. Or it may be the CEO accompanied by one or two others. In addition, there is no obligation to follow up on advice or criticism offered by the board. Business unit managers are free to take or leave the advice as they see fit.

You may ask, 'What is the point of this loose system?' The dozen business unit managers I interviewed all saw it as useful. They saw it as useful because they respected the advice of the CEO and the other members of the senior management team. The CEO had run several of ConsumerCo's businesses. He had spent many years on the front lines. He had established a reputation as one of ConsumerCo's most creative and effective managers. His warnings about the problems that a new product might encounter were taken seriously. And his suggestions of how to improve a marketing program were valued. In this case, junior managers viewed monitoring as an effective way to get advice and help from senior management.

Monitoring versus control Senior managers at ConsumerCo monitored decisions without taking control of projects. Even in the core business, responsibility for making decisions remained in the hands of the business unit or project team. Senior management could block the team from implementing a program they viewed as dangerous, but they did not make proposals. It was up to the team to propose things and then sell them to senior management.

This worked differently in several divisions of MGE. In Lawn & Garden, senior management took over management of a key project. This turned out to be disastrous. Senior management made numerous decisions, from pricing to distribution to the configuration of the product, which turned out to be wrong. They did not know the product or the market as well as they thought they did, and many of the assumptions upon which they based their decisions turned out to be wrong.

There are several key differences between the situations at ConsumerCo and at Lawn & Garden. First, managers at ConsumerCo do not take over. While they may comment on projects or even (in core businesses) block implementation of programs they view as dangerous, they leave primary responsibility for decision making in the hands of the project or business unit team. At Lawn & Garden, top management took over. It was they who made operational decisions, not the project team.

Second, managers at ConsumerCo stay in touch with their market. This was not the case with top managers at Lawn & Garden in the early 1990s. ConsumerCo managers at all levels go out on a sales route and visit customers at least one day per month. In addition, they regularly sit on product management boards, where they listen to product managers tell them what is happening in the market. Managers at Lawn & Garden did not visit customers. Nor did anyone else in the company other than sales people. There was no ongoing program of product meetings to keep senior managers informed of events in the marketplace.

Special monitoring and decision-making bodies

Up until this point I have talked about methods of decision-making in the context of operations. But many companies set up special decision-making bodies to handle special problems and special cases. Sometimes these special decision-making bodies deal with issues that are relevant to innovation.

Eastman Chemical, for example, has teams which manage nineteen key internal processes. One of the key processes is the innovation process. The innovation team observes the process and determines how to measure and monitor it. With the monitoring system in place, it identifies problems and fixes them. It also identifies opportunities for improvement and implements improvements.

Another team manages the company's competence base and its competence development process. This team first identified the key competences to be monitored. Then it identified who carried the competences and how they rated versus industry standards. It then set up a competence maintenance and development plan. This plan has been used to identify training and hiring needs.

The innovation team has a direct impact on innovation performance through its ability to improve the process. The competence team has a less direct, but still important, impact since it assures the continuity and development of the competences needed for planned innovations. (See Table 4.6 for a summary of key issues in decision-making methods.)

Table 4.6   Decision-making methods and their impact

Aspect of decision-making methods	Tool or variable . . . . Impact	
Unity of command versus consensus	▪ One person makes decision, versus consensus among a group	▪ Consensus forces communication (but must avoid false consensus, avoidance of responsibility)
Monitoring and appeals	▪ Method of handling blockages in consensus system, method of handling appeals ▪ Senior management monitoring of operational decisions	▪ Senior management can force team to be responsible by pushing appeals back down ▪ Monitoring (not control) of key decisions can help avoid mistakes, also allows senior managers to contribute as consultants
Special monitoring and decision-making bodies	▪ Teams to monitor, improve key processes that cut across organizational boundaries (innovation, competence management)	▪ Helps improve functioning of processes that fall across different people's territories

Corporate and Business Unit Management Tools 3: Personnel Management and Culture

So, once you have decided to innovate, how do you get your people to do it? In the 'Strategy and goals' section (Chapter 3), I described three things: how strategy setting guides innovation, how goal structures bring strategy to life at all levels of the company, and how mergers and acquisitions activity and competence management ensure that the company has the competences needed to achieve its innovation goals.

In the 'Structure and process' section (Chapter 4), I described three more things, how organization structure can facilitate innovation, how communications systems support innovation, and how aspects of the decision system can be managed in ways which facilitate innovation. But, complex as these discussions were, they do not tell the full story. We still have to motivate, guide and develop the people. That is the story of this section.

Motivating and guiding people involves a number of things. Monetary rewards and incentives are important in many companies. But there are more subtle methods of rewarding people as well. Additional guidance can be provided through evaluations and other personnel management systems. Personnel development is handled through evaluations, training and career path management. Finally, no company can specify in advance how a person should react to every situation. As a result, most companies establish general rules of behavior which guide a wide range of decisions and which eventually become part of the company's core culture.

I will discuss each of these topics in turn in this section. I will cover monetary rewards and other types of incentives in the section on 'Incentives'. I will cover evaluations, training and career path management in the section on 'Other personnel management systems'. Finally I will cover cultural issues in the section on culture.

Incentives

Incentives come in several types. The most obvious are monetary. But these are not necessarily the most effective type. In most companies, career incentives have an effect as large or even larger than monetary incentives. Another type of incentive that is often overlooked is social incentives. Finally, intrinsic rewards offer a kind of incentive to people who are very interested in their work. I will discuss each of these reward types in turn.

Then I will discuss which type of reward is used when. In good companies, the rewards for improving existing products are different than the rewards for creating new products. I will explore why this is the case. Other dimensions are important as well. In some situations, companies use group rewards. In others they use individual rewards. In still others they use no rewards at all. I will discuss why later in this section. Finally, companies sometimes reward effort, while at other times they reward outcome. I will discuss the logic behind this at the end of the section. (See Table 5.1 for a list of key questions on incentives.)

Monetary rewards

Companies pay salaries and compute raises. Often they pay bonuses. Raises and bonuses can be linked to innovation performance. Companies commonly link the bonuses and raises of people who are on innovation project teams to the success of the project. It is rarer to link the raises and bonuses of other people to their contribution to innovation performance. General managers, in particular, rarely have their raises and bonuses linked to the amount of innovation they contribute to. But innovative companies, like 3M and ConsumerCo, commonly link these monetary rewards to innovation performance. This is very clear at 3M, where managers have quotas to meet: the famous rule that at least 30 percent of sales should come from products developed in the last four years. It is

Table 5.1 Questions to ask about incentives

Types of incentive

- What kinds of incentives do we offer to people:
  - Monetary incentives?
  - Career incentives (promotions)?
  - Social rewards (recognizing people, making them heroes)?
  - Intrinsic incentives (letting them work on things they like)?

- Do we use all these different types of incentives effectively? Do we know when each is appropriate and when each is most effective?

Managing incentives

- Do monetary incentives and promotion patterns encourage people to resist innovation or to support it:
  - Are innovators promoted?
  - Or are people who play it safe promoted?

- Can innovators become heroes in the company?

- Can people who support or sponsor innovators become heroes?

- Or do people become heroes by playing it safe?

Who to reward

- Do we know when to reward individuals and when to reward groups?

- Do we know when it is best not to give any special reward at all?

- Do we know when to reward outcome and when to reward effort?

less obvious at ConsumerCo, where there are neither quotas nor significant bonuses. But innovation contribution is still a key factor in the evolution of a person's salary over the years.

Monetary incentives, while very clear, are not always the best way to encourage people to contribute to innovation. Research on scientists' behavior has found that overly large monetary incentives actually cause a decline in the creative output of many scientists (Angle, 1989). This surprising (to some) result may occur because scientists become distracted by large monetary incentives. They work less on what interests them (this is where they are most likely to find creative ideas) and they work more on areas where they think they will win the money.

When monetary rewards are used, they can be applied on an individual or team basis. Applying them appropriately is important. In situations where an entire team contributes to innovation, it can be damaging to give rewards only to a few individuals (for example, the team leaders) and not to the entire team.

Career incentives

At innovative companies like 3M and ConsumerCo, contribution to innovation weighs heavily in promotion decisions. No one can be promoted unless they have consistently contributed to innovation activity. The contribution may come from participating in innovation projects, or from supporting innovation activity from another position. No one can reach a high level in these companies unless they have consistently supported innovation for a number of years.

This is not at all the case in many other companies, including Industrial Chemicals and other units of MGE. For many years, participation in an innovation project was considered a 'kiss of death' for promotion opportunities at Industrial Chemicals. No one had ever been promoted out of an innovation project. People who participated in failed projects were often forced to leave the company.

The normal road to promotion was to run a small business, produce steady, predictable profits, and avoid surprises. Success with a small business would lead to a position running a larger business. Ambitious people avoided risky projects, since betting and losing would kill their prospects for a promotion. It is little wonder that business unit managers at Industrial Chemicals rarely supported speculative innovation projects.

Contrast this with the situation at ConsumerCo or 3M. At 3M, a technical person who has never failed at an innovation project may have difficulty getting promoted. Why? Because if they have never failed, that means that they weren't trying hard enough to innovate. Technical people at 3M participate in so many innovation projects, that failure is inevitable. It is also viewed as a learning experience. Someone who has never failed has never learned how to deal with failure. Nor has he or she learned how to deal with people who experience failure. Both lessons are important, and it is expected that anyone who advances to a senior position will have learned them.

Innovation project team members at 3M can increase their level of responsibility by bringing a major project to a successful conclusion. If they build a new business, they will be allowed to run it. This may involve a significant promotion, from project team member status to business unit management status. If they grow other business units from the first one, they may receive promotions to higher levels, all without competing with anyone else for these positions. At 3M, a manager can earn a promotion in place simply by growing his or her business.

Companies who want their people to support innovation should not just reward those who are directly involved in innovation projects. They should also reward those within the operating unit structure who have gone out of their way to support innovation. This will show that innovation is not just a matter for project teams. It will also ensure that there is an incentive for everyone to support innovation.

Promoting people who are involved in innovation and who support innovation accomplishes two things. It puts people who are experienced with innovation into senior positions. And it sends a signal to others that innovation is important to the company. Both of these factors will help build support for innovation throughout the company.

Social rewards

Social rewards are underused and underestimated. They can have an enormous impact on people, but few companies use them as well or as extensively as they could. Worse, sometimes they use them in perverse ways which discourage people rather than motivating them. Two stories will illustrate this point.

3M makes heroes out of its innovators. Someone who invents a new product will become a hero in his business unit. If he persists in working at a problem, despite early failures, and ultimately succeeds, he will be a bigger hero than someone who 'strikes it rich' early and easily. If he persists in working on his idea, despite repeated failures, and despite the opposition of senior management who don't want him to 'waste' further time, then he will be the biggest hero of all if he succeeds. He may, like Art Fry, the inventor of Post-It® Notes, become a public spokesperson for 3M. He may become widely known outside the company as well as in it.

The rewards of such personal recognition are great. People who are recognized feel good about themselves and they know they have a secure place in their companies. If they get social recognition for innovating, they will continue to innovate. Others around them will see that they are rewarded for innovating and they will try to do the same. As long as those who innovate keep getting rewarded, a positive dynamic develops and innovation will continue.

Other companies use personal recognition in a more perverse way. I attended a business conference on the subject of innovation recently where one of the speakers was from 3M. He talked about 3M's innovation system, including how innovators at 3M become heroes. A number of R&D managers from another company, which will remain nameless, were in attendance. They questioned the 3M manager in some detail. How did senior managers act? Didn't they take credit for innovations? No, responded the 3M speaker, they didn't. Hardly anyone outside 3M knew who 3M's senior managers were. They stayed in the background and facilitated a system where the technical people who were innovators became heroes.

The R&D managers from the other company were astonished. Things did not work that way at their company. If they, or one of their people, invented something, the senior management team would take credit. It would be the director of finance, or the CEO, who would make all the announcements, make all the public appearances, and collect all the awards. They were sorry to say it, but that was how things happened at their company.

They were demotivated when people at the top of the company took all the credit. Their teams were demotivated as well. But they couldn't stop their senior managers from taking credit. They were surprised to hear that senior managers at 3M did not act in such a self-centered way. They wanted their company to be more like 3M. They were crestfallen when they realized that this would never happen, since their own senior management team was what kept them from being more like 3M.

It is not always appropriate to treat innovators like heroes and to set them apart from the rest of the personnel in a company. This occurs at 3M when an individual or a small group has developed an innovation alone outside of their normal job. They are more likely to be recognized as heroes if they had to work against the opposition of senior management to get their project out the door.

But if 3M's people work as part of a team and they innovate as part of their normal job, they are not likely to be recognized as heroes. The team as a whole may be recognized. But even this may not be viewed as appropriate. The credit may be spread wider. An innovation team is normally supported by many people who are not part of the team. The team itself may believe that it is inappropriate for them to be singled out for special recognition. Such recognition may diminish the importance of those around the team.

Intrinsic rewards

Another often overlooked type of reward is the intrinsic reward. Some people are happy simply to be able to continue doing the job they are doing. It is reward enough to be able to continue doing it. This is an intrinsic reward. The activity itself is intrinsically rewarding to the person doing it.

Many of the best scientists are motivated by the intrinsic rewards of what they are doing. This is probably true of the best people in many jobs. There is evidence that innovations come disproportionately from people who are intrinsically motivated (Angle, 1989). There is also evidence that giving overly large bonuses and other financial rewards distracts intrinsically motivated people from their work (Angle, 1989). Companies, like 3M and ConsumerCo, which try to hire intrinsically motivated people, recognize this and limit their use of financial incentives accordingly.

Companies are well advised to distinguish between people who want to advance in the company, on one hand, and people who are largely motivated by the pleasure of what they are doing, on the other hand. The people who are motivated by what they are doing should not be promoted out of their jobs. Many companies establish separate technical career ladders for such people. They are able to advance in rank without moving into management. They are not forced to give up the work they love just to advance.

Improving existing products versus developing new products and businesses

There is a considerable difference between improving an existing product and developing a new product or business. People who improve existing products often work in the context of existing business units. They do a series of product improvements as part of their normal job. When they finish one project, they start another. There may be little or no change in the circumstances of their daily lives when they finish a project or when they move from one project to another. Innovation is simply part of their normal lives.

Most companies view it as inappropriate to give people exceptional rewards in this type of situation. If innovation is the job, then no special rewards should be needed. People who develop entirely new products and, even more so, new businesses are in a different situation. In many companies (the less innovative ones in particular), they may be putting their careers at risk by working on a speculative innovation project. Once the project is over, they may not have another job to go to. Since this type of project is fundamentally more risky for the people involved, companies tend more often to give them special rewards for participation.

When people develop new products and new businesses on the sly, that is, without their company's authorization, they may receive unusual rewards. This is the case at 3M. These wildcat innovators are valued considerably by the company, since they have often brought the company into lucrative new businesses. Other companies are not always so open to this kind of activity, particularly if they have organization structures which are so rigid that it is difficult for them to find a place for a growing new business.

3M has a flexible organization structure which can easily make room for new businesses. A new business will normally be attached to an established business unit. While the new business is small, it will share staff and infrastructure with the older unit. In effect, many of the new businesses staff will only work part-time on the new business. They will spend the rest of their time working in the old business. As the new business grows, they will gradually be detached and begin spending full time with the new business. Eventually when the new business is large enough, it will have its own staff and it will declare independence. The separation of the new business from the old will not involve any significant disruptions for anyone, since the new business's staff will already have completed the gradual transition from the old business into the new.

This practice eases the pain of developing a new product or business for people at 3M. The risk is less than at many other companies, since they have a secure position in an existing business unit. There are no sharp, difficult to manage transitions from one role to another. Rather, one role gradually evolves into another. Since there is little risk, there is little reason for an unusual financial reward.

There are rewards, but they are more of a career, social or intrinsic nature. The team that creates the new business will be given the responsibility for running it. The larger the business becomes, the more important their jobs. In effect, they receive promotions consistent with the success of the business they have created. They will become more prominent within the company as their business becomes more prominent. And they will be allowed to continue working on the product, which for many of them will be an intrinsic reward.

ConsumerCo also limits the risk and disruption involved with working on a new product. At ConsumerCo, new products are normally developed within existing business units. As at 3M, working on the new product is simply part of one's normal job. Existing business units develop radical new technologies in the same way. It is just part of the normal job. When one project is over, another one will start. So there is little personal risk.

In situations where innovation is part of the normal job, there is little need for special reward. And neither ConsumerCo nor 3M gave special rewards in these situations. Nonetheless, people were motivated to work on the innovations. They could see that it was good for the company, and thus for themselves, if they did so. In addition, they knew that if they didn't work on the innovations they would lose status. Failure to cooperate with innovation, in a company that values innovation, is dangerous. Everyone knew this at 3M and ConsumerCo. So everyone cooperated with the innovation projects.

Individual rewards versus group rewards versus no rewards

Once again, individual rewards are viewed as appropriate at innovative companies when individuals work outside the framework of the business they are in to develop an innovation. They are particularly important if the individuals involved had to 'rebel' against their senior management to develop the innovation. Clandestine innovations of this type can lead to considerable rewards at 3M.

Group rewards are used for people who work together as a team to produce an innovation. Group rewards are appropriate when success was clearly the product of a group effort, not an individual effort. They are most appropriate when the project is self-contained and it is clear who contributed and who didn't. They are less appropriate when the borders of the project team are vague and it is not clear where to draw the line between the team and the rest of the organization.

Earlier in this section, I discussed one situation where special rewards for innovation are viewed as inappropriate. That is when innovation is the full-time, normal job of the people doing it. Situations like this occur when groups of laboratory or marketing people have responsibility for managing innovations in a product line. ConsumerCo has such teams and they may be responsible for fifty or one hundred products or more. With such large numbers of products to manage, one product or another will always be in need of renewal. So there is always innovation work to be done.

At ConsumerCo, a division of labor develops among those who work on innovation. One entire team will be responsible for collecting information from customers. Another team will be responsible for technical experimentation and development. A third team may be responsible for regulatory and other tests. Representatives of the teams meet together frequently to coordinate their efforts.

Another situation where continuous innovation simply becomes part of the normal job is one which commonly arises at 3M. Many of 3M's businesses are industrial product businesses. They sell in markets which are dominated by a few large customers. I visited one 3M business unit which sold into such market. Ideas for changing and improving their products came from many different sources, from customers, from suppliers, from other parts of 3M, and from the team itself. Often the team had more ideas than it could try. But the team was motivated to develop as many ideas as it could, since customers would stop buying from them if they fell behind the leading edge.

The way this business unit managed innovation was the following. It set up a large network of people who were responsible for maintaining the pace of innovation in the business. Many people were in regular contact with customers. Technical service reps, part of the factory staff, were in contact with customers two to three days per week. So were marketers and sales people. The marketers also spent considerable time with the customers' customers, in an attempt to better understand how they could serve their customers. Technical people worked full time on technical development, although they often visited customers' factories as well. Both technical and marketing people maintained links with other parts of 3M. Technical people maintained links so that they could bring in technologies developed in other parts of 3M. Both groups maintained links so that they could keep track of what 3M was doing with this client in other businesses and in other parts of the world.

In both of these situations, at ConsumerCo and at 3M, innovation is a full time job for everyone. And no one, including the team members, see any reason to give anyone a special reward for doing something that is at the core of their normal job.

Rewards for outcome versus rewards for effort

Many discussions of rewards for innovation focus on rewards for outcome. If a team is successful in developing a product, and they receive a reward for being successful, that is a reward for outcome. The corollary is true as well. If they are not successful, and they are penalized (no promotion, no raise), that is a penalty based on outcome.

More innovative companies also reward effort. In fact, some innovative companies, such as ConsumerCo, seem to base their reward system primarily on effort. If someone is putting a lot of energy into an innovation project and doing good work, they will be rewarded whether or not the innovation is successful. Putting the effort in is seen as a good thing.

Innovative companies like 3M and ConsumerCo recognize that not all innovation projects will succeed. They are risky, so they won't all succeed. As a result, they do not punish the people on a project team when their project is not successful. They believe that penalizing people in such a situation would discourage effort. People would become less willing to participate in risky projects. Since the company wants to continue investing in risky projects, they reward effort. They may also reward successful outcomes, but they will not penalize people for unsuccessful outcomes, since that would discourage effort.

There are other reasons not to punish people when a project does not succeed. The success of a project is not entirely under the team's control. Technological problems are sometimes insoluble. Markets may change, contrary to the expectations of the team and the company. The regulatory environment may also change in ways that are unfavorable to the project. Project teams can influence such things, but they can't always control them. So some failures must be viewed as beyond a team's control.

If a person fails many times, questions may arise about his abilities. But occasional failures, or regular failures accompanied by successes, are viewed as normal at innovative companies. 3M, ConsumerCo and other innovative companies learn much from such failed projects. They retain much new knowledge by retaining the people who participated on 'failed' projects. By contrast, Industrial Chemicals sometimes fired people when project teams failed to meet their targets. They lost the knowledge the project teams had gained in the process. (See Table 5.2 for a summary of key issues in the area of incentives.)

Concluding remarks on incentives

In this section, I've discussed four key types of rewards: monetary, career, social and intrinsic. I've also discussed how these rewards should be used in different business situations. Monetary rewards are often overused, while the other types are underused and underappreciated.

Other dimensions of rewards are important as well. When an individual single handedly (or almost single handedly) develops an innovation, he should be rewarded individually. But when a group achieves an innovation, the whole group should be rewarded. However, when innovation is not something special or personally risky, but is simply part of the group's normal job, it may not be appropriate to give them any special reward at all. Their reward is that they maintain their status as key people in the company.

Innovative companies often reward effort, regardless of outcome. Less innovative companies sometimes punish project teams for unsuccessful outcomes. As a result, they discourage risk-taking and they sometimes lose the knowledge gained by the team.

Table 5.2   Incentives and their impact

Aspect of incentives	Tool or variable . . . Impact	

Types of incentive used	■ Monetary rewards:
	  – Bonuses, prizes, for individual or team
	
	  – Raises
		■ Signals value of innovation:
		  – Good for rewarding exceptional effort
		
		  – Good for rewarding long-term commitment

	■ Career incentives:
	
	  – Promoting innovators
	
	  – Promoting managers who support innovation
		■ Build commitment to innovation:
		  – Shows there is a career after the project, reduces risk of participation
		  – Ensures that the hierarchy will support innovation over long term

	■ Social rewards	■ Low cost, very high payoff to making people heroes, sets example for others
	■ Intrinsic rewards (let people do what they enjoy)	■ Key for inventors, others who are fascinated by technical problems, other problems
Improving existing products versus developing new products and businesses	■ Routine rewards for improving existing products (low risk activity) ■ Exceptional rewards for developing new businesses/ products (high risk activity)	■ Maintains commitment to what should be routine activity ■ Gives a powerful incentive for participation in high risk activity
Individual versus group rewards versus no rewards	■ Individual rewards for independent activity by a lone individual ■ Group rewards when a group (not an individual) has produced an innovation	■ Rewards lone inventor activity (best used only when individual largely acted alone) ■ Rewards group effort, retains group cohesion

(cont'd)

Table 5.2 (cont'd)

Aspect of incentives	Tool or variable . . . . Impact	
	■ No special rewards when innovation is normal part of job, or when large network of people involved (no one team can be singled out)	■ Giving special rewards difficult when innovators worked as part of a large network, all of whose members contributed, or when innovation is routine
Outcome rewards versus effort rewards	■ Outcome rewards, rewards which force individual to accept part of the risk of the activity	■ Unavoidable in start-ups; in larger organizations this may discourage participation, particularly in highest risk projects or in projects without direct financial outcomes
	■ Effort rewards, rewards which recognize effort, regardless of outcome	■ Encourages effort, makes it easier to participate in high risk projects in a large organization

Other personnel management systems

Many things besides incentives affect a person's interest in innovation. Goals, personnel development patterns, and evaluation systems can all affect a person's willingness to go out on a limb and try something new. Innovative companies also manage hiring in a way that brings in people who like to innovate.

Personnel systems can also affect a person's ability to innovate. The management of personnel development can have a particularly large impact on people's ability to generate ideas and follow up on them. But other policies, such as those which impact turnover, also have an impact.

In this section, I will discuss the impacts on innovation of each of these aspects of personnel policy. I will start with hiring, then move to personnel development, stability/turnover, individual goals, and evaluation. (See Table 5.3 for a list of key questions related to other personnel management systems.)

Table 5.3   Questions to ask about other
personnel management systems

Hiring
■ Do we hire creative people?
■ Do we hire a variety of people, people who will enrich the company with new perspectives?

Career management
■ Do we give the people we hire an enriching mix of experiences?
■ Do we hold on to our people? Or do we lose key competences?

Evaluations
■ Who does evaluations?
■ What kinds of data are used in evaluations?
■ Whose opinion counts in evaluations?
■ Do evaluations support people's development? Do people look forward to them? Or are they just a critique?
■ Are evaluations more than just salary reviews?
■ Do evaluations motivate people or demotivate them?

Personnel sourcing: hiring

Two things stand out in the hiring policies of more creative companies. The first is a focus on finding and hiring creative people. This
may not surprise anyone, but both ConsumerCo and 3M mentioned
this as a priority in hiring, while it was not mentioned as a priority at
less innovative companies. The second thing that stood out was the
preference for people with a variety of backgrounds. This was particularly important at ConsumerCo. 3M emphasized variety less in its
hiring criteria, but nonetheless it hires people from a wide variety of
technical backgrounds.

Hiring creative people Hiring creative people is an inexact science.
People come with degrees attesting to certain types of technical or
other training. They also come with CVs and references that attest to

certain types of work experience. There is no comparable certificate that attests to creative achievement. So, finding the most creative people among those who apply is a challenge for the personnel departments of innovative companies.

Both ConsumerCo and 3M deal with this challenge by looking for evidence of creativity in a person's past experience. Personnel managers at ConsumerCo, a marketing company, look at the way the person has done things. Is their 'creative flair' evident? Does the person do things in an unusual way? In his or her own way? Or does the person conform to existing norms and styles and produce good, but unremarkable work?

At 3M, which is a technical company, the questions are somewhat different, but the intent is the same. 3M also looks for evidence of creativity in past experience. But, in particular, it looks for practical, hands on experience. 3M wants people who are technically trained, and who are familiar with the theory of their field. But they also want people who have demonstrated that they can go beyond theory to build new things with theory. 3M particularly likes people who tinker with personal projects, people who build things on their own. 3M believes that such people are more likely to develop and follow through on an idea, rather than just talking or thinking about it.

Hiring people with varied backgrounds ConsumerCo is particularly keen to hire people with varied backgrounds. ConsumerCo hires people with a variety of core training. The people ConsumerCo hires are trained in a variety of core disciplines and in a variety of schools. Unlike other companies in its home country, ConsumerCo does not rely on the output of a few 'elite' schools to form its senior management team. It hires from a variety of schools with the expectation that the mixture of backgrounds will produce creative tension and a variety of ideas that would be lacking if it limited its hiring to a few elite schools.

ConsumerCo also looks for variations in geographic and national origin. Since consumer marketing is a key skill at ConsumerCo, hiring in different countries gives it insight into consumer markets in different countries. But, even more, it looks for a variety of different approaches to any business problem. People with different training from different countries are bound to come up with different ideas about all kinds of business problems. From this variety of ideas, ConsumerCo will find the best and pursue them.

ConsumerCo goes even one step farther in its hiring. At entry levels, about one hire out of ten is a 'wild card.' The personnel department has the right to hire interesting people who are not appropriately trained. For instance, they may hire a philosophy major and put him on a marketing team. The philosophy major will have no professional training in marketing, but he will, with little doubt, bring a new and unusual perspective to marketing problems. Such hires do not always work out. But they are a further source of varied input into ConsumerCo's idea generation factory.

Personnel development

Innovative companies not only try to hire creative people. They also develop them in ways which will increase their creative output. The first means of doing this is via rotation through a number of functions, businesses or territories. The second is through careful management of promotion patterns. The third is by establishing fixed common experiences that will give all people joining the company certain key experiences or key common perspectives.

Rotation ConsumerCo routinely moves people to a new job after three to four years in a post. The idea is that people bring new ideas and new perspectives to a post when they come in, but that, after a few years, they run out of ideas. At that point, the person should be moved to a new post, where he will again be productive and full of new ideas.

When ConsumerCo puts a person in a post, they expect him to react to it as follows. The first year he will be preoccupied with learning about the post. The second year he will begin to be really productive. The third year is the most productive year. By that time, he will know the post quite well, and he will still have new ideas he wants to try. By the fourth year his stream of ideas will begin to run dry. He will begin seeing everything in the same way. He will find it much more difficult to get 'out of the box' of the business he is in since he has been in it for so long. By the fifth year, the person will be stale and should be moved on to another post.

This is how rotation affects the individual's development. By moving around, the individual is regularly exposed to fresh ideas and fresh situations. This helps him take an original perspective on business problems and helps him to be more creative. But the individual's development is not the whole story; there is also the issue of how rotation affects teams.

Most work at ConsumerCo is done by teams. But teams can go stale. As Katz and Allen (1982) have shown, teams whose members stay on the team too long begin to reject ideas from the outside. They begin to reject any idea which is different from the norms they have established. The NIH (not invented here) syndrome becomes strong. By rotating people, ConsumerCo fights this tendency to reject ideas. ConsumerCo renews each team regularly. Each year, someone on each team will be new. Someone will bring fresh ideas.

At the same time, rotation assures that there will be a variety of perspectives on each team. A marketing team of six people may include someone whose original training was in finance. Another team member may have been trained as an engineer. The six team members may come from three different countries. They may have worked in five different businesses prior to joining their current team. This rich variety of backgrounds helps assure that the team will look at each problem from a variety of perspectives.

Promotion patterns At some companies there is one route to the top. In some companies, people move up functional silos through most of their careers. Only in the last years will they receive general management positions. In such companies, general managers often come from only one or two favored functions.

In corporations with many business units, people may be given general management responsibility at a much younger age. But again, general managers may come from only one or two favored functions. Or the management team may have a wider base, drawing in people whose initial experience was quite varied.

When the top team has a variety of backgrounds, this appears to help innovation. It assures that top-level problems will be viewed from a variety of perspectives. No one perspective or function can dominate. But when the members of the top team are all the same, other perspectives may not receive the attention they are due.

At 3M, technically trained people are quite numerous. Given the nature of the company's work, it would not be surprising if the entire top management team was made up of people with technical backgrounds. But this is not the case. 3M tries to maintain a variety of perspectives at the top. People from marketing backgrounds are there along with technically oriented people.

At ConsumerCo, most individuals at the top have experience in several disciplines. The 'royal road' to the top is through marketing. Since ConsumerCo is a consumer products organization, virtually all members of the top team have some experience in consumer products. But most of them have spent at least a few years in some other area. Finance, R&D and personnel are common stops on the way up.

Less innovative organizations sometimes have homogeneous teams at the top. One manager at MGE confided to me that the top three layers of the company, and of each division, were made up exclusively of technical people. Marketers had little or no chance to make it into top ranks. The few marketers who had made it to top levels had not lasted long. They were rejected, or just not taken seriously, by the others. What this led to at MGE was an overly narrow way of looking at the world. I tracked four projects in four different MGE divisions. All four projects suffered from too much focus on the technology and not enough focus on the market. Had the top teams at MGE included more marketers, there might have been a better balance between technical and marketing concerns.

Standard 'passages' during a career Some companies, including both ConsumerCo and 3M, view certain early career experiences as being key to the company's ability to innovate. At 3M, technically trained hires often spend several years in a technical service position. As technical service representatives, they are part of a factory staff. So they become fully familiar with the technical capacities and constraints of one of 3M's plants. But their job brings them into contact with customers two to three days per week. Because of the nature of their job, they are constantly hearing about customer problems and customer requests for changes in the product. They act as middle-men between the customer and the plant. They learn to use plant resources to solve customer problems.

At 3M, this is viewed as an extremely good preparation for later contributions to innovation. The technical service rep learns early that there are two sides to the business. On the one hand, there is 'what the company can do.' He or she learns the capacities and constraints of 3M as a technical institution. On the other hand there is 'what the customer wants'. The technical rep learns, in general, what customer needs are, how they express them, and how he or she can bring 3M's technical resources to bear in helping meet customer needs. This early training stays in the memory of 3M people for a long time. While people who have been technical service reps may go on to laboratory jobs where they have little direct contact with customers, they will not forget their early experience. They will remember that 3M works by serving customer needs, and they will retain some skill at listening to customer needs.

ConsumerCo puts its junior managers through a similar experience. All newly hired marketers must spend six to twelve months on a sales route as a normal sales person. People who rotate through marketing jobs later in their careers must do the same thing. This six to twelve month experience gives them a direct understanding of what customers want and of how to sell. In the words of one ConsumerCo manager, they will not be theorists or desk-bound managers after that. They will always remember the customers behind the numbers. ConsumerCo does not stop with the early six month exposure. The company expects each marketing manager and each general manager to spend at least one day each month on a sales route, talking to customers. This reinforces in everyone's mind that there is no more important job in the company than listening to customers. And it gives senior managers a regular contact with the marketplace which helps prevent them from losing touch with the market.

None of the other companies I visited had such fixed career paths. Both 3M and ConsumerCo viewed these early experiences as key to maintaining the company's innovative edge. At 3M, young technical people learned to link market needs with technical resources very early. The company hopes that they will continue to look for links between market needs and the company's technical capabilities for the rest of their careers (Dougherty, 1992). At ConsumerCo, young marketers and other managers learn early the importance of listening to customers. They also learn what sells. This experience is reinforced regularly, as they must spend one day each month for the rest of their careers talking to customers.

Stability of personnel and turnover

The most innovative companies I visited all experienced very low turnover. This was in line with management's wishes. Senior management at 3M, ConsumerCo and Eastman Chemical all wanted low turnover and a stable personnel base. Eastman Chemical experienced turnover in the 2–3 percent range. 3M and ConsumerCo had comparably low levels of turnover.

Why would this be seen as supporting innovation? In the first place, it reflects the companies' desire to maintain their skill base. People who leave before retirement take skills with them that the company could use. To keep the skills, the company has to keep the people.

But this traditional reason for limiting turnover is not the only reason. At these companies, each technical person and each marketer is an important part of the company's information and knowledge network. After a few years at the company, each person knows a lot of people. When an individual wants information on a particular subject, she knows where to go. When other people want information she has, they know they can come to her. If she leaves, a node in the network is lost. The accumulated knowledge of the company that she will take with her will be harder to replace than her technical knowledge.

In addition to the technical and network knowledge that the person takes with her, she takes away her fluency at speaking the company's common language. A newly hired person may have the same technical skills, but he will not necessarily be able to communicate as easily with others in the company. He will not know the company's experience. He will not know the examples which work and which motivate people. He will not know the values that underlie people's behavior.

ConsumerCo starts managing turnover even before people join the company. When it interviews candidates, it looks for people who want to spend their entire career at one company. A person who expresses the desire to stay with one company for her entire career is much more likely to be hired than one who appears to be shopping for a 'first job' that will lead to a second job with a different company.

3M is not so explicit about hiring people for life. But they want people to stay for life nonetheless. The company encourages people to stay by providing them with an environment that is more interesting than any alternative. The 3M environment includes unparalleled technical resources in areas like adhesives, coatings and surfaces. Technology, equipment and knowledgeable colleagues are all there, readily at hand. For anyone who is interested in exploring these areas, 3M is the best place in the world to be.

What's more, 3M lets people explore whatever new technologies they wish, with the full support of the company, as long as the company may at some point benefit from the work. 3M hopes that people who want to innovate will find this a very attractive place to stay.

ConsumerCo uses some of the same means to combat turnover. Like 3M, it provides an unparalleled technical environment in the areas it specializes in. In addition, it is one of the world's leading consumer marketing organizations. It offers outstanding opportunities both the technical and marketing side.

ConsumerCo also uses its compensation policy to fight turnover. Pay is linked to seniority. In effect, there is an informal deferred compensation policy. Outstanding young performers do not receive financial rewards immediately. They receive promotions. Their pay ramps up slowly as they prove themselves year after year. They know that there will be a financial reward. But it doesn't come immediately. It comes only if they show that they want to stick with the company.

I have made the point that innovative companies have low turnover. Some less innovative companies also had low turnover. MGE is a headquartered in a country where public policy and tradition discourage job-hopping. It is no surprise that the company experiences low turnover. The point is that the company makes no particular effort to maintain low turnover. It just happens because that is the way things are done in MGE's home country. In the 1980s MGE made no effort to take advantage of this fact by building stable, company-wide technology networks for instance. It experienced low turnover without trying to, and it failed to gain the innovation advantages it could have obtained from it.

Individual goals

Some companies allow their people to set their own goals to some extent. At other companies, senior management sets all goals. In between these extremes, there are several variants.

At one extreme, 3M allows technical people to do whatever they want with 15 percent of their time. The only constraint is that they work they do must have some possibility of benefiting the company at some future point. They can, clearly, set their own goals for what they do with their time. In addition, while doing company work they are allowed to decide for themselves how they will do it. The goals may come from their boss, but they can decide for themselves how they are going to reach the goals.

ConsumerCo does not have a 15 percent rule, but its scientists do have considerable freedom. Some do personal projects, but normally they negotiate the terms of these projects with their bosses first. Eastman Chemical has a similar, if more formalized system. A percentage of the whole R&D budget is reserved for speculative work. Any scientist in the company can apply for part of this money. Not all apply. In fact, less than half apply. Some end up working full time on the speculative projects they have proposed. Others, those who don't apply for the money, end up working on company projects.

None of the other companies in the sample had formal or informal methods of supporting personal projects. Some MGE units, including Industrial Chemicals, were talking of establishing 15 percent rules by the mid-1990s. But none had done so. Laboratory resources were fully allocated, and management feared that important work would not get done if scientists were allowed to work on their own projects. EurAuto laboratories were similarly fully allocated. No one had time for personal projects.

Evaluation methods

Companies vary considerably in how they evaluate people. One dimension of variation is the 'style' or 'focus' of the evaluation. Other dimensions are who performs the evaluation, and the criteria and data used. Finally, the supervisor who performs the evaluation may be either rather close or quite distant to the person being evaluated. I will discuss each of these dimensions in turn.

'Style,' or 'focus' of the evaluation In the traditional company, an evaluation looks at what a person has done, good and bad. A label is put on the person. Some are 'high performers'. Others are 'good contributors' or 'average'. Still others are 'below standard'. The high performers can expect promotions. They are identified as the future leaders of the company. The good contributors can expect a long career in the company, but not necessarily much advancement. Those who are below standard can expect to be pushed out of the company if they don't improve.

In this traditional system the supervisor evaluates the person's past performance and puts a label, good or bad, on it. The supervisor also sets goals for the future. But not all companies follow this traditional system. Not all put labels like 'good performance' and 'bad performance' on a person's past.

Eastman Chemical is one of the exceptions. It has developed an evaluation system that does not label past performance as 'good' or 'bad'. Eastman management believes that negative evaluations demotivate people. So they believe that their system motivates people more effectively than a traditional system.

One Eastman manager explained the logic of the Eastman system as follows. The result of a normal evaluation, in Eastman's view, is that the good performers will be discouraged. After being told that they are just 'average', they can have one of two reactions. They may decide that the person evaluating them 'just doesn't understand' the value of their work. Or they can resign themselves to being 'just average' and give up on ever making a significant contribution to the company. Eastman does not want them to give up. It wants them to continue trying to make an outstanding contribution. So it does not tell anyone that they are average.

What an Eastman manager will discuss with his subordinates is three things. He will ask each subordinate to list his or her accomplishments in the past year. He may add a few to the list. Then he will ask them what they hope to achieve in the next year. Again, he may add a few things to the list. Finally, they discuss future expectations for promotions and other opportunities. While they do not want to label people as 'average', neither do they want people's expectations to get wildly out of line.

Eastman does designate a few of its young managers as having 'high potential' for a future management career. These people do have a special career path. Over five to ten years, they are rotated through a variety of management positions. This gives them experience with many aspects of the company's operations. They then move on into general management positions.

But there are other ways to excel at Eastman. Those who are not on the 'high potential' track can still move into high-level functional positions. Or they may move into general management positions later. Like many technical companies, including 3M, Eastman has a dual-track career ladder. A bright technical person does not have to move into management to move up. So those who are not designated high potential still have other opportunities.

What the Eastman system does is maintain hope. It is designed to give each member of the Eastman team a chance to excel in his or her own way. The evaluation is designed not to kill this hope but to channel it in the direction where the person has the best chance of success.

Eastman's evaluation system is exceptional. I did not find any other companies who had thought through the psychology behind the evaluation in such detail. Other companies in the sample may have tried to avoid stigmatizing people in practice, but none of the others had worked out a way of systematically avoiding stigma.

Who contributes to the evaluation? In a traditional company, a person's boss may perform the evaluation without consulting anyone else. MGE for many years had such a system. The more innovative companies sought input from a much wider range of people. At a minimum, the person performing the evaluation talked to other people at his or her hierarchical level. At 3M, the evaluator talks, in addition, to the person's customers, both internal and external. At Eastman, there is a formal system of 360-degree evaluations. The evaluator asks people's bosses, colleagues and subordinates for input. At ConsumerCo, the evaluator may talk to many of the people the person knows.

The question, 'Who contributes to the evaluation?' matters because it tells the person evaluated what she should be paying attention to. If evaluators talk to customers, then she should be paying attention to how she treats customers. If they talk to subordinates, then she should be paying attention to how she deals with subordinates. If neither subordinates nor customers have input into the evaluation, then maybe their opinions, and how they are treated, are less important.

Intense self-evaluation Eastman's evaluation system has another unusual twist. After a few years at Eastman, anyone on a management track will be asked to spend one week at an off-site self-evaluation session. The session takes place at the Center for Creative Learning (CCL), a center which not only aids managers in their self-development, but also tracks them and does ongoing research on managerial career paths.

The session begins with managers being placed in a number of normal management situations. The CCL staff observes how the manager behaves in these situations. Later, it explores the manager's strengths and weaknesses in detail. Managers are encouraged to examine how they deal with people, when their methods works and why, when they don't work and why. They also look at their values, how their values affect the way they deal with people, and whether their current career choice really fits their deepest values.

After this session, Eastman managers report that they see their jobs differently. They are more sensitized to how they deal with people. In general, they think they deal with them more effectively. In addition, they have a new perspective on their values and their career. Some people leave the CCL session reconfirmed in their desire to advance at Eastman. Others discover that they would be happier remaining in technical positions or moving outside of a management career altogether. Eastman is happy whatever choice they make, since Eastman management believes that the company will be better off if its people are doing things which are in line with their basic values.

The managers who visit the CCL view it as a good experience. The evaluation helps them think through how to improve their management style. The opportunity to reflect on their career and their values gives them a longer-term perspective on their own development and the direction they want their career to go in. Eastman views it as good since its managers come back knowing better what they want to do and how to manage.

Criteria and data used in the evaluation All companies look at the contribution a person has made to the company's results when evaluating him. But what else they look at, and how they define contribution to results, varies enormously.

MGE had the simplest evaluation system of any of the companies. If a business unit manager achieved his profit goals for the year, he was doing a good job. If he didn't, he wasn't. Of course, if he destroyed a lot of capital equipment in the process, or alienated a major customer, he would hear about it. But short of such extreme behavior, all that mattered, really, was hitting the profit numbers. Promotion depended on that and on getting along with senior management or fitting the mold of what senior management thought the management team should look like.

ConsumerCo was at the opposite extreme. Here results mattered, but what mattered even more was how the results were achieved. It was well known at ConsumerCo that a manager could puff up her short-term results in ways that hurt a business's long-term position. She could dilute the brand's image by targeting products at the wrong audience. She could sacrifice R&D investment or market research. She could alter pricing policy in ways that undermined the brand's positioning. Many other variations on the theme were possible. So senior managers looked carefully at how their subordinates achieved their results.

ConsumerCo also considered other things. How well managers were developing their subordinates mattered. Whether or not they were investing in innovations mattered. How well they were managing the brand mattered. Cooperation with other units, in some cases, mattered. There are no specific overall evaluation criteria at ConsumerCo. Rather, managers are evaluated on their overall contribution to the company. The theory is that however they contribute, and wherever they contribute, it will be noticed, and it is the sum total of their contributions which will be evaluated, not a simple measure like short-term profit.

Most of the companies were in between MGE and ConsumerCo. At the more innovative companies, 3M and Eastman Chemical, contribution to innovation was a key criterion in evaluating people. Other companies did not cite innovation as a criterion. For some jobs at 3M, the criteria are 'whatever criteria the customer (internal or external) imposes'. EurAuto took a similar approach. But in general, the evaluation criteria at more innovative companies had three characteristics. There were more criteria. One of the criteria was 'contribution to innovation'. And the criteria tended to include more nonfinancial, qualitative elements.

Closeness of the supervisor to the person being evaluated Evaluations at MGE could, in theory, have been carried out from a considerable distance. Anyone who knew the targets that had been set for a unit could evaluate the management team by reading the unit's financial statement. People who had never visited the unit or even seen the unit's management team could do this evaluation. Things were not actually done that way at MGE. But at times they were done in ways that were not far from this description.

One MGE division manager told me about an evaluation he had received from the corporate executive committee. A senior manager who was only marginally involved with his unit looked at his financial statements and told him that his profits were too low. If he didn't raise them soon he would be fired. That was it. That was the evaluation. There was no discussion of what had happened or why. The supervisor knew a little about how he had been running the division. But he did not talk or inquire about what had happened. Nor did he offer to discuss the steps that could be taken to improve things. That the division manager had to worry about. By himself.

At ConsumerCo, by contrast, no one is ever left by themselves. Supervisors are intimately involved with their subordinates. ConsumerCo's consensus decision system assures that supervisors will not only know what their subordinates are doing, they will be brought into much of the decision-making, as it happens. As a result, supervisors at ConsumerCo are much more knowledgeable about what their subordinates have done than those at MGE. They are in a position to evaluate how they have done their job, how they have achieved their results, because they were there watching when they did it.

In general, more innovative companies had closer links and more communication between superiors and subordinates. ConsumerCo, 3M, and Eastman Chemical all had high amounts of vertical communication. This was less evident at less innovative companies like EurAuto and Industrial Chemicals. (See Table 5.4 for a summary of key issues in the area of other personnel management systems.)

Culture

Culture is, in part, a set of unwritten rules. Companies have rules. But no company has rules that will cover every possible situation a person will be in. At times people have to use their judgement. How they use their judgement usually depends, at least in part, on what they believe the company would want them to do. What the company would want can be communicated through statements of purpose and general principles, through stories, and through examples.

A culture can either be supportive of innovation or it can discourage it. It can encourage people to support innovation, or it can encourage them to avoid it, to 'play it safe'. The extent to which a culture supports innovation can vary considerably from company to company.

At ConsumerCo, 3M, and Eastman Chemical, everything is done to assure that the culture supports innovation. There are general statements of principle and purpose which support innovation. Managers regularly tell stories that illustrate the importance of supporting innovation. Managers themselves provide examples of responsible people supporting innovation.

Table 5.4   Other personnel management systems and their impact

Aspect of personnel management	Tool or variable . . . . . Impact	
Personnel sourcing: hiring	■ Hire individuals with 'creative flair', individuals with hands-on experience executing new projects ■ Hire people with varied backgrounds	■ Increases chances that personnel will have creative ideas, and that they will follow them through ■ Increased variety of viewpoints
Personnel development	■ Rotation across functions, product lines, geographies ■ Promotion to the top from several backgrounds ■ Standard passages: – Technical service – Sales route	■ More mixing of different perspectives, more new ideas ■ Broader, more balanced perspective in top team ■ Common experience or especially useful experience: – Sees technical and market issues at same time – Learns customer concerns
Stability of personnel, turnover	■ Keep people, low turnover	■ Retains skills, retains knowledge of company, knowledge of networks within company
Individual goals	■ Allow people freedom to select some of their own activities (15 percent rule)	■ Encourages entrepreneurial activity, allows quick reaction to new opportunity
Evaluation methods	■ Traditional style versus focus on what person will accomplish ■ Who contributes to evaluation	■ Traditional style can discourage people, focus on accomplishments motivates them ■ If more people contribute this forces the person to pay attention to a wider range of concerns

(cont'd)

Table 5.4 (cont'd)

Aspect of personnel management	Tool or variable . . . . . . Impact	
	■ Criteria and data used:	■ Influences what people pay attention to in their work:
	– Financial criteria only	– People will focus on financial results
	– Wider range of criteria, including how results were achieved	– People more likely to focus on long-term development, innovation
	■ Closeness of supervisor to person being evaluated:	■ Affects range of data that can be used:
	– Close, sees daily/weekly	– Can evaluate on a wide range of behaviors, skills
	– Distant, sees monthly or less	– May have to focus on measurable (financial) results

At MGE in the 1980s, the opposite was the case. No general principle supported product innovation. No one told stories which encouraged people to support innovation. By contrast, the stories that floated around the company indicated that those who took risks would be thrown out of the company if the risks didn't work out. So no one took risks. Managers weren't good examples for others since they didn't support product innovation themselves.

Culture has dimensions. In the first part of this section I will discuss eight dimensions of internal culture that have some impact on a company's innovation performance. Then I will look in detail at the issue of managing fear. Then I will discuss cultural issues that have an impact on the way the company relates to its customers. Finally I will discuss briefly the methods of passing culture. (See Table 5.5 for a list of key questions in the area of culture.)

Table 5.5   Questions to ask about culture

Storytelling

- What kinds of stories do managers (and others) in the company tell?

- Who are the heroes of the stories? How did they become heroes?

- Do the stories encourage people to innovate? Or do they encourage people to play it safe?

Mixed messages

- Does management send clear and unambiguous messages about innovation, or mixed messages?

Management attitudes

- Do we manage by fear? Or do we manage without fear?

- Do we try to give people a vision? Or do we just push them with fear?

- Are managers willing to listen to new ideas?

- Do managers give more weight to market considerations when making decisions? To technical considerations? Or are both market and technical issues considered when making key decisions?

- How do we apportion credit for success? Do we favor particular groups or individuals, thus discouraging others?

- How do we handle errors? Do we blame and stigmatize people? Or do we give them a 'right of error'?

Customer relations

- How do we handle our customer relations?

- Can customers trust us? Do customers trust us? Do we trust our customers?

- Do we understand what customers like and dislike about us? Do we have programs in place to preserve or enhance what they like and to suppress what they don't like?

Conscious management of culture

- Do we know what our culture is? Have we verified our opinions?

- Do we manage our culture consciously? Do we manage it effectively?

Dimensions of culture impacting behavior inside the company

People within a company may have a number of general 'attitudes' which can have either a positive or a negative impact on the company's innovation performance:

1. They may be resistant to innovation or supportive of it
2. Management may send clear messages about innovation or these messages may be very mixed
3. Management may manage by fear or manage without fear
4. Managers may be willing to question and change their beliefs and ways of doing things, or they may be unwilling to do so
5. They may be willing to listen, or unwilling
6. Some cultures are technically oriented while others are marketing oriented
7. Culture also impacts the way a company apportions credit for success
8. In some cultures there is a right of error, while in others there is not.

Each of these dimensions of culture has an impact on a company's ability to innovate.

Resistance to innovation versus support of innovation A company's managers may actively try to build support of innovation, or they may act in ways which build resistance to innovation. A common method of building support is storytelling. Managers at 3M constantly tell stories about heroes who succeeded in bringing new products to the market despite substantial technical and marketing difficulties, and, sometimes, despite the opposition of highly placed managers within 3M itself. They tell stories which illustrate the importance of innovation at 3M, the fact that the company has built its entire revenue base through innovation. They also tell stories about people who ran innovation projects which failed, but which nonetheless brought significant benefits to the company, in the form of knowledge or experience.

There are several messages behind these stories. One is that innovation is important. That 3M is built on it. Another is that innovation may be hard. Difficult technical and marketing problems may come up. But persistence may overcome them (another message). The final message is that failure is OK. Everybody who tries to innovate fails. Failure won't kill anyone in the company. In fact many people who have failed have gone on to great things. The implication of this last message is that taking risks is OK. No one will be punished for taking a calculated risk that doesn't work out.

The stories that floated around at MGE were quite different. People talked about the members of an innovation team who were summarily fired when their project failed to work out. They talked about senior managers who promoted people who played it safe, while passing over people who took risks. The messages of these stories were clear. Don't take risks and don't get involved in innovation projects if you want to stay with the company.

3M's management team manages the stories which float around the company. A 3M R&D manager told me:

Telling stories is an important part of a manager's job at 3M. We tell stories about innovation that will encourage people to take risks, stories that will encourage them go ahead and try it if they have an idea. That's what we want them to do, so we encourage them by telling them stories about people who have tried it and succeeded. We also tell stories about projects that fail, because then they will see that failing doesn't kill you here. You can try something and, if it fails, you can just try something else.

MGE managers did not manage the stories that floated around the company. They made no particular effort to tell stories that made any point about innovation. While, by the early 1990s, they wanted their people to innovate more, they did little to contest the stories which were floating around which indicated that innovation was risky and better avoided if one wanted to advance in the company.

Training programs are another method of building enthusiasm for innovation. MGE put hundreds of managers through training programs in the 1990s. In divisions where senior management followed through and brought their evaluation and other systems in line with the new preference for innovation, the culture changed. Risk-taking and participation in innovation projects became much more common and acceptable. But in other divisions management was less consistent and people continued to be risk-averse.

I must say that enthusiasm for innovation can be carried too far. Senior management at MGE's Lawn & Garden division was worried about the division's future. They did not have enough good new products in the product pipeline. So they decided to support several promising innovation projects. The problem was they went too far. They began suppressing dissent about the projects. They refused to hear bad news and they refused to let anyone else act on bad news.

One project that they invested much money and effort into failed to achieve more than a small fraction of its expected revenues. There had been numerous signs that the project was going to fail, but they ignored them all. This led to a serious public relations debacle. Division management had publicly promised customers that the new product would bring them substantial benefit. It did not. This failure to give what was promised harmed the credibility of the entire division.

Ambiguity: clear or mixed messages about innovation 3M managers give clear, consistent messages about innovation and participation in innovation projects. Both are good. No one has any reason to think that innovating or participating in an innovation project would be harmful to her career at 3M. Quite the opposite is the case. Both will help the person's career. Participating in an innovation project that fails will not harm the person's career. In fact, it may help it, since the company will appreciate and use what she learned.

MGE managers, by and large, do not give such clear messages. A statement that the company needs more innovations could be accompanied by a statement that last quarter's profits were below targets. So which should a manager work on: building up short-term profits, or investing in R&D for the long term? Most MGE managers thought the executive committee was more worried about short-term profits. So they worked on that.

Management by fear or management without fear In 1994, MGE's Ingredients business unit had a culture that was quite different from the mother company's. The unit had been acquired by MGE just three years before. The manager who ran it carefully maintained the unit's independence and its unique culture.

The most striking difference between Ingredients and MGE as a whole was the use or abuse of fear by the two management teams. At MGE headquarters, many people were visibly afraid of senior managers like Paul Thomas – introduced in the story of the Chemical Residues project, in my previous book (Christiansen, 2000). When he came into a room, they would tense up and stop talking. The head of Ingredients inspired no such fear. His subordinates talked to him as casually as they would to a close friend.

Paul Thomas spoke freely of using fear as a management tool. People who failed should be punished, he often said. There was no other way. And he let it be known that project teams who failed to meet targets would be punished. As a result, many of the people who worked under him were afraid to take risks.

The head of Ingredients never talked about punishment. He talked about managing without fear and ran his division with as little fear as possible. He tried to appeal to people's desire to contribute and found that they responded well to this appeal. He believed that people would be much more innovative if they were motivated by a desire to contribute rather than a desire to avoid punishment.

Recently, several popular books have recommended the use of fear as a motivator for innovation (Grove, 1996; Meyer, 1998). While fear is a powerful motivator, it is a two-edged sword. It can discourage innovation as much as it encourages it. Determining when and how to use fear is an important issue. As a result, I will devote an entire section to this subject later in this chapter.

Willingness to question and change beliefs and behavior The more innovative companies expect their managers to be willing to question and change beliefs and behavior. This works at the individual level at ConsumerCo. People are expected to question their own beliefs and to be willing to change them if there is evidence that they are wrong. They are also expected to be willing to alter their behavior when their behavior is not consistent with good management practice or with the best interests of the company. People without the ability or willingness to change their beliefs and behavior when necessary will not advance very far.

At 3M, this works more on a group level. People are expected to question the prevailing beliefs of the company. They are expected to act as individuals, to respect their own beliefs, and to persist in questioning common wisdom. This expectation provides a mechanism for bringing change into the system. If the company's beliefs are out of line with reality, individuals who point this out will receive some support, since they are exercising the principles of respecting their own beliefs and questioning common wisdom. How quickly the company will listen will vary with their persuasiveness, the data they are able to bring to bear on the issue, and the ability of those around them to listen. But their right, even obligation, to dissent will not be brought into question.

Eastman Chemical has a similar rule. But at Eastman, the key word is 'humility'. Managers are expected to be humble. This means two things. First, they are expected to recognize that they always have something to learn. They don't know everything about their business, so there is always more knowledge to be gained. No one individual can be the best in all aspects of management, so there are always ways to improve their individual skill at management as well.

The second aspect of humility applies to the company as a whole. Eastman managers are expected to recognize that the company always has something to learn. Complacency is out. Continuous improvement is in. Eastman managers tell stories that illustrate how complacency can hurt a company. They tell stories about other companies that lost markets through complacency.

One Eastman manager told me that Eastman had failed to recognize a flaw in the manufacturing process of one of its businesses. For many years, the costs of that business were out of line with those of its competitors. Eastman finally left the business. Only later did the company discover that a simple change in the manufacturing process could have saved the business. The manager used this story to illustrate the importance of two things: constant attention to detail and constant willingness to bring current practices into question and to improve.

Managers at the MGE divisions and at EurAuto did not put any emphasis on humility and questioning beliefs. It's not that arrogance and complacency were viewed as appropriate behavior. It's just that there was no particular emphasis on being humble or being willing to put oneself into question. No manager at MGE or EurAuto said that there was any expectation to be humble. Nor did they indicate that anyone was expected to question their companies' beliefs. No one's career would be held up if they weren't humble. But at Eastman, 3M and ConsumerCo, managers stated explicitly that these were important features of company policy. Humility was necessary at Eastman. Willingness to question one's own beliefs and behavior was necessary at ConsumerCo. And willingness to question the company's beliefs was a great advantage at 3M.

Criticism of current policies and beliefs can be suppressed at any company. At MGE's Lawn & Garden division, managers suppressed criticism of an important innovation project. They ignored negative signals about the project's prospects and encouraged the project team to ignore them as well. As a result, the project's failure was a complete surprise. The project's failure caused serious damage to the division's credibility in the market, causing long-term harm to its prospects.

Willingness to listen A manager in EuroChem's Innovation Office told me that managers at EuroChem needed to learn how to listen. He said that subordinates often came to their managers with half-formed ideas. If the manager listened to the idea and helped the subordinate develop it, something might come of it. But if he only half listened and dismissed the idea, the subordinate might return to his desk, 'put the idea in a drawer', and nothing would happen.

At ConsumerCo, managers are trained to listen. Many junior managers go through formal training programs in listening. They are trained in how to listen to their subordinates in ways that will help them develop their half-formed ideas. Some are trained to facilitate creativity in small groups. With such training, they are better able to help subordinates develop ideas, and junior people at ConsumerCo will be less likely to 'put their ideas in a drawer' after a meeting with their boss.

Marketing orientation versus technical orientation Some companies are run by marketers. The majority of senior managers in the company may have training and extensive experience in marketing. Marketing considerations may have predominant weight in all decisions. Marketers may have the most influential roles throughout the system, in fact. Such companies are 'marketing oriented'.

Other companies are run by technical people. The majority of senior managers may have training and extensive experience in technical functions. Technical considerations may have predominant weight in all decisions. Technical people may have the most influential roles throughout the system. Such companies are 'technically oriented'.

If I were to put the eight companies in my sample into two groups, I would put all but ConsumerCo into the technically oriented group. ConsumerCo would be marketing oriented. But three companies do not easily fit into the groups. These are ConsumerCo, 3M and Eastman.

ConsumerCo is the most difficult to classify. ConsumerCo is a consumer products company. As a result, marketing considerations have a high weight in any decision. And marketing is considered the 'royal road' to promotion at ConsumerCo. But two of the company's last four CEOs have had technical backgrounds. And technical considerations have, at times, outweighed marketing considerations in decisions about product development.

ConsumerCo has many mechanisms to ensure that both marketing and technical considerations receive weight in decisions. Marketing and technical people both sit on product management boards that meet monthly and make key decisions about how products are managed. Liaison people facilitate communication between the two functions and assure that each understands the concerns of the other. Finally, rotation between functions assures that many senior managers have experience both with marketing and with the management of technical areas. With these three mechanisms in place, both marketing and technical perspectives are represented in key decisions.

3M is famous as a technical company. But, on close inspection, it is quite good at industrial marketing as well. Its technical people often begin their careers in technical service jobs. These jobs bring them into contact with customers several days a week. For many of them, the contact with customers never stops. If they go on to work in a development laboratory, they will have contact with the customers they are developing products for. If they go on to positions in a factory, they will have contact with the factory's customers. Only if they go on into fundamental research are they likely to be insulated from customers.

3M's habit of placing most of its employees onto cross-functional teams assures that all technical people will be familiar with marketing issues. The reverse is true as well. All marketers will be familiar with technical issues. The company also practices excellent industrial marketing techniques, techniques that technical people become familiar with. It forms contacts with customer companies at many levels. It communicates in the customer's language. And it surveys both its customers and its customers' customers so that it can achieve a comprehensive understanding of its customers' markets.

Finally, 3M tries to maintain a mix of people at the top who have both technical and marketing backgrounds. This is another method of ensuring that both technical and marketing considerations receive weight in any decision.

So 3M, like ConsumerCo, does not easily fit into either the technically oriented or the marketing oriented group. If put on a scale, both would be near the middle, with 3M somewhat on the technical side, and ConsumerCo somewhat on the marketing side.

Eastman, like 3M, looks technically oriented at first glance. But again there are numerous mechanisms to assure that both types of considerations receive weight in any decision. High potential managers are rotated through technical and marketing functions on the way up. And the top team has a mix of backgrounds.

The way Eastman handles new product ideas is particularly revealing. Ideas often come from technical people, but they can come from sales people or marketers as well. Often they come from technical service people. By definition these are people with technical training who have continuous contact with customers.

As Eastman has plenty of technologists, the technical problems involved in developing an idea are likely to be recognized quickly. But the product development system forces people to think about market considerations very early as well. In fact, the first thing the person who generates the idea must do is to estimate the size of the potential market. Someone else validates this estimate for plausibility before it is entered into Eastman's idea bank. The estimate is refined and tested as development proceeds and more is learned about the product and its market.

So Eastman forces its people to think about markets as well as about technology. It, too, does not fit easily into the technology oriented group, although appears somewhat more oriented in that direction than 3M. This is not surprising, since Eastman is at the beginning of the chemical product chain (it produces primary chemicals) while 3M is part of the way downstream (it buys primary chemicals and turns them into other industrial products).

MGE, Northern Pharmaceuticals and EurAuto fit more securely into the technology oriented group, although each is trying to get out. MGE made no consistent attempt to bring market considerations into its new product development process until the 1990s. Scientists could work on any project that was of interest to them, as long as they could sell it to a laboratory or business unit manager. No systematic thinking about market attractiveness was required. Then, in the early 1990s, some new MGE products experienced serious problems gaining market acceptance. After that managers began requiring a serious study of a product's planned market before funding a project.

A more serious problem for MGE is the make-up of its management team. One senior manager confided to me that no one without technical training could make it in the senior management team. The corporate management team and the top three levels of each divisional management team were made up of people with technical training. Several marketers had been promoted into these ranks, but they had not been accepted and they had not survived long.

Another senior MGE manager said that most MGE managers did not consider marketing very relevant. The image marketers had in the company was the following. 'They are seen as people who sit in offices producing columns of numbers that don't have any relevance to anything. No marketer ever understands any market.' With such a reputation, it's not surprising that few senior people at MGE listened to marketers, or knew very much about the marketing side of their business.

Northern Pharmaceuticals began to embrace marketing earlier than MGE. Through the mid-1980s, product development was run by laboratory managers. Each laboratory manager had his favorite projects and those projects received funding. None of the laboratory managers was required to produce any documentation of the potential market value of projects he was funding. This technically oriented system began cracking in the late 1980s.

The first crack was, indeed, a major one. Consultants were brought in to reform the product development system. They analyzed each project on the basis of its technical feasibility *and its potential market payoff.* They recommended keeping those that had the highest potential for success, based on a combination of technical and market considerations.

Northern Pharmaceuticals adopted these recommendations and cancelled about two-thirds of its projects. For several years Northern's management team focused on managing these projects well. But the company still did not have a systematic means of bringing market considerations to bear on new project funding decisions. This changed in the early 1990s when the company hired a new head of R&D from the outside. The new head of R&D established a very clear set of criteria for funding new projects. The criteria included potential market size, potential profitability, existing competitors, and the number of competitors likely to appear before the product reached the market. To meet these criteria, project managers had to do serious studies of the potential market before beginning expensive stages of the project, such as clinical research.

EurAuto, like MGE and Northern, was clearly a technically oriented company until the mid-1980s. Then it lost money for several years. The board brought in a new management team, and the new team tried to get the company to pay more attention to market considerations. Before the financial crisis, EurAuto had managed vehicle development in a way that gave great weight to technical considerations. The development area was run and staffed by technical people. Marketing was not involved in product development until the car was designed. The main goal of development seemed to be to design the most technically perfect car, given economic constraints. However, the 'perfect car', in the engineer's view, did not correspond to the customer's view of the best car to buy.

EurAuto fell into a financial crisis because its cars wouldn't sell. It was as simple as that. For years consumers bought EurAuto cars because there wasn't much else available. All the European manufacturers were capacity constrained. People couldn't get enough cars. They would buy whatever the manufacturers put on the market. And, what's more, the government in EurAuto's home country protected it from competition in its domestic market. In that kind of environment, EurAuto thrived.

But that environment ended. After the second oil crisis (1979–80), European demand for cars flattened while capacity continued to go up. EurAuto's sales fell and the company went into deficit.

The effect on the development area was dramatic. For years they had been able to design whatever car they wanted and consumers would buy it. They had been very technically oriented. Marketing considerations had no weight in their design decisions. No marketing data was used in design decisions. There weren't even any marketers on design teams to give any voice to the customer. But suddenly this system wasn't working any more.

The leaders of the development area reacted like human beings often do. They thought the decline in sales was someone else's fault. Sales just wasn't pushing the cars enough. Or the customers weren't educated enough. They didn't know a good car when they saw one. The new management team that took over the company after the old CEO was thrown out didn't agree. They thought that there might be a connection between development paying no attention to customers and customers not buying the cars. This was a revolutionary thought at EurAuto and it led to some revolutionary reforms. The new CEO set up development teams led by managers who were sympathetic to marketing. Marketing and sales were represented on the team from the first. The basic concept and design of the car had to be approved by marketing before a full design project could begin. Marketing was part of the project team board that approved all changes in the car.

Marketing was not the only function affected. Manufacturing had never been involved in design projects either. They had always begun their work when development was finished. If the design was difficult to manufacture, they sometimes had to redesign the car. The new project team structure brought manufacturing in at the beginning. The result was far more manufacturable designs.

This story is not unique to EurAuto. It is the story of virtually every Western automobile company. All went through a transition from sequential product development (one function starting work only when the previous function finished) to simultaneous product development (all functions starting at the same time). They found that they could produce better cars, quicker and faster by having the functions work together. Some did better than others. EurAuto was not a leader. They were part of the pack. But they did improve. The quality of their cars improved dramatically. The cost went down as well. But the speed of product development did not improve very much. It still took them much longer than a Japanese manufacturer to design a new car.

I talked to a number of EurAuto's development engineers seven years after the change programs began. Their attitudes may explain why it was still difficult to get a car out quickly. They were still out to design the technically best car. While project teams included marketing representatives, the engineers were still very technically oriented.

EurAuto's engineers still talked like much like they had years before. They argued that customers just didn't understand how good their cars really were. They carefully explained to me that the Japanese were not nearly as ambitious as they were when they designed a car. EurAuto's cars were far more difficult to design and build. The idea that the Japanese were building cars the way people wanted them, while they were overdesigning and overbuilding them, had still not sunk in. EurAuto had survived the financial crisis, but people with a free choice preferred Japanese cars by a wide margin. Consumers in EurAuto's home market still did not have a free choice. So EurAuto made an effort to become more balanced in its orientation. Starting as a very technically oriented company, it gave increased consideration to marketing concerns after the mid-1980s. But its core design teams were still very technically oriented and the company's products reflected this.

To summarize this section, we have seen that the most innovative companies are neither purely technically oriented nor purely marketing oriented. They are somewhere in between. Their design teams give nearly equal weight to technical and marketing considerations. The less innovative companies among the eight were more technically oriented. Presumably a marketing oriented company that gave little weight to technical considerations would be less innovative as well.

Apportioning credit for success Companies vary in the way they assign credit and blame. Basically they can reward success or ignore it. They can punish failure, find something to praise in it, or ignore it. Which they choose can have an impact on how well the company innovates.

All companies I visited reward success. Or at least they say they do. Successful project managers are promoted and rewarded. But sometimes the teams behind them are ignored. In one MGE division, a project manager complained to me that that his incentive compensation was too high. A rare complaint, to say the least. But the logic behind the complaint was compelling.

This project manager would receive a huge bonus if his project succeeded. He would also receive a major promotion, skipping several levels. But what would his team receive? There would be no huge bonus for them. At best they would receive small bonuses. There would be no major promotions for them. More likely they would move horizontally into jobs at the same or a slightly higher level. Where was the equity? In the project manager's own view, it was the team that was doing the vast majority of work on the project, not him. He just coordinated it. Of course coordination was an important job. But it didn't mean that he deserved 95 percent of the credit.

The project manager thought MGE's reward system was demotivating for the team. Nor was it very beneficial for him. While he would not refuse the money, nor the promotion, what he really wanted was to lead another project. He was doing work he loved. He wanted to continue doing it. The promotion would take him away from what he loved and alienate him from the team he had worked with for many years. He just didn't like the way MGE managed its rewards.

Those who have read the section on incentives may recognize several problems. The project manager was motivated mainly by the *intrinsic* rewards of the job. What he wanted most was to continue doing what he was doing, because he loved doing it. The large *extrinsic* rewards he was being offered did not motivate him in the way management expected. They did not motivate him in part because they would have taken him away from what he loved doing. The promotion would have put him into a different job, one he did not particularly want. The money would not buy him what he really wanted, which was the chance to do another project. He was just not doing it just for the money. He was doing it for the love of the job.

The other problem was that the project team would not be rewarded for success. In the MGE system, all credit would go to the project manager. The project manager might take them out to dinner, but that would be it. Beyond that, success wouldn't boost their careers to any significant extent. The astute reader will have noted that MGE is using *individual* rewards here in a case when success is the result of *group* effort, not individual effort.

More innovative companies reward success more equitably. 3M distinguishes between innovations that are the work of individuals and innovations that are the work of teams. Individuals who push innovations through by themselves are rewarded individually. They receive bonuses. They become heroes.

Groups who work together to produce an innovation are rewarded as a group. They may be cited as heroes as a group. They may get a bonus shared by the group. Or they may have the opportunity to run a new business unit created to exploit the product developed by the group. This is a particularly common reward at 3M. A project team that builds a successful business will be allowed to run it, thus becoming business unit managers, a promotion. Note that this type of reward is a particularly ingenious one. It allows those individuals who are motivated by the pleasure of the work (intrinsic motivation) to continue doing what they are doing on a larger scale. Their reward is just what they want, to be able to continue doing what they love, but on a larger scale.

ConsumerCo and Eastman Chemical also reward more equitably. At ConsumerCo, innovations pushed by individuals are rare. Group efforts are far more common. The most common reward is a steady progression in pay, status and responsibilities. Intrinsic and extrinsic rewards are all there, although the financial rewards come slowly enough that they are not distracting. At Eastman there are a few heroes, individuals who have fought against the odds to get funding for a risky project which eventually succeeded. But most rewards are for teams, since teams do most of the work.

Blame, risk and the right of error Reaction to failure varies even more widely among companies. Suppose a new product development project is closed down before the product is even launched. It is closed down because the team (or management) figures out that the product is just not going to sell. What will happen to the people on the project team?

At ConsumerCo, people will hardly notice what happened. It happens all the time. Only if the project was one that the company invested major resources in will people notice. Then there will be disappointment. People will be sorry that the project didn't work out. There will be sympathy for the members of the team, particularly if they have spent several years on the project. Others will realize that they are feeling an acute personal disappointment. They have put much personal energy and commitment into the project, and now they are seeing it shut down. Others may protect them a bit. The protection will not be obvious, but they may be put on shorter, simpler projects for a few months, projects that are likely to succeed. This will help them get over their disappointment and rebuild their confidence, if their confidence needs rebuilding.

Is this what happens at all companies? No chance. I will describe the policies of a company which I can't name. I will call it Company X. In the early 1990s, people who worked on terminated projects were often fired. It was just too embarrassing for senior management to keep them around.

I heard the story of one project, I'll call it the Plastics project, from several Company X managers. Senior management of a chemicals division decided to invest in developing a new plastic. They invested lots of money for four years. At the end of the four years, the Plastics project had made little progress. A close investigation revealed that it was never going to make much progress, at least not in the foreseeable future. The technical problems the team was encountering were just too difficult. The project was terminated.

Ever since, people had spoken in whispers about the Plastics project. It was clear that senior management wasn't going to talk about the project and didn't want to hear about it. Rumors floated around. No one had seen the members of the project team since it was terminated. Some clearly had been fired. The rest may have left, sent to distant sales offices (Company X's equivalent of Siberia) or been fired. Their exact fate was not a subject of open discussion, but of rumor. Management was not willing to discuss what it had done with the people after terminating the project.

How do we explain this reaction to a failed project? And how do we explain the difference between ConsumerCo's reaction and Company X's reaction?

First, Company X had a culture where failure had to be blamed on someone. If an investment the size of Plastics failed, someone had to be a scapegoat. It was easy to blame the project team. They didn't have much power and they couldn't defend themselves.

The second issue is that Company X was not recognizing risk. Innovation involves risk. Companies like 3M, ConsumerCo and Eastman Chemical recognize that there is risk. When you try to innovate, sometimes it doesn't work. And there is no reason to blame someone. The task simply proves to be impossible. This fact was not accepted at Company X. Each failure was treated as something for which someone should be held personally responsible.

These explanations are for most purposes sufficient. But there is a rather subtle issue at work here. The fact that no manager was willing to talk openly about the project indicates that something deeper than simple failure to accept risk was at work. There was something else management was trying to avoid.

The management team itself had authorized the project. They had authorized the large budgets. The money was now gone, beyond hope of recovery, or so they thought. So the logic of the blame system indicated that some manager should be blamed for wasting that money.

But was any individual manager willing to accept blame? Of course not! That would seriously undermine his position in a company that only promoted and respected those people who had never made a public mistake. So it was better to simply suppress the whole issue.

Unfortunately, it was hard to suppress the issue when members of the project team were still around. They had their own story to tell. Their story was not consistent with management's story. They did not accept blame. So they had to be fired to protect management from being embarrassed by someone contradicting management's story.

This was the interpretation I heard from several junior managers at Company X. The facts were that the project had failed and the project team had been fired or forced to leave. Their interpretation of the facts was that the project team had been fired for two reasons. In part they were fired because they were blamed for the failure of the project. But in part they were fired so that management would not have to face the fact that management itself had authorized the project, and thus (according to the logic of the system) should also be blamed.

The implication the junior managers took out of this story was that management would punish anyone who worked on a failed project. Company X management confirmed this to me explicitly. Anyone who worked on a failed project could expect to be punished financially. They would clearly not receive a bonus. They would not receive an annual raise either. They would not be moved to a position of greater responsibility. At best, they would stay at the same level. If the failure were particularly egregious, they might be demoted.

Contrast this with ConsumerCo's reaction. At ConsumerCo, no one is blamed. The fact that life, and particularly innovation, fundamentally involves risk is something ConsumerCo managers accept. They know that innovation projects will often fail to meet their goals. So they are not surprised when it happens, and no one has to be blamed for it. The corollary at ConsumerCo is that no one is punished for failure. Failure is an accepted part of a career. Minor failures are hardly even noticed. If a technical person works on twenty small innovations during the course of a year and ten of them don't work, no one will be surprised. They will be more concerned about how to exploit the ten that succeed.

One phrase I heard often from ConsumerCo managers was 'right of error'. Everyone at ConsumerCo has the right to make a mistake. If a project fails, that is accepted. If a project fails because of someone's error, that is also accepted, at long as they learn from the error. Continuous repetition of the same error, indicating an inability or unwillingness to learn, is not accepted. But mistakes that are accompanied by learning are accepted.

Occasionally I heard the same phrase, 'right of error', at 3M. The phrase wasn't used as often, but it was clear the same rule applied.

Eastman Chemical had put considerable thought into the problem of how to institutionalize the right of error. Managers at Eastman were particularly concerned with what would happen to people coming off of terminated projects. In some companies, coming off of a project that had 'failed' would carry a stigma. Eastman went as far as it could to prevent any stigma being attached to participation in a 'failed' project.

First, the word 'failure' was banished from Eastman's vocabulary. Projects were 'terminated', they didn't 'fail'. The change in vocabulary was not merely cosmetic, but indicated a difference in the company's attitude toward the projects. The purpose of a project was defined not as 'developing a successful new product', but rather as 'finding out *if it was possible* to develop a successful new product, and, if so, to develop it'. Under this definition of a project's purpose, a team that finds out that an idea doesn't work has succeeded in its purpose. It has explored the avenue and discovered it leads nowhere. If it terminates its project quickly once this discovery is made, it should be rewarded for doing its job well. The company as a whole decided to explore the avenue. The team explored it and found out that it led nowhere. So the team has succeeded in fulfilling its purpose.

Eastman congratulates teams when they terminate projects appropriately. Team members each receive a letter from the CEO citing them for doing the right thing in terminating the project. Management carefully assures that all team members receive good assignments in their next project.

Such an attitude is worlds away from what we saw in Company X where an entire project team was fired to avoid having them around to embarrass senior management. Eastman managers deliberately follow a more sympathetic policy for two reasons. First, they reason that team members have competences that the company should conserve. They have learned things in the terminated project and in previous jobs that the company may need again. Second, Eastman wants people to be willing, even eager, to participate in innovation projects. But if people who participated in terminated projects are treated badly, then no one will want to participate in risky projects. This would make it far more difficult to staff innovation projects, since by nature such projects involve risk. The solution Eastman management has adopted is to bend over backwards to avoid having any stigma attached to participation in terminated projects.

This completes my overview of the dimensions of culture impacting behavior inside the company. In the next section, I will look in much more detail at the use of fear and its alternatives as a motivator. Then, in the following section, I will discuss dimensions of culture that impact people's behavior towards customers.

Motivation for innovation: building visions as well as running on fear

New perspectives on why we innovate Five years ago, most books and articles on innovation opened with a section on 'why innovate?' The argument usually went like this. If you don't innovate, your competitors will, and they will take your markets away from you. In other words, the reason to innovate is fear, fear of losing markets, fear of losing one's job. Andy Grove's famous (1996) quote, 'Only the paranoid survive', is perhaps the most eloquent expression of this concern.

The problem with this as a statement of why we innovate is that fear doesn't motivate everybody. And it is not the only motivation behind innovation. It is not even the most important motivation in many cases. Worse, sometimes fear stops innovation rather than starting it. If you're a manager, the issue is to determine when and where fear is appropriate, when you should use fear as a motivating factor, and when you should use something else. In some cases, it may be appropriate to create a general paranoia (Grove, 1996; Meyer, 1998). In other cases, this does not work.

An example One problem with fear is that it kills revolutionary ideas. Imagine you are a young inventor. You have an idea for a revolutionary new product. You are confident that the idea will work. In fact you have tested it and, technically, it does work. But you need to find partners to exploit it. Building and selling a commercially viable model demands more financial resources than you have at your command. You need to find a company willing to invest in your idea and bring it to market.

So you, the young inventor, go to all the high tech, innovative companies around and you try to sell them on your idea. You are surprised to discover that they don't buy it. You go to other companies, companies that sell products like the one you want to build, and they turn you down, too.

Why do they turn you down? Mostly out of fear. Fear that your product won't work, fear that it won't sell, or fear that it will cannibalize products that the company is already building. It is these companies' fear that prevents them from investing in your idea and helping you make a contribution to society.

Finally you find a small company that is willing to take a chance on your product. The small company has nothing to lose. While the investment is a major one, the small company is not a major player in the market your product will compete in. Its management team has enough courage to try something new. They see the commercial and technical logic behind your product and they decide to invest. They share your vision of what the product could do for other people. And, like you, they think it can be commercially successful. They are not motivated by fear, but by the vision of what they can contribute to the world, and by the rewards they can get for that contribution. They may be afraid that they will lose their money, that your product will fail, but they act in spite of this fear.

As a result of this vision driven investment, the small company becomes a big company, and its directors become quite rich. For your product is very successful. It is more successful than you believed possible. And all because, years before, you saw something that no one else had seen. And you had the courage to pursue your vision, alone, for several decades.

Were you, the inventor, motivated by fear? Was your innovation motivated by paranoia? Probably not. If you were afraid of losing your livelihood, you would never have spent so much time on your invention, for it had no relation to your immediate job. The person this story is based on spent many years trying to sell his invention. If you did the same, your obsession would very likely make you unemployable. Fear would have counseled you to drop the invention and concentrate on something you could be paid for in the short term. What kept you going was courage, a vision of what the future could be, desire to make a contribution, and desire to reap a reward from the contribution. Fear very likely had little part in it.

The man on whom this story is based is Chester Carlson. Born early in the 20th century, Carlson believed, long before anyone else did, that he could find a way to make photocopies of any document on plain paper. After years of experimentation, he succeeded in making plain paper photocopies in a laboratory in 1938 (Kearns and Nadler, 1992). He called the process xerography and obtained the first patents on the process in the late 1930s. As an American, he tried to sell his idea to the giants of American industry. He went to the most innovative, high tech companies of his day. He knocked on the doors of IBM, Kodak, and many others. They all turned him down. Either they didn't believe in his idea, or they were afraid they would lose business if it worked.

But Carlson persisted. In the late 1940s, he finally found a small company willing to invest in his idea. It was called the Haloid company. The Haloid company decided to rename itself Xerox and became the most spectacularly successful American company of the 1950s and 60s. It far outstripped its rivals in growth and profitability. Not until its key patents expired in the 1970s was Xerox's worldwide monopoly on the plain paper copying market broken.

Had Carlson been dominated by fear, he would never have persisted so long. But he was dominated by a vision of what he and his invention could contribute. In simpler terms, he saw a need that he could fulfil. So he persisted until his vision was realized. Had the management of the Haloid company been dominated by fear, they would never have invested in Carlson's invention. They would never have become Xerox. And perhaps the world would not have had plain paper photocopying until several decades later.

When paranoia is appropriate Of course, if Andy Grove reads this, he will say that the story proves him right. He would say that IBM, Kodak and the others should have been paranoid. They should have realized that if they didn't invest in Carlson's process, someone else would. He is right. This is where paranoia works.

The logic of the big company, faced with a new opportunity, should be Grove's logic. 'If we don't invest in this, someone else will. Regardless of what we may have to lose, we should invest in the new opportunity, because if we don't, someone else will, and we will lose a potentially major opportunity.'

When paranoia is not appropriate But paranoia doesn't work so well for inventors, for new businesses, or for new entrants in an old business. Here the issue is more how to nurture, develop and protect an idea until it is ready for market, in spite of the ever present possibility of failure. There will always be fear that the new product won't work, or won't be accepted by the customers. If the fear inherent in this situation becomes too overwhelming, it may drive people off or shut them down rather than motivating them.

Grove's 'paranoia' is based on fear of competitors. Speed does count for new businesses. New businesses often have to get their ideas to market quickly in order to pre-empt potential rivals. So the paranoia that can drive the rush for speed can be useful. But other things count as well. Sometimes it takes time to nurture and develop and idea. This can demand patience and moral support, rather than paranoia.

Vision as motivation If you are not just going to build on fear of losing markets, then how can you motivate your people? One answer, derived from the Carlson-Xerox story, is to build a vision. Show them something they can contribute to society, and show them that they can be rewarded for making that contribution. Appeal to their idealism and their greed, both at the same time. But, if you are trying to build something new, be careful how you play on fear. For if you remind your people too often that it might not work you may undermine their confidence and encourage them to go elsewhere to a safer, more stable job.

Vision building So where do you get a vision? Books and articles have been written on the process of vision building (Hamel and Prahalad, 1994, is an example). I will not go into a description of that process here. I will, rather, look at the nature of visions that lead to effective new products.

Carlson's vision included a specific technology and specific customers. He knew something he could technically do, and he had in mind specific kinds of customers who would value what he could do. Once he built the product, he was confident they would pay him for it.

Most successful new product visions are like this (Dougherty, 1992). They include a customer problem or opportunity and a technical solution or means to carry out the opportunity. Vision-building, in any particular market, involves identifying market problems or opportunities, and technical means to solve them. So, if you are looking for a vision, ask yourself if there are customer problems or opportunities you could address. In most markets, the answer is yes. Ask yourself if you have the technical means to address these problems. Most large companies have the means to begin work on some of them. Even smaller companies can usually find new product niches in markets they know well. The problem then is to identify the specific opportunities you want to work on, and then to get to work.

Letting people build their own visions, or helping people contribute The other approach to building a vision is to let your people do it. Some companies recognize that many of the people they hire already have visions. They have things they want to contribute to their companies and to society. Or they develop ideas, even visions, after they join their company. Some companies, like 3M with its 15 percent rule, encourage their people to work on these visions. They let junior people follow their ideas and develop their own visions of what the company's future could be. When the ideas and visions work, the company moves in that direction (Burgelman, 1983).

Culture in relation to customers

Companies deal with their customers quite differently. The key dimension we will discuss in this section is trust. When a company and its customers trust each other, information will flow more freely between them. It is more likely the customer will share ideas and useful feedback with the company. Given the increased information flow, more trust is likely to lead to more innovation.

There are at least three areas where management of customer relations can have a significant impact on customer trust. One is keeping commitments. Another involves methods of handling complaints. A third relates to the way the company sells.

Keeping commitments Both Eastman Chemical and 3M follow practices which allow them to build and maintain relations of high trust with customers. At Eastman, the company follows a policy of honoring any commitment made by a sales person to the customer. There is no after-the-fact review of whether the company will honor the commitment. There is no going back on a commitment. Commitments are simply honored. If a sales person overcommits the company or commits to something which is overly expensive to fulfil, he may receive some training or advice on what is reasonable to commit to. But there is no going back on the commitment.

Customers react to this very favorably. In customer surveys, they have identified this as one of the key reasons they like dealing with Eastman. They can trust what the sales person says. The communication is clear. The commitments are clear. They know that there will be no second guessing or mind-changing once the sales person has said something will happen.

Handling complaints 3M has developed methods of handling customer complaints which help build trust. A 3M manager told me about a cultural change that occurred in his part of the company in the 1980s. His division was very technically focused and, in the 1970s, it often responded to customer complaints by arguing with the customer. If the customer complained that a particular product batch was of poor quality, the sales person would argue that the product was actually of very good quality. The customer, of course, would disagree. Sometimes the customer won the argument and sometimes the sales person won, but the relationship risked becoming adversarial.

The cultural change occurred when the division started treating such situations as learning opportunities. If the customer saw something wrong with the product, that was an opportunity to learn how to improve it. It was also an opportunity to engage in joint problem-solving with the customer. Joint problem solving is, in turn, a key to relationship-building.

One 3M manager explained to me his philosophy for trust building. He said that in most cases, if 3M trusted its customers, the customers would trust 3M. One way he showed customers he trusted them was the following. When they say that there is a problem with a 3M product, he believes them. He doesn't argue with them. He believes them. The one thing he asks them to do is to look carefully at whether they can use the product despite the problem. Often they can.

A defect may affect only part of a 3M product batch, meaning that the customer can use the remainder. Some defects have no impact on the final product, but do impact the production process. In these cases, the product may be usable if the customer runs his machinery a bit more slowly. In such cases, 3M will let the customer set his own rebate. 'Customers are fair', said my informant. 'They charge us with their extra costs and no more.'

3M gets several benefits out of this. It does not have to scrap as much product. And its customers are more prone to become partners, not adversaries. The terms of the partnership are open sharing of information, some sharing of risk, and trust in financial matters. What the customers get is a supplier who takes their word for it when they say something is wrong. What they also get is a supplier who is willing to take more risks in developing new products and product variations for them, since the supplier knows that mistakes will not be punished any more severely than necessary.

Selling methods In some cases, companies have a choice of taking a cooperative or an adversarial stance in selling their products to customers. MGE's Advanced Plastics business unit, for instance, sells many products in a regulated industry. At one point, the unit had devised ways of making some of their customers' products safer through the use of new raw materials. But they were unable to sell the new materials to their customers, since the customers denied that there was any safety problem with the old materials.

The unit's management had a choice between two ways of approaching their customers. They could take an adversarial stand, publicly pointing out the dangers inherent in the old materials still used by their customers. Or they could take a cooperative approach, trying to engage their customers in constructive problem solving. They chose the latter. They believed that the adversarial approach would permanently burn their relationships with the customers, while the cooperative approach held some hope of building productive selling relationships. This decision was soon rewarded when the team succeeded in signing up its first customer.

Conscious management of culture

Corporate culture is often viewed as a near-permanent feature of a company. Corporate cultures, being based largely on unwritten rules and habits, are slow to change. Nonetheless, some companies manage their cultures.

Eastman Chemical, for example, has done an inventory of its own culture. The company appointed a team that systematically attempted to understand how people in the company behaved and the impact of their behavior on the company's results. This team surveyed people inside the company as well as people outside the company (customers, suppliers, partners). They asked their respondents to iden-tify what was distinctive about how Eastman people behaved and what impact it had.

Through this process Eastman discovered several valuable features of its culture that it may not have discovered any other way. One of these was the habit of honoring commitments made by sales people. I discussed this practice earlier. Once Eastman discovered that this was something distinctive that customers valued, the company developed a plan to preserve the practice. The practice was discussed frequently and new sales people and new managers were trained to continue following it.

I did not find any other companies that approached the problem of culture management as consciously as Eastman. ConsumerCo talks about and deliberately replicates some features of its culture, such as the habit of consensus decision making, confrontation of opposing viewpoints, and regular contact with customers at all levels. But ConsumerCo has never done the sort of thorough inventory of its cultural practices that Eastman did. The advantage of a deliberate culture policy is that the company may discover, as Eastman did, that some of the practices that it paid no particular attention to are actually of considerable value to customers. The opposite may also be the case. (See Table 5.6 for a summary of key issues in the area of culture.)

This concludes my discussion of personnel management and culture. It also concludes my discussion of company-wide manage-ment systems and practices. In the next section, I will look more specifically at how companies manage ideas and innovation projects.

Table 5.6   Culture and its impact

Aspect of culture	Tools or variables . . . . . Impact	
Type of behavior encouraged inside company	■ Resistance to innovation versus support of innovation	■ Open senior management support of innovation smooths the way for lots of projects
	■ Clear or mixed messages about innovation	■ Mixed messages discourage people from supporting innovation
	■ Willingness to question beliefs and behavior, willingness to change	■ Helps people and organization maintain flexibility
	■ Willingness to listen	■ Helps managers to develop others' ideas
	■ Marketing versus technical orientation	■ Balance most effective
	■ Apportioning credit for success	■ Giving credit to all involved, not just a few individuals, most effective
	■ Blame, risk, right of error	■ Blame makes people risk-averse, right of error supports entrepreneurial activity
Methods of motivation	■ Fear, 'healthy paranoia'	■ Fear of competitors keeps leaders on their toes, but too much fear can discourage entrepreneurial effort
	■ Vision, desire to make a positive contribution	■ Motivates people to make positive contribution
Type of behavior encouraged in customer contacts	■ Keeping commitments made by sales people	■ Clients trust sales people, believe what they say, clearer communication
	■ Listen to complaints, deal with them (versus ignoring them, arguing with them)	■ More trust, better communication
	■ Cooperative sell (versus adversarial sell when regulator could force customer to buy)	■ Improves relations with customer, but may slow penetration
Conscious management of culture	■ Analysis, conscious management of own culture	■ Helps identify, maintain valuable features of company culture

Corporate-level Tools for Managing Projects and Ideas

The tools I have discussed so far impact an entire company. Culture impacts business units and innovation projects alike. So does organization structure. So do incentives. So does strategy. But there are other management tools that are less broad in their scope. Some tools, like a project funding system, impact projects without having any perceptible impact on a company's ongoing business. Others are even smaller in scope, impacting only one project at a time. Supervisory actions, like replacing members of project team, fall into the latter category. In this chapter, I will discuss tools which impact a company's project management system. In the next chapter, I will discuss tools which impact individual projects.

Idea management

Idea generation is a relatively unexamined part of the innovation process. For each book and article on idea generation, there are probably one hundred which focus on development or project management. Early studies of innovation (for example, Morison, 1966) noted that idea generation was part of the innovation process, but often the analysis did not go much further than that. Morison (1966) cited the preconditions to idea generation, such as a pregnant situation, a prepared mind, and a triggering event. But few took the analysis further. There have been many books on creativity, but few on focusing specifically on the problem of generating ideas for new products or processes within business organizations.

Recently, a few books on business creativity have appeared (Ray and Myers, 1986; Kao, 1996; O'Keeffe, 1998) which have begun to fill the gap. The authors of these books make useful suggestions on methods companies can use to increase the production of ideas. The suggestions generally are drawn from the authors' experience of working with companies. They are not drawn from a systematic study of business practice in a sample of companies. It is the latter that I will provide here.

I gathered data on idea generation methods by interviewing nearly 100 managers in eleven organizations. The organizations were drawn from a variety of industries, including chemicals, pharmaceuticals, consumer products, diversified manufacturing, automobile assembly, financial services, government. Within each organization, I asked managers to describe to me any methods their company used to generate ideas. I also asked them to give me examples of ideas their companies had developed in recent years. I then traced the origins of many of these ideas in an effort to determine how they were generated.

In the end, I identified more than two dozen methods used by the eleven companies. I then classified these two dozen methods into eight groups. The eight groups are the following:

1. Direct request
2. Setting up a rich context
3. Setting up incentives
4. Other aspects of personnel management
5. Tracking and linking with locations where ideas can be generated
6. Tracking and pursuing different types of ideas
7. Looking for ways to exploit a technology
8. Identifying and linking with sources of idea pull.

I will describe the methods below. (See Table 6.1 for a list of key questions in the area of idea management.)

I do not discuss goal setting in relation to idea generation here. As idea generation goals are sometimes applied to business units, I discussed them in Chapter 3, in the section on goal setting. But at times they will apply only to independent R&D areas or to other areas of a company that are separated from operating units. In these cases, such interventions could more properly be classified as project management interventions, not business management interventions.

Table 6.1   Questions to ask about methods of idea generation

General
■ Do we understand how the process of idea generation works in our company?
■ Do we manage the process of generating ideas consciously and effectively?

Specific methods of generating ideas
■ Do we ask people for their ideas?
■ Do we periodically force them to rethink what they are doing in a way that will help give birth to new ideas?
■ Do we enrich people's environments in ways that will help them come up with interesting new ideas? Do we understand all the methods we could use to enrich their environments?
■ Are there incentives to generate ideas?
■ Do we know how to manage small groups in ways that stimulate idea generation? Are first-line managers trained in how to stimulate idea generation?
■ Do we encourage and expect idea generation throughout the company? Or only in a few favored areas?
■ Do we track and pursue a number of different types of idea sources? Or are we stuck in a rut, using the same types of ideas over and over again?
■ Do we systematically look for multiple ways to exploit a new technology?
■ Do we systematically survey consumer demand and look for ways to fulfil it?

Asking people for ideas

Some of the methods of idea generation that managers described involved managers simply asking for ideas. The request could be a very simple, verbal request. Or it could involve setting up a dedicated team and giving them the job of looking for particular types of ideas. In each case, the main activity was the simple request that some person or group find an idea. The request could be general, in which case any idea would do. Or the request could be very specific when the goal was to find ideas in a specific area.

I identified six methods of managing idea generation which fit best in the direct request category. These are itemized below.

Direct request to individuals or groups A 3M manager told me that senior managers routinely ask for new ideas when they visit business units. He described one instance where a visit by a senior manager resulted in a half-day brainstorming session where all the people in the business unit got together to brainstorm about what kinds of new products and services they could produce. He found the exercise quite valuable. The meeting produced many interesting ideas. He only regretted that the team had insufficient time and support to follow all of them up.

An MGE senior manager, Paul Thomas, had a substantial effect on the practices of one of his business units by asking a simple question. He asked Frank Kelly, the head of his Advanced Plastics business unit, whether his unit had any interesting innovation ideas afoot. Until that point, Advanced Plastics had hidden all its ideas and projects from corporate view. There was a reason for this. Advanced Plastics had four different owners in a six year period. Several of the owners had viewed Advanced Plastics as a divestiture candidate from the beginning. They had told Kelly to eliminate all spending on R&D projects to increase profits and cash flows.

Kelly didn't openly refuse. He simply hid all the projects in the business unit. People assigned to projects were never assigned full time. They always had other jobs. So if anyone from corporate ever came by and inquired about what they were doing, he could legitimately say they were working on something else. All project expenditures were charged to the accounts of the ongoing business. This limited the amount of resources Advanced Plastics could put into projects. Large expenditures could not be hidden. But the unit was able to continue investing in innovation while not leaving any traces for corporate to discover.

Shortly after MGE acquired Advanced Plastics, Paul Thomas asked Kelly whether the unit had any interesting innovation projects. After verifying that Thomas's interest was genuine, Kelly told him about several projects. He was soon able to take them out of hiding. With corporate support, he began investing more substantial resources in them.

The Advanced Plastics case may be extreme. But the same effect can be observed on a smaller scale in many companies. When managers like those at 3M ask for ideas, they get them. People make special efforts to generate ideas and to share them with senior managers. On the other hand, when senior managers don't ask about ideas, people make no special effort to generate or share them. This is an instance of the general principle that senior managers get what they ask for. They encourage efforts in the areas they monitor. The corollary is that they don't get things they don't ask for. If they don't ask for ideas, people may believe that they don't want them, and they may not get them.

Publication of the need for new ideas Managers have other ways of asking for ideas besides direct, face-to-face request. Eastman Chemical, EuroChem and other companies routinely publish the need for new ideas in internal newsletters. OptiCo puts posters all over the corridors of its buildings. The posters relate to innovation and competition. No one who can read can avoid getting the message that the company wants to be competitive and that it wants innovation.

Seminars (often off-site) to stimulate creativity ConsumerCo periodically sends business unit management teams to off-site seminars where they are encouraged to develop new ways of looking at their businesses. This is most frequently done with older, established business units where products and advertising themes have been stable for a few years. The company brings psychologists or other creativity experts in to facilitate discussions and to get managers to identify and examine their own assumptions about their products and customers.

One ConsumerCo manager described a session to me. He and his team were off-site for several days. Their facilitator asked them to describe in detail how they perceived their product, not just how they objectively perceived it, but how they felt about it. As they were each users of the product, he asked them to think about how they felt using it. What associations did it have? What were these associations linked to? After a few hours of exercises that helped them surface their unconscious thoughts and beliefs related to the product, they went back to examine how they designed and advertised the product. They discovered that there were several key psychological themes related to the product that they were not exploiting. They resolved to redesign their marketing program, and perhaps the product itself, to take account of these themes. (Some of the methods used in seminars of this type are described in Ray and Meyers, 1986; Adams, 1986; Proctor, 1995; Nadler and Hibino, 1998.)

I never heard whether the new themes resulted in increased sales. But it was clear that the directed reflection that occurred in the seminar had produced new ideas.

Directed efforts to rethink/redesign a product/service/process ConsumerCo sometimes takes managers out of an ongoing business and tells them to redesign a product. Sometimes they are asked to design a product to fit a particular market niche. Sometimes they are given a new brand. Or they may be asked to design a line extension to an existing brand. The results are often original. The new products do not correspond to anything in ConsumerCo's existing catalog, but represent real new approaches to the marketplace.

There are well-publicized examples of other companies taking similar approaches. Sony chairman Akio Morita famously told his engineers to develop a stereo system that he could carry with him in his pocket on the golf course. His engineers responded by developing the Walk-Man™. Honda engineers developed the City car in the same way. Eastman Chemical, like many other companies, has set up dedicated teams to redesign processes. Such teams often achieved process cost savings which well exceeded the cost of the project.

Kim and Mauborgne (1997a) have developed a method generating ideas that involves redesigning a product or service. They recommend that product management teams look carefully at the key dimensions of value in the product or service. They suggest that companies can often generate considerable value by identifying dimensions of the product where they can add considerable additional value to the customer, while, at the same time, identifying areas where they are offering more than the customer really wants or needs. By offering more in areas where the customer wants more, and by offering less where the customer doesn't care, they can construct a more valuable but often less costly product for the customer. Kim and Mauborgne cite Formula One hotels in Europe and Cineplex Cinemas in Belgium as examples of products which have gained high market shares using this method.

Establishing a 'future design group', or a dedicated team to look for ideas MachineCo, a manufacturer of industrial equipment, has set up a future design group. That is the group's name, the 'Future Design Group'. The group is charged with searching the world for technologies and other things that may in some way affect the company's products. The group surveys new and evolving technologies and tries to discover ways in which they can be used to improve the company's products and processes. The group has a direct line to the company chairman, as it has the same status as any other department, including manufacturing, marketing, sales and R&D.

ConsumerCo hires experts whose sole job is to devise ways of improving the company's packaging. I talked to one such expert, who said that as far as he knew, ConsumerCo was the only company in its industry which dedicated any people solely to the problem of improving packaging. The other companies in the business relied on their packaging suppliers for such innovation. ConsumerCo benefited from its investment. It was the first to have several significant packaging breakthroughs. And it was able to maintain a monopoly in several of these packaging breakthroughs through a good patenting strategy.

Eastman Chemical and other companies also dedicate people to the problem of scanning the horizon for technologies and other developments that may impact the company's products. ConsumerCo is somewhat exceptional in that it conducts searches in areas which its rivals do not view as key areas for technical innovation.

Establishing routine methods of testing (for example, testing chemicals) for the purpose of generating ideas Pharmaceutical companies routinely screen thousands of chemicals each year for possible use in medical therapy. In effect, these screening programs are searches for new ideas. The company knows of a medical need. What it has to discover is a technical means of filling that need.

Chemical companies screen molecules in much the same manner that pharmaceutical companies do. They identify areas where there is a need for a new material. They then screen thousands of materials in an effort to find one that can fulfil the need.

The opposite procedure can also occur. A company may know of a material which is in abundant supply. It may then look for niches in the market where the material can be put to use. Such searches for a need to fit a technology may be routinized, but they are, nonetheless, searches for an innovation idea.

Enriching people's environments to stimulate idea generation

Managers often encourage idea generation less directly. They set up the organization so that people are in an environment that stimulates or encourages idea generation. I identified eight methods managers used to manage context. These are:

1. Providing interesting colleagues
2. Regular inter-functional contacts
3. Setting up a 'key crossroads' job where individuals routinely obtain information from several complementary sources
4. Appointing liaison people to facilitate information flow between key functions
5. Increasing horizontal contacts within functions or professional groups
6. Rotation
7. Flattening hierarchies
8. Stimulating bottom-up feedback

I will discuss each of these methods in turn.

Providing interesting colleagues Good knowledge workers often join companies where they know they can learn things, where they know they will have colleagues with whom they can discuss interesting ideas. By providing such colleagues, a company can go a long way toward building a stimulating creative environment. A group of bright, interesting, communicative specialists in an area can often serve as a magnet that will attract the best young (and old) talent in an area to the company. The people in the group may also feed off of each others' ideas, meaning that the group as a whole will develop many more good ideas than the people in it would if each was working individually.

Companies often know in which technical areas they are strong. They consciously build or maintain their strength in these areas. They know that if they lose their edge, their position on the leading edge, they will no longer be able to attract the best people in the area.

Regular inter-functional contacts Contacts between functions are often more difficult to manage than contacts within a function. People know how to talk to colleagues within their function. They share common training, common values, and a common technical language. By contrast, when they meet people from a different function, they are likely to discover that their training is different, they have different values, and they don't even speak the same language. No wonder companies have such trouble constructing effective cross-functional teams.

Nonetheless, cross-functional contacts are valuable. At some stage in the innovation process, they are usually essential. A new product idea is often born through contacts between marketers who know of a market need and technologists who know of a potential solution. A company which encourages cross-functional contacts is likely to stimulate more such ideas.

So how can companies encourage cross-functional contacts? They can bring different functions together in cross-functional teams, training programs, or other exceptional meetings. They can locate people in different functions together, rather than isolating them onto different floors or into different buildings. They can also rotate people between functions. This is so important and so useful a tool in some companies that I will deal with it in a separate section.

Setting up a 'key crossroads' job Some companies create jobs which stand at the crossroads of several key information flows. 3M's technical service representatives are an example. They are trained in technical disciplines and spend one-half their time on 3M's factory sites. This puts them in constant touch with the flow of technical information around their products. But they also spend half their time talking to customers. As a result, they are plugged into a conversation flow that focuses on customer problems and needs, rather than on 3M's technical issues.

The resulting mix of technical and market information that the tech reps are exposed to is a quite rich one. Each technical rep must, on the one hand, pay attention to 3M's technical problems and opportunities. On the other hand, he/she must also pay attention to customers' problems and needs. Both of these things are essential to the daily performance of the job. As a result, the tech reps are unusually well placed to identify new business opportunities for 3M.

A 3M manager gave me an example of a new business opportunity uncovered by a 3M tech rep in Europe. The rep in question dealt regularly with automobile body shops and other customers who faced difficult, customized painting problems. One problem these customers had was in masking gaps between two surfaces to prevent paint from getting into places where it shouldn't be. 3M had sold masking tape for generations, but it was often quite laborious to apply masking tape to gaps.

While talking with a customer, a 3M tech rep had a new idea. Why not create a kind of spongy masking tape which would fill the gap? He knew 3M made spongy materials and it made masking tape, so why not combine the two? He came back to his laboratory with the idea. While there were numerous technical problems to be solved, like how to cut a spongy material to shape, eventually the problems were solved, and 3M had a new product.

In concluding the story, the 3M manager told me, 'Technical reps are a major source of ideas for us'. He anticipated that the technical reps would continue to be a key source of ideas for 3M's future.

Appointing liaison people between key functions ConsumerCo believes that links between R&D and marketing are so important that it appoints liaison people between these two functions in each business unit. The job of the liaison person is to assure that these two functions communicate effectively. They do this by participating in and managing meetings between the two functions. They also carry messages between functions between meetings.

The liaison people have multifunctional backgrounds. Often trained in technical subjects, they typically acquire marketing competence on the job. Familiar with the specialized vocabularies and values of both marketing and the technical specialties relevant to their work, they are able to assure that communication flows smoothly across the marketing-technical divide.

Increasing horizontal contacts within functions or professional groups Many companies have technical or other functional groups that are spread over a wide geographic region. Technical service representatives are an example. They typically serve customers in widely scattered regions. So they are often located in widely scattered offices. They may never, in the course of their normal work, have any occasion to meet or talk with each other.

But technical service reps often have a lot to say to each other. They can share their understandings of customer problems, of technical issues at their plants, and how to solve them. By organizing regular meetings of such widely scattered people, companies can stimulate useful exchanges of ideas.

3M has many technical networks that function like this. Many interest groups exist, each focusing on a different technology. Regular meetings of these interest groups stimulate new ideas and idea exchange.

ConsumerCo has similar groups at several levels. Sales people have their networks. Technical people have their networks. Managers also have their networks. One business unit manager described the network he belonged to. At least once per quarter, the fifty-odd managers at his level met to discuss what was happening in their businesses. A number of them would make presentations. They would talk about what was happening in their marketplace and how they were dealing with competitors and customers.

It was clear that these club meetings served several purposes. One was information exchange. But, in addition, the club meetings serve to direct people's attention towards innovation. Each member of the 'club' makes a presentation at least once each year. Most talk about innovations their business units have developed. The manager who doesn't have an innovation story to tell would be viewed as 'not contributing to the company's future'. Questions would be asked about her management ability and priorities, and her status in the group would decline. The group meetings, as a result, served as a powerful incentive for business unit managers to keep their eyes directed toward producing innovations.

Rotation Rotation of people through several jobs serves two purposes. It is a means of enriching the individual's experience. But it is also a means of enriching the environment for those who work in the area(s) which receive him later in his career. Once an individual has worked in several jobs, he will bring a richer variety of experience to his new job. His broad range of experience will enrich the environment for his new colleagues.

Rotation typically works on three dimensions: function, business unit and geography. ConsumerCo rotates people on all three dimensions. It is normal for a ConsumerCo manager with fifteen years experience to have worked in both technical functions (or finance) and marketing. He or she may have worked in other functions, like human resources or manufacturing, as well. In addition, he or she is will have experience in several business units, and possibly in several countries as well. I once met a ConsumerCo manager who said he could speak nine languages. Five of them were languages he had learned on the job in his rotations through six countries. At ConsumerCo, the more senior the manager, the more likely it is that she or he will have rotated through a number of positions. In fact it is not possible to reach senior ranks at ConsumerCo without having worked in several functions, several business units, and several countries. Those who are unable or unwilling to rotate are unlikely to rise beyond mid-level positions.

The logic behind ConsumerCo's rotation policy, like those of other companies, is as follows. There is no better way to encourage cross-functional understanding and cooperation than by having people work in several functions. While young managers who join ConsumerCo normally have training in only one function, within five years they are expected to begin broadening out their experience. A manager who moves up should, after ten years, be able to work in two functions. This minimizes the number of cross-functional misunderstandings and miscommunications. It also stimulates idea generation, since managers with broad and unusual mixes of experience are more likely to have unusual ways of looking at things.

Rotation between business units and across geographies also serves two purposes. It gives the individuals who move richer and more diverse experiences. Market situations in one country may be quite different from those in another country. When a manager is forced to deal with several countries, her flexibility, skill level and experience base will all increase. She will have a richer variety of experiences to bring to any new problem, and she will be more likely to come up with original ideas about how to solve problems.

The second reason for rotation between business units and across geographies is to build networks within the company. People who have worked together for several years do not forget each other. Even if one of them is later moved to another country, they will have a relationship. One can pick up the phone and call the other at any time. They will remain colleagues and will be able to exchange information and ideas whenever appropriate. By rotating people, ConsumerCo assures that no business unit or distant geographic outpost will remain isolated from the rest of the company. Managers within each unit will have tight links with managers elsewhere. This helps ensure that there will be a free flow of ideas and a free discussion of problems throughout the company.

Another benefit of rotation is that it freshens each group that people move into and out of. With people moving into or out of virtually every management group each year, there is no chance for any group to develop the 'not invented here' syndrome. Management groups do not fall into the trap of developing a stable 'common wisdom' and beginning to reject ideas from the outside. They can't do this, since a new member, with new and interesting perspectives, is added to each group each year. Groups are obliged to remain open to new ideas, since the personnel in them are constantly being renewed.

The rotation policy at ConsumerCo means that most people outside of highly technical areas move every few years. But the pace at which they move varies with their age. Young people move more often than older people. People in their twenties may move every two or three years. People in their thirties may move every three or four years. But people in their forties may stay in positions for five or ten years. The company prefers to have more stability in senior positions for several reasons. First, stability in senior management positions gives more stability to senior management policy. Second, the company recognizes that older people cannot move as easily as younger people.

People in certain highly technical posts are to some extent exempt from ConsumerCo's rotation policies. It takes many years to train people for certain highly technical jobs in chemistry, physics and other areas. People with this training are rarely, if ever, rotated out of their specialized area. They are too difficult to replace.

Management positions in laboratories, by contrast, are subject to rotation. It is not unusual for a laboratory to be headed by someone with marketing or other nontechnical experience. This is possible, since laboratory management is primarily an administrative and people management job, not a technical job. Putting a marketer in charge of the laboratory is viewed as a good way to accomplish two things. The marketer will learn a lot about the technical and other problems laboratory people face. Meanwhile, the laboratory people will better understand how marketers and customers view things. Both will learn from the contact with people from another background.

This example points to another feature of ConsumerCo's rotation policy: the way people are selected for jobs. A person's ability to *do* a job is often not a primary criteria. In fact, it is sometimes not a criteria at all. A person's ability to *learn* a job is a criteria, since there is often no expectation that he will be able to do the job on the first day. Job rotation is used as a way to train people in new skills. The new appointee's lack of experience doesn't matter as long as the management team he is joining has enough experience to carry him as he learns the job. He will be expected to learn the job within a year. After that, he will be expected to contribute as much as any experienced person.

Since it uses jobs as training grounds, ConsumerCo in part determines what job a person should have by looking at what she most needs to learn. In part it also looks at what types of diverse past experience she will bring to a new job, that is, what she will be able to teach her new colleagues. This view of rotation as a two-way growth-stimulating process was somewhat unique to ConsumerCo.

Many companies have rotation policies that are similar to ConsumerCo's, but I did not find any others whose rotation policies were as extensive or as thoroughly thought out. EuroChem and FoodCo (both pseudonyms) are European manufacturers of chemical and food products, respectively. EuroChem rotates people as a means of avoiding the 'not invented here' syndrome. By moving people every three to five years, it keeps the groups they join, and the individuals themselves, open to new ideas.

FoodCo rotates people to develop multifunctional skill. Like ConsumerCo, FoodCo expects people to be competent in several functions after ten years with the company. Neither company has the extensive international rotation policy found at ConsumerCo.

Eastman Chemical also practices rotation. Rotation is virtually obligatory for junior managers whom the company thinks will advance rapidly. It is a means of giving them experience in a wide range of functions and a wide range of the company's businesses before they receive significant general management responsibility.

Flattening hierarchies According to the business press, many companies have 'cut bureaucracy' and 'flattened hierarchies' in recent years. Managers at MachineCo, Eastman Chemical and MGE said that this had occurred at their companies. All believed that this had increased idea generation. People were less concerned with following bureaucratic rules and less concerned with pleasing the boss. They had more time for customers, more time (and more need) for horizontal communication at their own levels, and more responsibility for solving customer problems themselves, rather than merely reporting them to a higher authority.

These managers reported two additional positive effects of flattening hierarchies. Each company had constructed horizontal technical and marketing boards at lower levels to replace the communications functions formerly performed by middle managers. The companies found that news of innovation ideas spread more quickly through these horizontal contacts than they had through the old layers of management. The company also found that more legitimacy was given to ideas from lower levels than had been the case in the past. Since there was less differentiation in status, the status of the person originating the idea mattered less, and the quality of the idea mattered more, than had been the case in the past.

Stimulating bottom-up feedback It is often people at the lowest levels of a company who notice changes first. It is they who are in constant contact with customers. It is they who are in constant contact with the company's technology. It is often they who have contacts with colleagues in other companies, who hear first about new technologies that may threaten the company's position. But in some companies, what they hear and see is ignored. Senior managers may believe that the world doesn't change, that what they learned when they were junior people is still true. Or senior managers may have their own ideas and pet projects to push, meaning that they will not listen to ideas or projects proposed by others. When either of these situations is the case, junior people will not have the authority or power to insist that their voice is heard. Ideas and insights they produce will be lost.

Junior people at one company I visited said that the 'official' criteria for selecting projects for funding meant nothing. They described the formula that was 'actually' used to determine which projects would get funding. They said that the funding decision was based on a rating given to each project. The rating equaled the merit of the project times the hierarchical weight of the person proposing it cubed (that is, taken to the third power). A nearly valueless project with high-level support would far outrank a very valuable project that did not enjoy such support.

Managers at other companies were not so cynical. Many companies fight the tendency to ignore lower layers through two general mechanisms. Flattening hierarchies is one of them. By eliminating middle management layers, companies bring junior people closer to the top. They simultaneously eliminate the middle managers who may be pushing their own ideas and ignoring ideas from those lower down.

EuroChem and Admin (a European government agency) used a second method. Both these organizations had established 'Offices of Innovation'. The purpose of these innovation offices was to encourage people lower down to share ideas. The offices provided an ear outside the hierarchy. If a junior person's boss rejected an idea, the person could bring the idea to the innovation office. If the idea looked good, the office could send him somewhere where his idea would receive a more favorable hearing. Or it could give the idea preliminary funding itself. Both offices had large enough budgets to fund preliminary investigations on several dozen ideas each year.

Setting up incentives for idea generation

Some companies set up incentives for generating ideas. Earlier, in the section on business management systems, I discussed three types of incentives: monetary, social and intrinsic. All of these incentives can be used to encourage idea generation.

Bonuses and raises can be used to encourage idea generation, as can prizes and other forms of social recognition. Promotions and opportunities to engage in interesting work can be used as well. Bonuses and raises can be tied to idea generation by making the latter part of the personnel evaluation screen. If people who share good ideas are known to receive larger bonuses and raises, this will help focus people's attention on two things: the need to generate ideas, and the company's willingness to reward those who generate good ideas.

Prizes and other forms of social recognition can also be tied to idea generation. Special prizes can be awarded for good ideas. Some companies, like MGE, award an annual prize to the team producing the most important innovation. A single prize may not be very motivating, since only one team each year can win it. A better system might give many project teams prizes or some other form of recognition so that anyone making regular contributions to innovation could expect to be recognized at some point.

Promotions are a powerful incentive for ambitious people in most organizations. Promotions can be used in two ways to support idea generation. The first and most obvious is that people who generate ideas can receive priority for promotion. But this is not the most important way to use promotions. People who generate ideas are often people who like being immersed in technical or marketing problems. They may not welcome promotions into a managerial ladder if this means that they will no longer be able to continue doing what they are doing. In addition, management positions demand quite different skills from technical positions. Successful scientists may fail quite miserably as managers. Many companies have found it better to reward technical people with promotions up a technical ladder, promotions which do not remove them from the work they love and do well.

In many organizations it is more important to promote managers who visibly support innovation. Promotions up the managerial hierarchy should be a reward for those who use their management positions to support innovation. For promotion up the managerial hierarchy brings power. And, if the organization wants to be more innovative, power should only be given to those who use it to support others' innovation activities.

Methods of managing individuals and small groups

Many other aspects of personnel management also affect a company's ability to generate ideas. I will discuss hiring, personnel assignments, supporting creative individuals, and facilitating group creativity here.

Hiring Individual creativity varies. Some individuals are more willing than others to consider new ways of doing things. So, if a company wants to be more innovative, it should hire more creative individuals.

Not surprisingly, 3M and ConsumerCo both look for evidence of creativity when they screen candidates for positions. When hiring for technical positions, 3M looks for engineers who have invented things or done things differently than their peers. 3M also looks for people who are not simply theoreticians, but are practical enough to have implemented their ideas. ConsumerCo looks for people who have done things with 'a creative flair'. Other companies in the sample put less emphasis on creativity in hiring.

Personnel assignments Once people have been with a company for a while, the company will have some idea of how creative they are, of how willing they are to find new ways of doing things. Several companies in the sample identified creative people and put them in positions where creativity was needed. Innovation projects, obviously, need creative people. But these companies also put creative people into management positions in business units which needed to find new ways of doing business in their markets. Putting creative people into positions where change is needed is a way to facilitate change.

Supporting creative individuals Putting a creative person into a job is not the end of the story. Creative people can be starved of resources and surrounded with people who are unwilling to change. If this is the case, then no matter how creative the individual, little will change. On the other hand, creative people can be given enough resources to do their jobs. They can be teamed with people who will support their efforts. If a company supports creative people this way, they will get far more out of them.

At 3M and ConsumerCo, many people are creative and virtually every workgroup is supportive of creativity. So normally there is no need for special efforts to manage a workgroup to support a creative individual. It is at companies with less tradition of innovation that this becomes an issue. A EuroChem manager told me that supporting creative individuals was key at his company. The head of the innovation office at Admin, the European ministry, said the same thing. In their organizations, it was not safe to assume that a creative individual would be supported by her colleagues. Managers interested in innovation needed to pay attention to resource allocations and to the social environment in a workgroup to be sure that people interested in change received adequate support.

Facilitating group creativity Junior managers at ConsumerCo are often trained in how to facilitate small-group creativity. Marketing managers in particular are often in charge of small marketing teams. Team meetings are frequent. ConsumerCo offers creativity training for these managers. The training teaches methods of assuring that group meetings produce the maximum creative output. Managers are trained not to focus on their own ideas, but to focus on helping others' surface and develop their own ideas.

Tracking and linking with locations where ideas can be generated

A EuroChem manager told me that innovation was quite uneven in his company. Some functions and some geographic areas produced far more ideas than others. He was not sure what the reasons for the difference were. He was hoping he could make 'less innovative' units more innovative by giving them more resources or more attention from senior management.

Managers at other companies also said that some groups within their companies were more creative than others. But they did not always identify function and geography as the key dimensions which divided more innovative groups from less innovative. In total, I identified seven different dimensions on which creativity of individuals or groups within the company could vary. These were:

1. Function
2. Geography
3. Rank

4. Tenure and seniority within a group
5. Age
6. Internal users of products versus nonusers
7. People involved in a process versus people not involved.

Function The EuroChem manager said that his company tracked new product and process ideas. Many ideas came from technical areas. Marketing and sales also produced numerous ideas. The functions which rarely innovated were the administrative functions, such as accounting, finance, and those involved in back office processing or other administrative work. He said that these support functions often acted as a brake on the innovativeness of the other groups. They resisted any change which would force them to alter their practices. Since introducing new products and processes sometimes required changes in administrative functions, the latter frequently got in the way of change.

EuroChem's management had not yet dealt with the problem of how to make the support functions more innovative. Possible approaches included increasing contacts between administrators and line functions, increasing contacts between administrators and customers or other outsiders desiring change, and rotating people between administrative and line jobs.

Geography The other dimension the EuroChem manager identified was that of geography. Business units in the home country produced more ideas than those located in foreign subsidiaries. EuroChem management was not sure of the reasons for this difference. They had two hypotheses. One was that the foreign subsidiaries had lower quality resources than those near corporate headquarters. They were not producing as many new products and process because they did not have the right people, or because they did not have the resources to pursue the ideas they had. The other hypothesis was that the foreign subsidiaries were not very well connected with headquarters. They had ideas, but headquarters didn't hear about them and, thus, didn't support them.

EuroChem management was acting on the second hypotheses. Managers in corporate headquarters were attempting to build closer ties to people in foreign subsidiaries, so that any ideas that came up in those subsidiaries would receive enough corporate support.

Status, or hierarchical level Managers at several companies said that people at different hierarchical levels produced ideas at different rates. One noted, as a general observation, that American companies often acted as if technically trained engineers would produce far more ideas than people working on shop floors. This idea, he believed, is a heritage of Taylorism. He noted that Japanese companies expected far more ideas to come from workers on shop floors.

True to form, several European and American managers told me that education did make a difference in idea production. In their companies, people with university education produced more ideas than those who were not trained. One hypothesized that this might be due to the fact that university educated people are trained to think more abstractly about what they are doing. His company was trying to increase the number of ideas produced by shop floor workers by training them in the theoretical principles behind their work. Other companies, like EurAuto, had tried quality circles and found that they had a positive impact on idea production at the shop floor level.

Tenure and seniority within a group Managers at several companies observed that new people in a post had more ideas than senior people. They viewed this as a natural result of experience. People with little experience bring fresh ways of looking at things. People with more experience have often become habituated to looking at things in a single way.

Companies that recognized this difference used it in two ways. They assured that workgroups would not go stale by adding new people to them regularly. If, in a group of five people, one was replaced each year, the group would remain fresh and open to new ideas. Companies also moved people as a way of keeping them fresh as individuals. A EuroChem manager said:

> People stop having ideas after a few years in a job. They go stale. If they stay too long in a job, they get rigid. They stop being open to new ideas. So we move them. After about five years in a job, people have to move on. They have to do something new. This helps keep them fresh.

Age A ConsumerCo manager told me that keeping a mix of ages in each workgroup was important. Himself in his late forties, he said that people over forty were good at organizing people and they were good at implementing ideas, but they were not so good at generating new ideas. Younger people, particularly people in their twenties, were far better at generating new ideas than the managers in his age group. The young people in his business unit had many more ideas than he or his peers did. Having observed this, he said that a key lever he used to keep ideas flowing was to bring young people into the group regularly. He hired at least one new graduate a year into his business unit so that there would always be someone around who was taking a totally fresh look at things.

Internal users of products/services versus nonusers In some businesses, internal users of a company's products are a useful source of information and ideas about the products. 3M secretaries used Post-It® Notes in ways that Art Fry had never thought of. Xerox secretaries and former secretaries saw the usefulness of the personal computer and the mouse before Xerox executives did (Smith and Alexander, 1988). Internal customers can test a product before the company does riskier tests with external customers. Information can flow continually from internal users to a development team. This can be much more difficult to achieve with an external customer.

Some companies provide themselves with internal test sites by buying a customer. Eastman Chemical makes some chemicals used by paint companies. Eastman executives have sometimes considered buying a paint distributor to gain more information about the key issues in the paint business. This has not happened at the time of writing this, but the fact that it has been considered illustrates the importance of downstream information in stimulating and guiding innovation.

3M is larger and more diverse than Eastman. Its businesses often have internal customers. A 3M manager told me that these internal customers often provide valuable early information on how products work and how they can be improved to better serve customers' needs.

People involved in a process versus people not involved Soichiro Honda, founder of the Honda Motor Company, believed that the people involved in a production process knew far more about the process than anyone else, including the engineers who designed the process. His willingness to tap into this wisdom was one of the reasons why the Honda Motor Company came from nowhere to become one of today's leading automobile assemblers. EurAuto began trying to copy Honda's success in the 1980s.

Before 1985, EurAuto made no serious attempt to tap into ideas from people on the factory floor. The company reversed that in the mid-1980s when it initiated a quality movement. Management set up quality circles in each factory in an attempt to help junior people generate and implement ideas.

In the early 1990s, manufacturing managers said that the quality circles and other initiatives were generating many ideas, more than the company could implement in fact. Boards had been set up in various manufacturing areas to determine which ideas to implement first.

Involving factory floor people in innovation was not a major concern in other companies in the sample. Most of them did not have the large manufacturing volumes that EurAuto did. They manufactured smaller volumes of many more products. At 3M, manufacturing personnel were broken up into smaller, product-based teams, rather than being organized into large assembly lines. Members of these small teams could share their ideas within the teams as easily as EurAuto people could share their ideas within quality circles.

EurAuto, Admin and EuroChem had suggestion box systems. These produced some good ideas which were implemented. But it appeared that quality circles and other initiatives that involved people more directly produced more ideas per capita.

Tracking and pursuing different types of ideas

Some companies with stable product lines realize that innovation within these product lines fits into several patterns. An assembled product may be made up of a set of relatively standard components. Remixing and rearranging these standard components may result in new variations on the product which are attractive to consumers in certain niches. Alternatively, the technologies on which the components are based may change, leading to fundamentally new types of components. Other ideas may come from new understandings of consumer behavior.

Companies unwilling to challenge conventional technological wisdom may miss changes which involve remixing or rearranging existing components. Companies more oriented toward consumers than technology sometimes miss changes in component technologies. Technically oriented companies often miss changes in consumer markets. But a smart company will have sensors set out to detect changes in each of these areas. A smart company will tie these sensors into its product development process so that any potential improvements are rapidly realized as new products.

ConsumerCo's marketers are in weekly contact with customers. Its laboratory scientists scan developments in every technology that they believe might have an impact on ConsumerCo's markets. Its development personnel regularly try new ways of mixing and remixing the components in ConsumerCo's range of products. Each of these groups sits on ConsumerCo's product development teams. Any ideas they generate or detect can be immediately integrated into ConsumerCo's product development process. If there is any stone left to be turned at ConsumerCo, it is hard to imagine what it would be.

3M covers as many bases as ConsumerCo. The company's many laboratories look at every technology the company can imagine will impact its products. The company's marketers and tech reps are in regular contact with customers. The product development teams regularly try new mixes of components in their efforts to improve products. Once again, few bases are left uncovered.

Other companies in the sample were not so thorough in covering different innovation types. MGE's coverage of technologies related to its products was spotty. When George Marsh was looking for help to exploit his water treatment idea, he found that the company had none of the relevant competences. At the same, the company's marketers and sales people were not well tied into the product development process. Technologists did not seek their input on new ideas developed in MGE laboratories until very late in the development process. In some cases, key market trends were missed, leading to failed product launches or declining sales in key product areas.

I have talked about companies tracking ideas involving reorganizing or remixing components, new developments in component technologies, and new understandings of consumer behavior. Ideas in these categories seem relatively easy to track and integrate into the product development process. A product development organization can relatively easily remix existing components, scan the horizon for technologies which will impact existing components, and track trends in existing consumer groups.

What is harder is to foresee entirely new technologies or radically different components that cause fundamental reorganizations in product architecture (Henderson and Clark, 1990). Companies tried to keep up with this by tracking what competitors were doing and by plugging into customer and supplier information networks. But these out-of-pattern innovations are just harder to predict and track, and no known monitoring system can pick up and deal with all potential threats of this type.

Looking for ways to exploit a technology

Innovations are sometimes described as stemming from technology-push or from consumer-pull. Technology push innovations represent a technology in search of a market. Consumer pull innovations represent a market need in search of a technology capable of filling it. In this section I will describe methods of generating ideas through a technology push strategy. In the next section I will look at the somewhat more complex problem of generating ideas through a consumer pull strategy.

Some companies specialize in one or a few technical areas, become the best in the world in that area, and look for markets to serve with the technology. Here the idea generation effort involves systematic search and testing of potential markets. This is a 'technology push' idea generation strategy. The effort that led to the Chemical Residues project at MGE (see Chapter 2) followed this pattern.

Methods of searching for markets for a product are not well established. Such searches often take the form of looking for things already in the market that the new technology can replace. In such a search, the search team will carefully document the characteristics of the new technology and the products it can produce. Then the team will look at the industries and customers that might find these characteristics useful. Usually a few ideas will surface. The team will then test the technical and economic feasibility of the ideas. Finally, the team will manufacture a few sample products and do market tests with them. If the tests are successful, the team will then launch the new product.

This type of work is most easily performed in a larger company with a number of related business units. Such a company will normally have a considerable information base on many related markets. The search team can tap into this information base, rather than having to do all its own market research. Such a diverse company will also have the skills and assets necessary to bring any new products to the market quickly, once a viable market is identified. Smaller, less diverse companies are less able to provide needed information and other assets. As a result, smaller companies with useful technologies often link with larger companies in the same or related industries. The larger partner provides complementary assets and information, while the smaller partner provides the key technology.

Such partnerships are very much in evidence in the pharmaceutical industry, where small biotech companies with key technologies are linking with pharmaceutical companies. The much larger pharmaceutical companies are better positioned than the biotech startups to shepherd new products through regulatory screens and to sell them once they have regulatory approval.

Identifying and linking with sources of idea pull

Some companies, particularly those in consumer markets, pay close attention to sources of consumer pull. Specific demands may come from customers, from regulators, or from other standards setting bodies. Standards setting bodies may represent the public at large, as when a government sets standards. They may represent customers. Or they may represent manufacturers themselves. Sometimes companies follow standards set by lobbying groups, such as environmental groups, even though the standards have no force of law.

Linking with sources of pull, or consumer demand, as a means of stimulating idea generation is a standard topic in marketing courses. The ideas in the remainder of this section will be familiar to those who have worked in marketing. Nonetheless, it is useful to translate the familiar marketing concepts into a language more directly related to this discussion of new product development.

To use existing consumer demands as a means of stimulating idea generation, companies need to do four things. First, they need to identify the nature of the demands they are subject to. Second, they need to identify the sources of these demands. Third, they need to link with the sources of demand and track changes in the demand. Finally they need to find ways to fulfil the needs represented by the demands. If they do that, they will have a means of generating frequent innovations in areas of consumer need.

Unidirectional and multidirectional pulls To help identify and deal appropriately with consumer demand, it is useful to classify demands into two groups. Some demands are unidirectional: more (or less) is better. Cost-related pulls behave this way. In nonluxury markets, lower cost is better, no matter how low the cost goes. Product reliability is unidirectional. All things being equal, more reliability is better than less.

But some consumer pulls are multidirectional. More is not always better than less. In cars, bigger is not always better. For some people, like rural people with large families, bigger cars are better. But for single city dwellers, small cars are better than big cars. Here preferences are not unidirectional but multidirectional along the same dimension. Some prefer big. Some prefer small.

Multidirectional pulls reach an extreme in fashion-driven businesses. The clothing business is a classic example. Style is important. Consumers want more fashionable clothes. But what is fashionable depends greatly on the eye of the beholder. Preferences for color, shape and cut may vary. Producers must guess where on a particular dimension buyers will be found.

Companies must deal differently with uni- and multidirectional pulls. Unidirectional pulls, once identified, can be a continuous stimulus to product innovation. Companies can spend years introducing initiatives to reduce cost or increase performance, all of them appreciated by customers. In order to take advantage of unidirectional pulls, companies need to identify them, they need to find means of improving their products on the relevant dimension, and they need to track customer response to improvements. Companies dealing with unidirectional pulls often build research units dedicated to improving products on the relevant dimension. They also link with consumers to track consumer response to improvements on the dimension. Response information will give them an idea of how valuable improvements really are to the customer.

Multidirectional pulls require a different response. When customers have different preferences for product performance along a single dimension (for example, some want big cars, others want small cars), there is the possibility of creating multiple niches. Here the challenge is to develop products that are customized for broad or narrow bands of consumers along the dimension. Companies try to identify where consumers' preferences are along the dimension, they select which consumers they want to serve, and then they develop single products or ranges of products aimed at the target consumers. Ongoing management problems include tracking changes in consumer taste and adjusting products to fit (for example, building smaller cars when consumers begin wanting smaller cars), and improving the product on other dimensions (for example, cost, see below).

The kind of product development organization a company builds when dealing with a multidirectional pull depends on the company's strategy. If the company chooses to serve only a single narrow band of consumers, the organization may be quite simple. Sales and other customer contact people link directly to these customers and feed information into a single R&D unit. The goal is to track consumer response to any changes or improvements and to develop a product customized to the needs of the chosen consumer group.

If the company chooses to serve a wider range of customers, product differentiation will be necessary. If the range of customers to be served is wide, the company may set up independent business units to serve different customer groups. The product development process, and the organization behind it, may become much more complex. A fundamental research laboratory may look at technologies that could profitably be used to serve all customers. Several development laboratories may be set up to apply common technologies to the different customer groups served. Marketing organizations will track needs of all groups. Marketing will also be concerned with defining and redefining products and niches, determining whether several customer groups can be served with the same product, or whether a group currently served with one product could be more profitably served by replacing the single product with several more specialized products.

Dealing with multiple pulls In a single product, there may be multiple, conflicting consumer demands. The 'pulls' may not pull in the same direction. The manufacturer must make trade-offs between multiple dimensions in designing the product. The automobile business provides an example.

A motor engineer at EurAuto said that his company had identified at least six types of pull related to automobile engines. Consumers generally want more power, more fuel economy, more acoustic comfort, more reliability, and lower price. In addition, regulators, who represent the public at large, want reduced emissions. But adding power generally reduces fuel economy, increases noise, and increases price. Fuel economy, if gained through use of expensive, lightweight materials, will conflict with price. So, while more may be better on each dimension, automobile companies cannot simply give consumers more of everything. The economics, physics and chemistry of the automobile engine don't work that way.

As a result, companies must make trade-offs between different pulls. The result is product differentiation. Companies make different products with different combinations of these characteristics in an attempt to appeal to different consumer groups.

Effective innovators will make choices based on two things. The first is evidence from past sales trends or consumers' preferences as expressed in surveys or comments to the company. The second is educated or, sometimes, inspired guess. No one has ever developed a comprehensive and completely reliable formula for how to make trade-offs among different consumer demands, since consumer demands themselves are not always reliable and predictable (conjoint analysis being the best attempt). But market mapping tools, such as those found in any good marketing text, can make the process more precise.

Consumer pulls in the automobile industry are relatively well understood, although the EurAuto engineer's discussion of pulls related to engine performance may have over-simplified the actual state of things. The engineer described all the pulls as unidimensional. But do all consumers want more power, and more acoustic comfort, without limit? Probably not.

As an illustration, would all consumers buy a car with a high-powered, sports car type engine if it were cheap and quiet enough? Probably not. Some would be afraid of its power, or they would feel they would never use it, and would prefer a less powerful engine, even at the same price. As another illustration, do people want cars to be as quiet as possible? Probably not. In the quietest possible car, the driver would not be able to hear the engine or any road noise. Many drivers would not like this. They would feel cut off from the road, cut off from their own vehicle. They might, correctly, view the super-quiet car as dangerous. So while people want acoustic comfort, this does not mean they want more quietness without limit. A car can be too quiet as well as too noisy. Different consumers would put the 'optimum sound' point at different points on the sound chart.

Once a company has identified existing sources of pull and determined whether they are uni- or multidimensional, they still have several challenges. One is to find ways to satisfy current consumer pulls. If important consumer pulls are consistent over long periods, a company may set up a dedicated research organization to look for ways of satisfying the pull. The other is to forecast future consumer preferences or pulls. Will consumers want the same things tomorrow that they want today? Or will they want something different?

Some companies, such as ConsumerCo, establish special units to think about future consumer demands. Others leave this task to the same product management teams that handle current consumer demands. In the latter case, there is a danger that the product management team will focus on current demands and ignore speculative questions about what customers will want several years down the road. After all, they have customers in front of them demanding things now.

If there is no special team charged with taking a more speculative look at the future, this type of work may fall off the agenda altogether.

Consumer pull across industry I have classified consumer pulls as uni- or multidimensional. But they can usefully be classified on other dimensions as well. There are systematic differences in the nature of consumer pull across industry.

Many consumer products have *fashion or taste-driven demands*. There is an overall demand for increased sensual appeal. But how that demand can be fulfilled can vary from year to year. In style-driven areas, there is a problem of boredom. Styles can wear out irrespective of the function they represent.

Customer demands in industrial product areas are much more driven by *technical characteristics* of the products. Industrial products companies sometimes lead their customers by introducing new features (a form of technology push). This has novelty value. Customers may try the new feature out of interest. But if there is no measurable performance payoff, the new feature will not last long.

Consumer demands can limit change as easily as they can stimulate it. This is most evident in personal care products. Producers of lipstick have occasionally tested lipsticks made from fundamentally different materials to those in standard lipsticks. While these products have had a equal or better appearance than standard lipstick, with the bonus of greater durability, consumers have universally rejected them. Why? The products do not 'feel' the same way that standard lipstick feels. Consumers like the feel of standard lipstick, or they are simply habituated to it. Up to this point, products with a different 'feel' have been rejected.

Familiarity can also play a role in industrial products. A manager at a printing machinery manufacturer explained to me how his company had introduced a new technology in the 1920s. First it designed a new printing press which took full advantage of the strengths of the new technology. It demonstrated the new press to customers, showing them that the new technology could print more sheets faster than any previous press. Yet customers refused to buy the press. Why? It looked quite different than the old presses and this made it difficult for them to understand or have confidence in the workings of the press.

The press manufacturer got around this barrier by redesigning the new press to look, from the outside, exactly like an older press. All the visible gears, levers and controls were in the same place. Customers were familiar with it and appreciated the fact that it performed better than the old model. So they bought it. Once the new technology had gained a foothold in the market and customers became used to it, the manufacturer began changing the design of the presses more effectively to take advantage of the new technology.

To take full advantage of consumer pull as a stimulator of ideas, a company would be well advised to do the four things noted at the beginning of this section. First, it should identify the nature of the demands its products are subject to. Second, it should identify the sources of these demands. Third, it should link with the sources of the demands and track changes in them. And fourth, it should set up dedicated research programs to address the needs behind the demands. It is the fourth item, the dedicated research program, that would allow the company to improve its products. The other items on the list should be done to insure that the research is appropriately directed. (See Table 6.2 for a summary of key issues in the area of idea management.)

Laboratory management

Many ideas are generated in laboratories. In many manufacturing industries, crucial steps in product development occur in laboratories. As a result, how laboratories are managed is a key issue in idea generation and in project management. I will discuss laboratory management in three parts. First I will look at issues in the overall management of laboratories. Then I will look at laboratory communication and finally at laboratory personnel management. (See Table 6.3 for a list of key questions in the area of laboratory management.)

Management of laboratory personnel's time

There are two key questions to ask about time management:

- Who controls laboratory research programs and time allocations?
- Do laboratory systems allow spontaneous, unplanned investigations into interesting phenomena?

I will deal with each of these questions in turn.

Table 6.2   Methods of idea generation and their impact

Method	Tool or variable . . . . Impact	
Direct request	■ Direct request to individuals or groups ■ Publication of need for new ideas ■ Seminars to stimulate creativity ■ Directed efforts to rethink or redesign a product, service or process ■ Establishing a future design group, or other dedicated team to look for ideas	■ All forms of direct request show top managementís interest in innovation; stimulate generation & sharing of ideas among those receiving the request
Setting up a rich context	■ Establishing routine methods of testing, screening, to search for ideas ■ Providing interesting colleagues ■ Regular inter-functional contacts ■ Setting up a 'key crossroads' job ■ Appointing liaison people between key functions ■ Increasing horizontal contacts within functions or professional groups ■ Rotation ■ Flattening hierarchies ■ Stimulating bottom-up feedback	■ All forms of creating a rich context involve increasing the stimulation any individual will receive; in most cases this will increase the number and quality of ideas generated
Setting up incentives	■ Create incentives (monetary, career, social) for generating, sharing and developing new ideas ■ Hire creative individuals	■ Signals top management's interest ■ Creates a reward for risky activity
Personnel and small group management	■ Put creative people in positions where creativity is needed	■ Increases ability to generate ideas ■ Increases probability that ideas will be generated where they are needed

(cont'd)

Table 6.2 (cont'd)

Method	Tool or variable . . . . Impact	
	■ Support creative individuals, assure they are supported by colleagues ■ Train managers to facilitate group creativity	■ Allows removal of barriers to creativity ■ Increases generation of ideas within work teams

Tracking and linking with idea generation locations	■ Dimensions of organization that can be monitored:
	  – Function
	  – Geography
	  – Status, hierarchical level
	  – Tenure or seniority in a group
	  – Age
	  – Internal users of products/services
	  – People involved in a process
		■ Can identify areas which develop few ideas, investigate why
		■ Can also improve links with areas that generate lots of ideas to improve exploitation

Tracking and pursuing different types of ideas	■ Monitor potential changes in product components ■ Monitor potential changes in the ways existing components are mixed or used ■ Monitor potential changes in product architecture ■ Monitor potential changes in consumer markets ■ Monitor technologies that may someday impact the market	■ Broader range of monitoring increases probability the company will be among the first to see and exploit a change
Looking for ways to exploit a technology	■ Survey consumer/ industrial markets to find areas where a new technology can be applied profitably	■ Helps exploit technologies in other markets, beyond the ones they were originally developed for
Identifying and linking with sources of idea pull	■ Link with sources of consumer demand, to track demand more closely and react to it more quickly	■ Quicker reaction time to changes

Table 6.3   Questions to ask about laboratory management methods

Control issues
■ How tightly or loosely do we control laboratory personnel's time?
■ Who controls laboratory personnel's time? Do laboratory people themselves have some control over their own time?
■ Are spontaneous, unplanned investigations possible?

Efficiency and effectiveness
■ Do our laboratories perform routine operations efficiently?
■ Do our laboratories have goals that are science-related? Business-related? Or both?

■ How effectively do our laboratories communicate:
   – With each other?
   – With operating units?
   – With customers?
   – With outside technical resources?

■ Do we have an optimal mix of laboratory personnel?

Who controls laboratory research programs and time allocations? The answer to this question gives some indication of who has a license to innovate in a laboratory. If laboratory managers tightly control all time allocations, it is likely that only a few centrally approved ideas will be investigated. If laboratory personnel control some of their own allocations, however, then they will be able to investigate their own ideas, as well as any ideas coming from the outside which strike their fancy.

In some companies, project managers who are not part of the laboratory team determine time allocations. The project managers use money from their budgets to 'buy' laboratory people's time. In this case, the people who determine which ideas will be investigated are those who allocate money to project managers. There may still be room for independent work by laboratory personnel, however, if the system leaves some of their time unallocated.

A system which leaves laboratory personnel in control of some of their own time will likely increase idea generation and overall innovativeness. But, in industries where development is very expensive and only a few ideas can be pursued, tight control of development laboratory time is usually the rule. Research laboratories in such industries may preserve some flexibility. But development laboratories will normally be run as efficiently as possible.

Are spontaneous, unplanned investigations possible? The answer to this question gives another indication of how likely the laboratory is to generate viable ideas. In tightly controlled laboratories, unplanned investigations are impossible. A scientist who works in an independent, government-supported laboratory in Europe once described the difference between his laboratory and the corporate pharmaceutical laboratories he often worked with. In his lab, if someone had a good idea, they could drop whatever they were doing for a few weeks to investigate it. He had done this himself. The fruit of one of his spontaneous investigations was a widely used anticancer drug. In a normal pharmaceutical company's lab, procedures would have been less flexible, and the discovery may never have occurred.

In pursuing his anticancer idea, the scientist and two of his colleagues had worked as an independent team for many months. The project had taken many unexpected twists and turns. They had done much physical and chemical work with the raw materials from which the drug is extracted. Had they been forced to deal with a large lab's procedures at this stage, the project would never have reached its goal, he said. They would not have had time to deal with time allocation procedures and with obtaining authorizations for needed laboratory materials. They would have given up, or run out of time, long before discovering the active molecule.

Efficiency in routine or repeated operations

Another key question in managing a laboratory is: *are there efforts to make routine or repeated operations more efficient?* The answer to this question reveals whether a laboratory is likely to produce more or fewer new ideas in the future. In some laboratories, no repeated operations are performed. In such laboratories there may be little change in output from year to year. Or at least variations in output will not be explicable on efficiency grounds. But in laboratories that repeat certain fundamental operations, efficiency gains may lead to an increase in the generation of viable ideas. When a pharmaceutical laboratory succeeds in reducing the amount of resources that must be devoted to routine screening, it should generate more viable ideas *per capita*.

Laboratory goals: science-related or business-related?

Yet another key question is: *is the goal of the laboratory science or business?* Scientists are professionals. As such they belong to professional groups that extend beyond the boundaries of the organization that pays them. As a result they have mixed loyalties. While they may be loyal to the company that pays them, they often hold a greater loyalty to their professional group. The reasons why are clear. Most scientists can leave their company and get a similar job elsewhere. The company is replaceable. But they cannot leave their professional group. They have invested years, even decades, in building up skills and a reputation within their professional group. They cannot give this up. It is part of them. Their profession is their life.

As a result, scientists are sometimes very concerned with their professional accomplishments and their reputation in their professional community. They are sometimes more concerned with their status in the professional community than they are with the success of the company they work for. A symptom of this is when scientists in a company's laboratory are more concerned with getting papers published and getting patents in their name than they are with developing saleable products.

Northern Pharmaceutical's laboratories suffered from this problem throughout the 1980s. As the company's R&D head said a few years later, Northern's scientists were not in any way concerned with whether they were producing saleable products in the 1980s. The company was making plenty of money (or so they thought) from the products produced by a previous generation of scientists. So why not do what was really important in life: good theoretical research that would allow them to publish lots of interesting papers?

When a commercially oriented scientist was brought in from the outside to head Northern's laboratories in the early 1990s, this changed. He told the scientists that they were there to produce commercially viable ideas. Papers could be a byproduct, but the commercially viable ideas had to come first. He explained, as if they didn't know, that their paychecks came from the commercially viable ideas. He also explained that the patents that the company made its living from were running out. Viable new ideas were needed if the money was to continue flowing.

To enforce the message, the new R&D head set up production quotas for every lab. Development areas were expected to reduce the time needed to develop a molecule by 50 percent. Discovery (research) areas were expected to come up with a specified number of testable new molecules each year. The latter, especially, was a revolution. Some managers in the discovery laboratories were not able to adapt to the new, much stricter, management regime. They were replaced or moved into staff functions.

The message for other companies is to watch carefully what laboratory scientists are really trying to do. If the goals of the laboratory relate more to papers than to producing viable products, it may be worthwhile to change management style to focus people's attention more on products and less on papers.

Laboratory communication

Laboratory communication can be broken into two types, communication within a laboratory and communication between the laboratory and people on the outside. Both can be important to innovation performance.

Communication within and between a company's laboratories Horizontal communication within a laboratory matters because colleagues in a laboratory can share and develop ideas together as well as alone. Having interested, knowledgeable, inquiring colleagues can help a scientist develop her ideas beyond what she could do alone. Sometimes ideas come out of discussions among colleagues as well.

In some laboratories, tight control of people's time and activities causes the laboratory to become compartmentalized. People do not have time to discuss their work with colleagues who are not directly involved. Laboratory management may even discourage communication across workgroups in the mistaken belief that such communication 'distracts scientists from their real work'. Few laboratories would be so backward now. But some laboratories blocked horizontal communication until the early 1990s.

In a large organization with multiple laboratories, communication between laboratories is an issue. Communication between laboratories can be as stimulating for new ideas as communication within a laboratory. If the company's laboratories work on related technologies, cross-fertilizing them can result in a heady mix of new ideas. Companies can encourage communication between laboratories (or within large laboratories) by holding conferences or 'science fairs' where laboratory people show off their work. Laboratories can also be connected at the top, as when laboratory managers meet regularly to discuss the work being done in their laboratories and the opportunities being uncovered.

Vertical communication within a laboratory is another issue. Here what is most important is the content of the communication. Do laboratory heads ask subordinates for new ideas, for new approaches to things? Or do they simply tell them to go about their work? Laboratory heads who ask for new ideas are more likely to get them than those who don't.

Communication with technical resources outside the company Studies by Tom Allen in the late 1970s showed that the success of a project varied with the extent to which project team members communicated with people outside the team (Allen, 1977). Communicating with other people in the laboratory aided success, as did communicating with people outside the laboratory, whether in the company or not.

Communication with marketers, sales people and customers all help laboratory members keep track of what customers need. This makes it more likely that their ideas and the products they produce will be viable in the marketplace. Communication with people in laboratories outside the company is important in many industries. University laboratories, government laboratories, and independent laboratories may all do research which is relevant to the company's work. The company's scientists need to keep abreast of this work to ensure that they can take full advantage of it and not fall behind. In industries where such independent work is important, companies routinely give outside laboratories research contracts, second their scientists to such laboratories, or invite scientists from the laboratories, especially from university laboratories, to act as consultants to the company.

Not all industries attract the attention of university and other publicly funded researchers. In these industries, there may be no reason to maintain close technical ties with public laboratories. The only people outside the company doing any research relevant to the company's work may be working in competitors' laboratories! In such industries, secrecy, rather than links with the outside, may be the rule. Nonetheless, scientists in such industries would be well advised to stay in touch with any basic research relevant to the industries being done in publicly funded laboratories.

Optimizing the mix of laboratory personnel

Another problem Northern Pharmaceuticals' laboratories experienced in the 1980s was a shortage of chemists. There was a mismatch between the tasks that needed to be done and the skills available to do them. This is an issue in laboratories where the work done by different disciplines is interlocked. Biologists, microbiologists and biochemists did work which chemists needed to follow up on. But there weren't enough chemists to do all the necessary follow-up.

Optimizing the number of personnel along a scientific pipeline is mathematically similar to optimizing equipment in a factory line. When a certain type of equipment is overloaded, it becomes the constraint and the output of the operation will slow to the speed of the constrained operation. In a factory, the ways to increase speed include (Goldratt and Cox, 1992):

1. Adding more of the constrained equipment
2. Getting more out of the equipment in place
3. Substituting something else for the constrained equipment.

Similar tactics work when there is a shortage of scientific personnel.

In the Northern Pharmaceuticals example, the company could hire more chemists, it could use the chemists it has more efficiently, or it could train nonchemists to do things chemists currently do. Northern tried to develop new screening methods that would allow it to use its chemists' time more efficiently. Hiring new chemists was difficult, because the company as a whole was laying off personnel, and the laboratories were nominally under a hiring freeze. Northern was also looking for ways it could use nonchemists to perform some of the work done by chemists. (See Table 6.4 for a summary of key issues in the area of laboratory management.)

Table 6.4   Laboratory management methods and their impact

Method	Tool or variable . . . . . . Impact	
Management of laboratory personnels' time	■ Who controls laboratory research programs and time allocations: – Central control, control by laboratory head – Laboratory personnel have considerable flexibility and choice ■ Allowing spontaneous, unplanned investigations	■ Affects amount of entrepreneurial investigation, amount of diversification: – More focus, but less flexibility to take advantage of unexpected opportunity – Less focus, but much more reactivity, more diversification ■ Supports quick reaction to unexpected opportunities
Efficiency in routine or repeated operations	■ Identify routine and repeated operations, develop ways to perform them more efficiently	■ Improves laboratory efficiency and increases output
Laboratory goals: science- or business-related?	■ Ensure technical people see business-related goals as primary	■ Ensures laboratory work will focus on topics of potential value to the company
Laboratory communication	■ Horizontal communication within and between a company's laboratories ■ Communication with technical resources outside the company	■ Supports cross-fertilization of different skills, idea generation ■ Supports learning and import of new technologies
Optimizing the mix of laboratory personnel	■ Identifying links and dependencies between laboratory functions, optimizing mix to maximize output	■ Improves laboratory efficiency and increases output

The project funding system

Project funding systems are key to the success of any company's innovation program. Perhaps more than any other single feature, the project funding system, if badly designed, can bring a company's entire innovation system to a halt. Getting it right is a key task for all companies.

Fortunately, project funding systems are easier to chart and understand than other key functions, like idea generation. Most companies know how they fund projects. Most can identify and change features of the project funding system with relative ease. By contrast, many companies have only a vague understanding of how they generate ideas and how corporate policy influences idea generation.

In an effort to clarify how effective project funding systems are run, I will discuss four aspects of funding systems overall. The first is the structure of funding systems. When I use the word structure in this context, it refers to the issue of who can fund projects and where they are located on the organization chart in relation to the sources of project ideas. The second aspect is the information used in funding decisions. The third is when funding decisions are made. The fourth is the more obvious one of the level of funding allocation relative to the number and cost of ideas generated. (See Table 6.5 for a list of key questions in the area of project funding.)

I do not discuss goal setting in relation to funding here. As such goals are sometimes applied to business units, I discussed them as business management interventions in Chapter 5. But at times they will apply R&D or other independent funding boards that are separated from operating units. In these cases, such interventions could more properly be classified as project management interventions.

Funding structure

One key issue in any funding system is the location of funding sources. 'Who has the power to fund projects?' is a key question in any innovation system. Closely related to this is the number of funding sources which will be available to the typical person who has a project idea. A second issue is the nature of the links between funding sources and the sources of ideas. How long are the links?

Table 6.5   Questions to ask about project funding systems

Structure of the funding system
■ Who funds projects?
■ How many funding sources are available to any individual?
■ How much time does it take to get a funding decision?
■ Does information get distorted by being passed through too many people?
■ How much information do decision-makers really have about the projects they fund (or don't fund)?
■ How formal is the decision process? Is the level of formalization appropriate?
■ Are decisions made at the appropriate level?
■ Are the right kinds of information being used in the decisions?
■ How frequently during a project's life do funding reviews occur? Is this frequency appropriate?

Level of funding
■ How generous is funding?
■ Do all projects that deserve funding get funded?
■ Do we frequently fund projects that should not be funded? Why?
■ Are too many projects funded?

That is, how much time is involved in transmitting information and making the decision? And how much distortion will the information undergo between the idea source and the funding source?

A corollary of this is how much information those who make project funding decisions have. Are they close enough to the action to be immersed daily in technical and market information relevant to the projects they made decisions about? Or are they far removed from daily contact with product technologies and markets? Other issues are the level of formalization of project funding decisions, the types of information used in the decisions (covered in a separate section), and the match between the importance of the decision and the level of responsibility of the person who makes it.

Who funds projects? Some discussions of innovation management refer to a decision funnel. Many project ideas come into the funnel and only a few are chosen. A corporate or business unit board does the choosing.

The funnel analogy is very appropriate in pharmaceutical and motor vehicle companies, where the company can afford to fund only a few of many potential products. In more diversified companies, the funnel concept must be applied far more carefully. The issue is that diversified companies can have far more than one funnel. There may be many sources of funding in a diversified company and having only one funnel may actually be a sign of a system that is not working at its optimum level.

It is useful to list potential locations where a diversified company may have funding sources. First, business unit managers or a business unit level board may fund projects. Second, there may be funds available at the group or division level. Third, corporate may have special funds for 'corporate projects'. Fourth, there may be specialized funding boards that have the authorization to fund particular types of projects no matter where they originate within the company. Fifth, funds may be obtained through supplier–customer relations within the company. In this case, someone with a project idea must negotiate with someone downstream (for example, in a regional marketing unit) for funds. The downstream units fund only projects that they think will produce products that will sell in their region. Sixth, small teams, such as groups of technical reps, factory engineers, or a product management team, may be authorized to fund their own projects, within some limits. Seventh, individuals may be authorized to fund their own projects, within some limit. And eighth, companies may authorize project teams to try to sell early prototypes or early product runs on the market to raise money to continue development.

How many funding sources are available to any individual? A further source of variation involves how widely, in the horizontal dimension, companies allow their people to search for funds. MGE in the 1980s allowed people to look for funds only in units they belonged to. 3M, by contrast, allows people to look for funds anywhere in the company. An MGE person in the 1980s could look for funds only in one business unit, the one he worked in. A 3M person could, in theory, look for funds in any 3M business unit. The 3M person, thus, had hundreds of potential funding sources to choose from. The MGE person had one. No wonder 3M developed far more new products.

In the mid-1990s, when I interviewed managers at both companies, 3M was using seven of the eight types of funding sources. MGE Industrial Chemicals had used only one in the 1980s. By 1992, a second was added. By 1995 a third was under consideration. Is it any mystery that 3M was the more successful diversifier?

Time needed to get a decision One factor that determines the time needed to make a decision is the number of different people or boards that need to approve the decision. Historically, some companies were very slow because of the need for multiple approvals.

To illustrate, in the 1960s Bower (1970) studied funding processes at an American chemical company. He found that ultimate funding power for significant investments rested in a corporate board. Project ideas, which normally originated in functional areas in the company, had to pass through two intermediate screens, at the business unit and division level, before receiving final approval. The process of getting approval for a project was quite time consuming. Information had to be transmitted from the idea source to the business unit funding board, then from the business unit board to the division board, and finally from the division board to the corporate board, before receiving final approval. Then, of course, notification of approval had to be passed down the ladder. Notifying people of a decision normally happened quickly. But the process of moving information upward, and waiting for decisions, could take several months.

I have not found any business organizations in the 1990s that use such a cumbersome process. Most have learned that speed matters and they have cut the number of approvals even for large projects. In most companies business units can fund their own projects, with no need to go to higher levels for review, except for very large projects. Pharmaceutical and automobile companies, where all projects are very expensive, normally have only one central funding board. All project proposals go to the same board, where they are either accepted or rejected. In either case, the funding decision involves only one step.

As a note, some public and quasi-public organizations still have very cumbersome funding processes. I am aware of a European, publicly owned corporation where investments larger than $15 million must be approved by seven separate boards. Under certain circumstances, nine separate boards must approve the requests. Not surprisingly, the organization in question is known for being very slow on its feet. It loses many opportunities to private sector competitors that respond to opportunities much more quickly.

Another factor determining the time needed to make a decision is the time involved in communicating information. The time involved is partially a result of how many people the information must pass through before the final decision is made. When three different funding boards must approve a request (Bower's example), information must be transmitted three times.

Another factor determining the time is the distance, physical or otherwise, between the person with the idea and the person making the decision. If they work in the same laboratory and communicate daily, and oral requests are sufficient, the communication time will nearly be zero. If, as at 3M, people are allowed to fund work on an idea themselves via a 15 percent rule, then no communication will be necessary and communication time will be zero. But if the person with the idea must write the idea down in a specific format, back it up with voluminous supporting information, and then transmit written copies to a distant office, the time involved in communicating will be large.

It is easy to ignore things that slow the decision process down. So I will itemize the various steps in the process which take time. I will use, as an example, a funding system where funding requests must be written down in a specific format.

First, the person with the idea will need to assemble the information needed. If she has never submitted an idea before, she will have to educate herself as to what information is needed and how to collect it. Then, second, she will have to write the information down in the required format. Third, she may need to discuss the proposal with her supervisor or another experienced person and rewrite it to fit the specific biases of the funding board. This rewriting process may occur several times. Several levels of the hierarchy may be involved. Then, fourth, she must communicate the proposal to the funding committee.

Fifth, she may have to wait for the funding committee to meet. Sixth, the funding committee may take time to consider the proposal by not making a final decision at the first meeting. Seventh, the funding committee has to communicate its decision not only to the person making the request, but also to those who need to provide her with resources. Eighth, she may have to wait for those controlling resources to allocate resources to her. Ninth, she may have to wait a little more for the allocated resources to come free and begin work on her project. All these steps can add up to months of waiting time.

By contrast, look at what can happen in a small, entrepreneurial corporation. Someone has an idea on a Monday morning. He talks to the CEO, whose office is down the hall, and gets authorization to work on the idea. If he needs help, the CEO talks to the people he needs help from and work begins Monday afternoon.

Companies like 3M match the speed of small, entrepreneurial corporations through mechanisms like the 15 percent rule. Again, a laboratory person has an idea on a Monday morning. She begins working on the idea immediately, since she can allocate 15 percent of her time to any project she wishes. She can ask anyone nearby for help. If they are convinced of the value of the idea, they can help immediately, since they can also allocate 15 percent of their time to any project they wish. If the idea is directly related to the business they work in, they may be able to work on the idea full time with, at most, the approval of their boss.

Distortion of information in the decision process When information passes through many hands, it becomes distorted. If funding requests pass through many hands and are translated or edited by many people, the original thrust of the request may be lost entirely. In most companies, the person or group who originated the idea must follow the idea throughout the process to avoid such distortion. When funding requests must be sponsored and presented by a senior person and adapted to the funding board's bias, this may not occur.

Information held by decision makers The quality of a funding decision is determined, in part, by how much the decision makers know about the technology and market involved in the idea. If they know a lot about the technology the proposed product would use, they will make better decisions than if they know nothing about the technology. If they know a lot about the market the product would be aimed at, they will make better decisions than if they know nothing about that market. When decision makers are in the same business unit or laboratory that the idea originated in, they are likely to know a lot about the relevant technologies and markets. If they are far away in a corporate center, they may know very little.

Level of formalization of decisions Decisions can be made very informally, via simple oral request. Or they can be made via written request. In the case of a written request, there may or may not be a required format for the request. The written request may have no particular information requirements. Or the fund seeker may be required to provide answers to dozens of detailed questions about the technology, the market, competitors, the regulatory environment, and other issues that may be key to the project.

The most innovative companies do not have the most formal systems. In fact, they may have quite informal systems of resource allocation at some levels. Both 3M and ConsumerCo provide R&D areas with considerable funds that can be spent on a discretionary basis. But this does not mean that all companies should have informal funding systems. When large investments are involved, all companies, including the most innovative, look carefully at a wide variety of variables.

MGE's funding processes were very informal in the 1980s. The problem was that funding boards tended to ignore market considerations. In the early 1990s, most of the company's divisions introduced much more formal funding systems. The formal system forced people to answer questions about the market viability of ideas. The company's managers used the formal system to teach people what they needed to think about.

With these examples in mind, it is likely that the level of formalization follows an inverted U-curve (see Figure 6.1). The lowest levels of formalization occur in companies where little attention is paid to innovation. When these companies begin to focus on innovation, a much higher level of formalization may be used to teach people what they should pay attention to. In companies which have been emphasizing innovation for many years, some procedures are formalized, but the level of formalization found in the mid-range companies is simply not necessary. People know what to do, so they don't need so many rules to guide them.

Match between decision importance and the decision maker's hierarchical level 3M can let laboratory workers make decisions about where to allocate development money because the funds involved are not very large. 3M is in an industry where many inexpensive ideas can be generated and explored. Automobile companies and pharmaceutical companies cannot afford to let their laboratory technicians decide which cars or which molecules they will invest in. The quantities of money involved are so large that senior corporate officers must be involved in these decisions.

The challenge companies making large bets face is to ensure that decisions are made promptly and that decision-makers have enough information about the product and its market. It is not surprising that

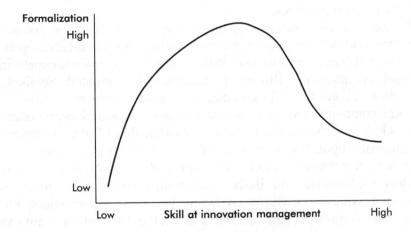

Figure 6.1   Level of formalization of
information requirements

companies that make large bets are often single industry businesses. The senior management teams of pharmaceutical companies know the pharmaceutical business very well, since it is the only business they are concerned with. The same goes for senior management teams in automobile companies. Such companies may be conservative, since they can only take a few bets. But knowledge of the industry should not be a problem.

Information used in funding decisions

Companies vary widely in the amount of information required for funding decisions. I will begin this section by discussing the types of information that may be required. Then I will discuss why companies differ on this dimension. Later I will look at the issue of managing risk.

Types of information required As may as eight types of information may be required in a detailed funding request. Any funding system will ask for a description of the product, process, or product variation. Most will ask about the intended customers. Most will also ask about the technology or technologies to be used to develop the product.

Beyond those three items, the other questions asked will depend on the industry the company is in, its position in the industry, and the company's own practices.

Monopolists don't need to ask about competitors. But most companies have competitors or potential competitors. So potential competition is a key issue in most companies. Many companies compete in unregulated industries. But other industries are regulated. So likely regulation is a key issue for companies in those industries.

Some companies have guaranteed, inexpensive access to raw materials. Or they produce products/services that don't have significant raw material input. But most companies are dependent on suppliers in some way. For those companies, the supply of raw materials for a new product is a key issue. Similarly, some companies distribute products directly to consumers. But many others go through distributors. For them, how to push the new product through the distribution chain can be a key issue.

Finally, some companies are so good at executing innovation projects that the issue of how to organize a project team is not considered at the funding stage. It is simply assumed that the right people will be available and that they will be organized in the right way. But many companies cannot afford to make such assumptions. Those companies sometimes require people to include an organization, staffing and execution plan in their funding request.

Beyond these basic issues, there is the question of whether the funding board asks for one set of financial projections, or whether it asks for several sets of projections based on different scenarios. In situations where many projects compete for funds, and where the funding board cannot hope to become familiar with all the issues relevant to each project, it can be useful to ask teams to think through several scenarios. A promising approach pioneered by SmithKline Beecham (SKB) and documented in a recent *Harvard Business Review* article (Sharpe and Keelin, 1998) provides an example.

At SKB, the funding board asks each project team to provide four budgets. In the first budget, the team indicates how they would continue present activity. In the second budget, they are asked to show what they would do if the funding was significantly reduced. In the third budget, they must show what they would do with a significant increase in funds. In the fourth budget, they show how they would close the project, preserving as much as possible of the learning they have achieved. The funding board asks the team to specify in detail what it would do under each scenario. With all this additional information, the funding board is able to understand far better what the impact of cutting or raising each project's funds will be. This improves the quality of funding decisions and limits the politics involved.

Formalization of information requirements In the previous section, I noted that some companies have much more formal funding systems than others. In some companies, there is a very formalized procedure for requesting funds. In others, funding requests may involve nothing more than a brief meeting between a person and his or her supervisor.

The level of formalization does not just impact the procedure. It can also impact the type and amount of information required. In very formal systems, all funding requests may be required to provide answers to a variety of questions covering, in the extreme case, all eight of the basic categories above. In very informal systems, there may be no specific requirements for information. The information required may vary for each request with 'common sense' being used to determine what information should be required for each proposal.

MGE's Industrial Chemicals division went from one extreme to another. In the 1980s, there were no specific information requirements. Business unit heads could demand as much, or as little, information on a proposal as they wished. This changed. In 1992 corporate management introduced a much more formal funding system. Each potential project head was required to submit information on the proposed product, the intended customers, the value for the customers, the technology, likely competitors, likely regulation, suppliers and the organization of the team. In short, Industrial Chemicals went from having no specific requirements to requiring seven of the eight categories of information listed earlier in this section.

Industrial Chemicals established a more formal funding system as its managers tried to make the company more innovative. The management team used the formal system to ensure that all relevant aspects of a project would be considered in the funding decision. But not all innovative companies use formal funding systems. Funding systems at ConsumerCo and 3M are not as formal as the one established at Industrial Chemicals in the 1990s. At both companies, many everyday funding requests are dealt with quite informally.

ConsumerCo and 3M can use informal systems for smaller requests successfully because their people generally know what kinds of information should be evaluated in a funding decision. They don't have to have a formal information request to be reminded.

Since both companies deal with a variety of projects, with different issues being relevant for different projects, it would be inefficient to enforce a uniform information requirement for each project.

In addition, ConsumerCo and 3M managers are immersed in flows of information about the technologies and markets that they supervise. When their subordinates make funding requests, they are, in many cases, already familiar with the technical and market issues involved. Only in the case of particularly new or unusual requests is a new information search necessary.

As noted in the previous section, formalization of funding systems and information requirements appears to follow an inverse U-curve. Companies inexperienced with innovation may have funding systems that are quite informal. As these companies become more experienced with innovation, they may establish much more formal funding systems to assure that all relevant information is taken into account. But the most innovative companies are not so worried about assuring that all relevant information is taken into account, at least in the case of smaller projects. They are more confident that their people know what information to consider while evaluating a project idea. Formalization would simply slow the investment process down without improving the quality of decisions.

For large projects, the situation is different, even at the most innovative companies. When the company has a lot at stake, senior management will assure that all relevant information has been collected and evaluated. As a result, large projects are evaluated as formally at ConsumerCo and 3M as they are at Industrial Chemicals.

Using information to manage risk A key reason for collecting information on project proposals is to identify and manage areas of risk. Projects face many kinds of risk. Each of the classes of information listed above relates to a particular type of risk.

Some of the key risks facing a project are the following:

1. *Technology risk*: will we be able to produce the planned product at a reasonable cost?
2. *Market risk*: assuming we can produce the product, will it sell? Will it sell at a profitable price?
3. *Competitive risk*: assuming the product sells, will we be able to keep the gains?
4. *Internal risk*: do we have the organizational capacity to carry the project through?

Other types of risk, not all of them carried by all projects, following:

5. *Regulatory risk*: will regulators allow the product to be sold as we envision it?

6. *Supplier/partner risk*: will suppliers be able to supply needed raw materials or components? Will needed partners be found? Will raw material and component prices be low enough for us to make a profit? Will partners be in a position to bargain away our profits?

7. *Distribution risk*: are appropriate distribution channels available? Will they carry the product? Will we have enough bargaining power versus distributors to retain profits?

By gathering and analyzing relevant information, a project team can determine where the most significant areas of risk are for the project. They would be well advised to set up the project plan in such a way as to resolve areas of uncertainty or high risk as early as possible, before significant funds are spent on the project. For example, if the risk of technological failure is high, the team may be able to set up early tests to determine if the technology is feasible. Or developing the technology to the point at which it can be tested may be the first priority. Similarly, if market risk appears to be the key issue, perhaps early market tests can be set up to enable the company to better gauge likely market response.

Producing early prototypes is a way to test a number of different types of risk. Producing the prototype tests the company's technical capabilities, as well as the availability of key raw materials. It also tests relationships with partners and suppliers. Finally, trying to sell prototypes or early production versions can give important information about market response.

Project funding boards can force project teams to identify key risk areas. They can force project teams to address areas of high risk, and to try to reduce or resolve the risk, as early as possible. In fact, forcing project teams to identify and manage risk is one of their most useful functions.

When funding decisions are made

Large innovation projects are rarely funded on an all or nothing basis. Preliminary funds are granted for exploration. If the exploration turns up positive results, additional funds may be granted for preliminary development. If positive results continue, the company's commitment will grow until finally there is a decision to launch the product. In the case of a large project, there may be several dozen interim funding decisions. A formal specification of processes to be completed and milestones to be reached before additional funds are released may be in place (for example, phase-gate, or stage-gate systems, discussed in Meyer, 1998).

Small projects, those that last at most a few months, and which absorb relatively small amounts of resources, may be completely funded from the beginning. But even such projects may be shut down early if negative results appear. At any point the project team could let senior management know that there was no further reason to pursue the project and shut it down.

All or nothing funding is rare for large projects. Vehicle development projects come closest to this model. When an automobile company decides to fund a new vehicle development project, it is unlikely that the project will be cancelled. While there may be preliminary studies that explore potential alternative designs for the vehicle, at some point early in the process the company commits itself. Vehicles are so expensive to develop that automobile companies do not go half way. Beyond inexpensive preliminary studies, vehicle development is an all or nothing proposition. No company can afford to waste money designing a car half way and then abandoning the project.

Pharmaceutical projects have a different profile. If a molecule enters clinical trials, the company is, for all practical purposes, committed to bringing the molecule onto the market *provided it successfully passes its clinical trials*. Clinical trials are so expensive that no company will put a substance into clinical trials unless it fully intends to market it if it successfully passes the trials. But here there is a risk factor. The company knows that 80+ percent of drugs will fail their clinical trials. If early tests show a lack of efficacy, the company can pull the plug and avoid spending the $100+ million that it takes to bring a substance all the way through clinical trials.

The situation is relatively straightforward for pharmaceutical companies. If a substance fails its trials, funding stops. The issues that companies in many other industries must deal with are the following. How often should they review the funding of projects? And precisely when should they review funding?

Calendar-driven review There are several common solutions. One is to review project funding at regular, calendar-driven intervals. Some companies may review projects every three months. Others may review them every six months or, in the case of longer projects, once each year. Short intervals, such as quarterly reviews, are common for all but the most long-term projects.

A calendar-based review is somewhat arbitrary, since the calendar dates set may not correspond to any key events in the project. But it does allow an easy fit with the corporate budgeting and review process. If there are lots of projects to review, the calendar method may allow a more simplified and efficient administrative process.

Milestone-based review The other common solution is to set milestones for each project and to review funding after each milestone. If a project is supposed to achieve X at time T, the company will conduct a review at time T to see if X has occurred. If X has occurred, and other signs are favorable, the project will be refunded. If X has not occurred, the project review board will ask why. If the reason for the failure casts doubt on the project's feasibility, further funding will likely be denied. But if there is a logical explanation, and the failure to reach milestone X does not cast doubt on the project's feasibility, then funding may continue. See, for example, discussions of phase-gate funding processes, such as in Meyer (1998).

A milestone-based review fits more naturally into the rhythm of the project. Key events in the project, those events that actually have bearing on the project's future and likely outcome, can be identified, and the reviews set up around these events. This allows quick corporate reaction to events in the project. If the project is consuming large amounts of resources, milestone based review may be essential. If, on the other hand, the company has large numbers of small projects, it may not be adminstratively feasible to arrange milestone-based reviews for all of them. As a result, milestone-based review is more commonly used for larger projects, where the resources involved are significant for the company as a whole.

Frequency of review One issue the funding source needs to consider is the following. How often does it want to have the option of stopping the project? A corollary issue is: How often does it want the option to increase funding for the project? The answer to this question should determine how often project funding is reviewed.

As a general rule, high-risk projects should be reviewed frequently, while low-risk projects need not be reviewed very often. The size of the project budget may also influence the decision on how often it should be reviewed. A company may wish to review expensive projects more often than inexpensive projects, simply because catching a problem early may allow the company to save a substantial amount of money.

Ongoing review by the project team A third approach to funding reviews is to encourage the project team to review its own project's chances of success in an objective fashion. Normal project review systems assume that the project team will be biased towards continuing the project. In most companies, this is probably the case. Ending a project may hurt the careers of the people running the project. So they won't want to end it. As long as there is any chance of reaching a successful conclusion, they will continue to pursue their goal.

By comparison, an objective review of the project by the project team could save the company considerable money. If the team notifies management that the project is unlikely to succeed as soon as this is the case, rather than waiting until all possible hope is lost, they may save the company months, even years of wasted investment.

Here companies with much experience running projects have an advantage. 3M and ConsumerCo run so many projects that project failure is common. No one is surprised when a project fails. It is just a part of normal, everyday life. So there is no stigma attached to project failure. And there is little reason for a project team to hide negative signals from management when project success seems unlikely.

The same effect can occur when projects take only short periods of time. No one will be very concerned if a project that has run three months fails. No one has invested that much of their lives in it. But if a project runs a year or more, the story is different. In the latter case, the project team members have invested a significant portion of their lives in the project. They will not want to see it die, particularly if their careers will be marked by a stigma if it does die.

Eastman Chemical runs many long innovation projects. A few years ago Eastman managers compared the average total costs of projects that failed with the average total costs of projects that succeeded. The analysis revealed that projects that ultimately failed cost as much as projects that ultimately succeeded.

Eastman management explained this by hypothesizing that project teams were continuing projects even after it became evident that the projects would fail. Why would they do this? Because they believed that there was still a small chance that the project could succeed. To avoid the stigma of working on a 'failure,' they would just continue the project as long as there was some small ray of hope that it would succeed.

Eastman management decided to fight this tendency by removing, to the extent possible, the stigma attached to 'failed' projects. For one thing, the word 'failure' was removed from the Eastman vocabulary. Projects that would have once been called 'failed', were now called 'appropriately terminated'. The difference was more than cosmetic. It implied a change in the mission and role of project teams. They were no longer expected to 'make the project succeed'. Rather, their mission became to 'determine if the project can succeed', and to 'make it succeed if possible'. When a project ended, team members were congratulated for having appropriately terminated the project. Senior management would ensure that their next position was a good one.

Level of overall funding allocation

The ratio of overall budget size to the cost of pursuing all the opportunities available varied considerably across the laboratories of the companies in the sample. ConsumerCo laboratories through the early 1990s had enough money to pursue virtually any idea they or their marketing departments thought of. How could this be possible? Well, for one thing, ConsumerCo had been putting a high priority on innovation for generations. The priority was backed up with a high spend on R&D. The company's management believed that a high proportion of ideas should be pursued, to maximize the chances of finding the best ideas.

This being said, in the early 1990s ConsumerCo management began asking laboratories to be more selective about which ideas they pursued. Marketing departments were told to screen their own ideas before presenting them to the laboratories. Management believed that too many ideas were being pursued, that the company was spending money on ideas that weren't really worthwhile. Some laboratory managers and marketers I interviewed agreed. They did not think the increased selectivity about which ideas to pursue would harm the company in any significant way.

3M's laboratories also appear to be generously endowed. I heard few complaints about lack of funds for innovation when I spoke to 3M managers. Managers at Eastman Chemical told much the same story.

The same was not true elsewhere. Resources appeared to be constantly short at MGE's laboratories. Northern Pharmaceuticals kept cutting projects because it didn't have the resources to pursue all of its ideas. At EurAuto the situation was even worse. Technical development people told me that the company had no money, none at all, for experimentation during development projects. No vehicle development team could afford to take a risk on an unproven technology. If the technology was not proven to work early in the vehicle design phase, it could not be included in the vehicle design.

The more richly endowed laboratories shared several characteristics. They operated in areas where there was little or no government regulation. They did not have to pay for extensive, regulation-driven tests. The technologies they dealt with were relatively simple, and thus inexpensive. The overall cost of pursuing a project was relatively low.

By contrast, most of the laboratories with limited budgets operated in businesses where mega-projects were the rule. In pharmaceuticals, even pursuing a few ideas can be prohibitively expensive for a small or medium-sized company. To make matters worse, some of these businesses, like automobiles, are cyclical. In these cyclical businesses, laboratory budgets can come under extreme pressure during downturns.

This pattern was reflected in the sample companies. Some of the chemical projects MGE pursued had multimillion dollar budgets. Northern Pharmaceuticals faced project bills of over $100 million for a product at launch. EurAuto was a mid-sized player in an expensive, cyclical business. Its development teams were so constrained that even small technological investments were unthinkable if there was any risk that they would not succeed.

Another feature of the more richly endowed laboratories was their flexibility. If an interesting new idea came up at 3M or ConsumerCo, it could usually be pursued immediately. Projects were short and numerous, so there was always someone coming off of a project. They could be immediately allocated to the new idea.

The more constrained laboratories were less flexible. The inflexibility was more acute since these laboratories handled fewer, larger projects. People rarely came off projects, since projects lasted for years. When an interesting new idea came up, the company might wait for months to pursue it, since people would not be available.

MGE sometimes dealt with this inflexibility by allowing project managers to hire new people or to contract out research. George Marsh used both these routes to pursue the Chemical Residues idea. In fact, the project would have never got off the ground if Marsh had been obliged to use available MGE resources. Laboratory people were committed to other things when the idea originated, and there was no way to reallocate them to Chemical Residues in the MGE system. The project made progress only through the use of outside resources. (See Table 6.6 for a summary of key issues in project funding systems.)

Project structure

Another key issue in the management of projects is the structural position of the projects and the structure of the project teams themselves. One issue is the structural links between project teams and the rest of the organization. Another is the structure of the teams themselves. A third is the links between teams and other parts of the company. A fourth is links between teams and the outside world. The last issue I will consider in this section is the role played by those who supervise the project. (See Table 6.7 for a list of key questions in the area of project structure.)

Where projects fit in the company's structure

Three issues are key here:

- How much power to project chiefs have?
- Who do they report to?
- How permanent are their teams?

I will deal with each issue in turn.

Project chiefs' power Companies have different kinds of middle- and senior-level managers. Some manage projects. Some manage business units or groups of business units. Others manage functions.

Table 6.6   Variations in project funding
systems and their impact

Issue	Tool or variable . . . . . . Impact	
Structure of funding system	■ Who funds projects:	■ Affects speed, distortion of communications:
	– People close to source of ideas (front-line people themselves, or their immediate supervisors)	– Quicker, less distortion
	– Distant from source of ideas (higher levels in corporation)	– Slower, more distortion
	■ How many funding sources available to any individual:	■ Affects ability to diversify:
	– One (for example, his/her immediate supervisor)	– Limits diversification, maintains focus, order
	– Many (supervisor, BUs, groups, corporate, and so on)	– Facilitates, even encourages diversification
	■ Level of formalization of decisions	■ High formalization can be used to teach people what to think about in making funding decision
	■ Match between decision importance and hierarchical level:	■ Trade-off between fiscal responsibility of corporate leaders and allowance for diversification, quick reaction:
	– Major bets affecting overall company results made at corporate level	– Fiscal responsibility requires corporate oversight of major bets
	– Smaller investments decided at lower levels	– Allows more experimentation, diversification, quicker reaction
Information used in funding decisions	■ Types of information required (can be few or many)	■ Affects focus, depth, range of discussion

(cont'd)

Table 6.6 (cont'd)

Issue	Tool or variable . . . . . Impact	
	■ Formalization of information requirements	■ Formalization assures consideration of key issues, but limits flexibility and speed
	■ Use information collected to identify and manage key areas of risk	■ Forces project team to think through risks involved and address them early
When funding decisions are made	■ Calendar driven	■ Simplifies process, allows easy fit with annual budgeting process
	■ Milestone driven	■ Allows funding decision to be linked with key events in project's history
	■ Frequency	■ Each review gives company option to increase/ decrease funding, frequent reviews desirable for expensive projects
	■ Review driven by project team, team signals problems, opportunities	■ Allows quickest response to problems, it team can be relied upon to honestly face problems
Level of overall budget allocation	■ High overall budget	■ Allows much experimentation, more ideas can be explored
	■ Low overall budget	■ Forces teams and management to carefully consider and evaluate options, limits experimentation

Table 6.7   Questions to ask about project structure

Power, prominence, continuity
■ How powerful are project chiefs?
■ What level do innovation projects report to?
■ Do they have visibility at top levels?
■ How are reporting levels determined?
■ Are project teams permanent, or do they come and go?
Cross-functional cooperation
■ Is cross-functional cooperation built into the structure of innovation projects?
■ Do we have methods of adapting and habituating people to cross-functional work?
■ Can we measure the effectiveness of cross-functional cooperation?
Links between project teams and others
■ Are our innovation teams effectively linked to the rest of the company?
■ Are they effectively linked to the outside world?
■ Are our projects effectively supervised?
– By whom?
– At what level(s)?

The relative power of each type can have an important impact on innovation performance.

In companies where functional chiefs are strong, innovation projects may suffer. Functional chiefs may have the power to give and withhold resources from project teams. If teams have to beg for resources and resources are allocated in whatever way is optimal for the *function*, projects will be slowed and at times starved of resources.

The relation between project chiefs and business managers is less problematic. But there may still be disputes over corporate allocations of funds. Business unit heads who supervise innovation projects may starve them of funds. This will allow them to invest more in their ongoing businesses. Alternatively, they may simply keep the money and show larger profits in their ongoing businesses.

Some companies defuse all these rivalries by making some of their project chiefs completely independent of business unit and functional constraints. They set up projects with direct reporting lines to corporate management. Automobile companies give project managers power by giving them direct reporting relationships to senior management. Pharmaceutical companies do the same. Even MGE began giving some projects direct reports to senior management in an effort to make sure that they received sufficient resources to pursue their opportunities.

Whom projects report to The issue of what level project teams report to is more complicated than this. Project teams can report to low-level supervisors in laboratories. Or they may report to laboratory heads. Projects located in business units may report to low-level functional supervisors within a business unit. Or they may report to product managers or to the business unit head. Projects outside of business units may report to divisional or group heads, or to corporate management itself. And, of course, a project may report to several levels at once.

Several factors determine where a project reports. One is where the idea originated. Project teams tend to be formed first within the unit where the idea originated. When an idea originates in a lab, the team built to explore it will report to a laboratory supervisor or to the laboratory head.

A second factor is the location of competences or resources needed. If a project team is using marketing competences located in a business unit, it is likely to have a reporting relationship with someone in the business unit.

A third factor is the project's importance to the company. A project viewed as key to the entire company's future may have a direct reporting relationship to the CEO, in addition to any other reporting relationships. A project of no great importance to anyone will report to a low level manager in a laboratory.

The fourth factor is the project's need for high-level support. Some projects use resources located in several different business units (for example, technological resources from one business unit, marketing competences from another). A senior manager may be involved in these projects to be sure they get the resources they need. He may also assure that the efforts of the two business units are properly coordinated. He may be involved because his presence is necessary to ensure that the project gets done, even though the project is not viewed as key to the company's future.

Permanent versus nonpermanent project teams Some project teams live longer than the projects they work on. They may work on multiple projects, adding new projects as old ones are finished. Or they may move from one project to the next, with the team largely intact. Keeping a project team together allows a company to conserve intellectual capital. A team experienced in running one gastrointestinal (GI) pharmaceutical project may be kept together to run another project of the same type. Or it may be given several GI projects to work on at once.

Another advantage of keeping a team together is that the cost of building a team for the second and subsequent projects is avoided. The process of building a team is a cost that some managers don't notice. People must get to know each other. They must learn to speak each others' functional languages. They must establish effective working relationships. All this takes time. During the early stages of a project, while these relationships are being worked out, the project team may function at a fraction of its subsequent efficiency. These start-up costs can be avoided by keeping the team together.

3M has permanent innovation teams in many of its business units. So does ConsumerCo. These teams do project after project, routinely working on several at once. These companies do so many different projects, some major and some minor, that forming a different team for each project would be unfeasible. By establishing permanent teams, they build up specialized expertise in innovation in each area, and they minimize the start-up costs associated with building new teams.

In all companies, some projects are so large, complicated, or unusual that a new team must be formed. This particularly applies to projects that require full-time commitment for a long period of time. In these cases, dedicated resources must be found to staff the team. Only in unusual cases will there be a whole team available, having just finished its previous project, with all the right resources.

The structure of project teams

The main issue in team structure is the extent of cross-functional relations. Large teams in automobile and pharmaceutical companies are sometimes divided into independent functional units. Little cross-functional contact may occur, meaning that coordination across functional boundaries may prove difficult.

In other industries, the same problem may occur. Even though a team may be smaller, its members may be dispersed across different functional or business units. They may never see each other. They may coordinate their work via written messages or via the intervention of a manager higher up.

Cross-functional coordination is important because the lack of it slows a project down. Most innovation projects involve multiple tasks. Usually these tasks must be performed by specialists from several functions. If the specialists cannot coordinate their work, they may have to perform it sequentially. This slows a large project immensely. As a result, companies have been trying for more than a decade to speed projects up by establishing more effective cross-functional relations. One solution to the coordination problem is to give the project a chief with a lot of power. The chief can then command the functions to work together effectively. I've discussed this solution above. Automobile and pharmaceutical companies have used it extensively. But the brute force solution is not the only one available. There are subtler ways to accomplish the same goal. The subtler ways, which involve quiet learning more than brute force, arouse less resistance. They are likely to be more effective in the long run. In recent years many of companies, including automobile and pharmaceutical companies, have been using the more subtle means as well.

Before discussing the other approaches, I will discuss what is required for effective cross-functional cooperation to occur. After this I will discuss approaches to building cross-functional cooperation. Then I will look at the problems of adapting personnel to cross-functional work and of measuring the success of a cross-functional team. Finally, I will look at differences across companies and industries in the problem of encouraging cross-functional cooperation.

Requirements for cross-functional cooperation Until the late 1980s, Northern Pharmaceuticals ran drug development projects in the classical 'sequential' way. When one department finished with a project, it would 'toss the project over the wall' to the next department, at which point the next department would begin work. In general, no two departments worked on the project at the same time. This was the classic 'before' situation described in numerous books and articles, such as those by Wheelwright and Clark (1992) or Clark and Fujimoto (1991).

When Northern Pharmaceuticals realized that this sequential development system was costing the company much time and money, management decided to force the departments to work in parallel. Stringent completion time goals were set up and project managers were given strict control over laboratory resources so that they could enforce cross-functional cooperation. Eventually cross-functional cooperation happened, but it was not easy.

Laboratory managers to some extent were uncomfortable with the change, as it represented a loss of power for them. But there was not that much of a problem in implementing the change. Everyone knew that the patent life of pharmaceutical products was limited, and that losing time meant losing money. Everyone could see the logic behind cross-functional cooperation. But it was not that easy to do. Northern's development departments ran into three related problems as they began trying to work together. The first was that they didn't share the same *language*. The second was that the departments did not have the same *values and concerns*. The third problem was the difficulty of *planning and coordinating work*.

Each department had its own technical *language* for talking about pharmaceutical products and pharmaceutical development. No department knew any of the other departments' languages. Toxicity had many words and procedures related to testing toxicity. Clinical development had many words and procedures related to clinical testing. Neither knew the others' vocabulary. To be able to work together, these two departments had to communicate about the product in depth and effectively. This was not possible until each department had learned some of the other department's language. Since a dozen different departments were involved in the development of each product, much learning had to occur before they could all work together.

In addition to learning another department's language, each department had to learn something about the *values and concerns* of the other department. To be able to work together effectively, each department had to have some idea of what was important to the other departments. What kind of outcomes were the other departments seeking? And what, for them, constituted a problem?

Then, there was the issue of *planning and coordinating work*. Besides speaking different technical languages, the different departments each had a different way of tracking the progress of a chemical through their procedures and tests. The checkpoints used by different laboratories rarely corresponded. Rather than track hundreds of checkpoints, the laboratories had to agree on a few checkpoints that would be enough to serve the purposes of all laboratories. Once the checkpoints were agreed, the laboratories then had to work out how to use the checkpoints to manage the progress of a project. If there was a delay in meeting a checkpoint, who needed to be notified? What special actions needed to be taken? If, on the other hand, a checkpoint was met early, how could the laboratories take advantage of this?

Learning each others' languages, values and concerns took months. Developing common means of tracking and managing projects together took additional months. This work of determining how to work together took much more time than anticipated. Making the decision to establish a cross-functional work capability was only the beginning. The real work occurred when people tried to work together for the first time.

Methods of building cross-functional capacity Companies have developed several methods of building cross-functional work capability. Perhaps the best known is to establish what Wheelwright and Clark (1992) call a 'tiger team'. There are three key features that distinguish a tiger team:

1. It is headed by a strong project manager
2. It controls its own resources
3. It is independent from business units or functional departments, often reporting directly to senior management.

Some tiger teams are physically separated from the rest of the corporation and located in 'skunk works', or sites far removed from the influences of other departments.

The extreme solution of the tiger team is used most often in companies that have the most difficulty establishing cross-functional cooperation. These are typically older, well-established organizations with strong functional groups, or (less often) strong business units without any history of cooperating with each other. In such organizations, the powerful project chief and the isolation of the tiger team are needed to break down long-established barriers between functions.

Many companies, where the barriers to cross-functional cooperation are not so high, use less extreme solutions. In effect, they use some of the features of the tiger team, without using all of them. For example, rather than isolating the team from the rest of the organization, they may simply *co-locate* them. Team members remain in a corporate building, where they will rub elbows with colleagues from their old functions. But they sit together and have more contact with fellow team members than with anyone else. Co-location greatly facilitates communication, as researchers from Allen (1977) on have discovered. And the more team members communicate, the more they will understand each others' language, values and concerns. And the more they will be able to effectively coordinate their work.

A second more subtle method to get people to cooperate is to give them a *common problem* to work on. They do not have to be co-located to work on a common problem, although it helps. When faced with the same customer, expressing the same problem, they will have an incentive to work together to solve it. If their bonus, their next promotion, or their future with the company will be determined by the outcome of the project, their incentive to work together will be that much stronger. In the process of working together, they will communicate a great deal. They will learn each others' languages, values and concerns through constant communication. In effect, all will become multilingual. Business necessity will force them to develop whatever tools or common capabilities are necessary to work together.

Another way to get people to cooperate across functional boundaries is to make *cross-functional teams* (rather than functional teams) the *primary organizational unit*. Moving from a functional structure to a business unit structure is a large-scale version of this. But some companies, 3M among them, do virtually all their work through cross-functional teams. Down to the lowest level, down to the most minor task, teams are not unifunctional but cross-functional.

A fourth way to encourage cooperation is to *build special-purpose horizontal links between functions*. Liaison teams, coordinating groups, or teams for specific tasks can be built up, even if most of the work is done by unifunctional teams.

A fifth way to encourage cooperation is to bring people in different functions into contact with each other outside of the normal work environment. This can perhaps most effectively be done through *educational programs*. If all managers in a company pass through an intensive, multiweek educational program that trains them in several functions and mixes them with members of other functions, they will acquire language and relationships that will equip them to work far more effectively with people from other functions.

The above techniques work particularly well in companies where much of the work can be done by small cross-functional teams. Other methods are useful in companies which use large teams to perform highly complex and functionally specialized tasks. Senior managers in such companies can create a *strong project leader who controls the compensation and advancement* of the people on his team. The project leader may be backed up by a strong project management structure that allows him to carefully track the contribution of each team member. Such a leader should be able to elicit cooperation, even if team members are not co-located.

Second, the *project leader may control a budget* that he uses to hire resources from functional areas. Here the functional areas may maintain nominal control of their people. But they do not have a budget to support their people. They 'earn' money by supplying people to project teams. If they don't have the kind of resources the teams need, or if they don't provide them when the teams need them, they will find that they no longer have any money to pay their people.

Third, the large project teams themselves may include a *coordinating group within the team* that coordinates the work of the various functional subunits within the team. Some automobile design teams are organized this way. Specialized subteams design the chassis, the body and its components, and the engine and drive train. A separate unit within the team coordinates the work of the others. The coordination team has four main tasks. It identifies conflicts between the designs produced by the various subteams. It facilitates resolution of the conflicts. It evaluates the overall design of the vehicle, particularly on dimensions like noise and economy, which are affected by the work of many subteams. And finally the team develops propositions for meeting goals on overall design when the work of the subteams does not adequately meet these goals.

Fourth, companies with larger teams and more complex tasks may *change their organization structure to establish cross-functional links at lower levels.* EurAuto has a new materials development laboratory. At one time, the head of new materials reported to a boss who headed all experimental laboratories. There was no direct hierarchical connection with the vehicle development areas below the CEO level. Disputes with the development areas regularly arose, but they could not be resolved because the CEO would not pay any attention to them.

A typical dispute involved what the new materials laboratory should be working on. The engineers in the new materials laboratory were regularly frustrated when their innovative and useful (they thought) proposals were not accepted by the automobile design unit. Meanwhile, the design teams were unhappy that the new materials people kept bringing them proposals that did not take account of the constraints they were under. To resolve this difference, and to avoid further wasted effort, the new materials unit was made part of the design unit. It was expected that the head of design would assure that the new materials people worked on things that the design teams would actually use.

A simpler variation of this theme occurs when a *company shifts the balance of power between project heads and functional chiefs*. A company may operate through a matrix, but give most of the weight in the matrix to the functional chiefs. If the functional chiefs control personnel allocations, compensation and promotions, the project chiefs may actually have little influence over how quickly or how efficiently their projects get done. If the project chiefs are given responsibility for personnel allocations, compensation, and/or promotions, they will find that they have more control over their teams.

Adapting personnel to cross-functional teamwork When companies begin working in cross-functional teams, the issue arises of how to adapt the company's personnel to cross-functional work. There are two quite different issues here. First, if the company has long been organized in functional silos, the task of adapting the more senior members of the hierarchy to the change may be quite difficult.

Equally important, but generally less difficult, is the task of adapting younger, less experienced people to cross-functional work. If the company has just moved from a functional to a team oriented structure, the young people may have a few years of experience in the functional structure, years of experience which may have to be unlearned. But even if the company has always operated with cross-functional teams, the problem of adapting young people will still be there.

Most young people companies hire are already specialized in one function. New hires in their twenties rarely have experience in more than one function. Even graduates from generalist programs such as business administration are notoriously narrow in their viewpoints and their experience. While they may have taken courses in a variety of disciplines, they will typically have experience in only one. And they may have reinforced this bias in their education by taking all their elective courses in the same functional area they worked in (as when a finance specialist does an MBA, specializing in finance).

The reason why it is more difficult to adapt older people to cross-functional work should not be explained through clichés such as 'the stubbornness of the old' or 'the inability of the old to learn'. Older people are often quite flexible and they can still learn. The key issue is that they often have far more to lose in an organizational change than young people do.

A fifty-five year old functional chief in a functional organization has spent more than thirty years of his life building up his functional skill. His authority is based on two things: his knowledge in his function, and his ability to manage other specialists in his function. Now, as he experiences a shift to cross-functional work, his world is turned upside down. His high level of functional skill no longer brings him a high position in the hierarchy. His role may be reduced to that of a simple scheduler for his people. They no longer come to him with their most complex and interesting technical problems. Rather, they work out the answers in their cross-functional groups. His job becomes much more boring as a result.

Worse, perhaps, is the fact that much younger people, with skills he neither respects nor recognizes, suddenly become the 'darlings' of senior management. People who were 'barely out of diapers' when he was already a senior engineer have responsible management positions on project teams. These people have no particular functional expertise. They are the ones who always talked about 'problems that crossed functional boundaries'. They did not do very well in the functional hierarchies, since they didn't buy into the functional way of looking at things and doing things. Now, after being sidelined for years, they are suddenly on the 'fast track to top management positions'. They are on first name terms with senior management.

Our senior functional manager may still not have figured out what skill these younger people have that allows them to be promoted so quickly. But he does not like being sidelined. Nor is he happy to discover that the skills he has carefully built up over thirty years are now worth far less than they were just five years ago. Management no longer values his skills as highly as they once did. His sense of equity and fairness are offended.

All this is to say that the senior functional manager has a lot to lose when an company moves from a functional to a project-based organization. No wonder functional managers often resist. They are the losers. They usually need to be compensated with interesting coordination jobs or other perks to gain their full cooperation. It is not unusual for them to leave. A company planning a change should determine carefully how likely its senior functional managers are to cooperate. If it is likely that they will not cooperate, it should carefully calculate the cost of losing them. It should, in fact, construct contingency plans if they do leave. If management decides to push through the change, and they do not cooperate, they may have to be pushed aside or even pushed out.

The problem of adapting younger people is less difficult, since they have far less to lose. A thirty year old has invested, at most, ten years in his function. He or she still has plenty of time to learn other functions, or to learn cross-functional coordination skills. Good thirty-year-olds will often see a shift to cross-functional work as refreshing. The shift puts them in a position where they will learn more. It also, in many companies, puts them in a position where they have more responsibility and where they are more independent of the functional bosses who previously dominated their work and their careers. If the shift is presented as something that will offer them greater and more interesting opportunities, while simultaneously improving the performance of the company, it is likely they will buy in.

Measuring the effectiveness of cross-functional cooperation Managers sometimes try to measure how well their cross-functional teams are working. When they bring people who have never worked with anyone outside their function together, they are justifiably concerned as to whether the new team will work. They look for ways to measure success.

In general there are two ways to measure success, outcome measures and process measures. Outcome measures simply measure how well the team is doing its job. Is the work done and is it done on time? Does the cross-functional team do the work any better than the previous independent functional organizations did? Often, cross-functional teams acquit themselves quite well on these dimensions. But managers may not want to wait two years to see the outcome of a project. They may want interim measures as well.

Obviously projects can be tracked formally. Managers often set up milestones and track the team's progress against the milestones. If the milestones are met quickly, they assume things are going well. If they are not met, they assume the team is not functioning well.

But milestone measures are still outcome measures. A team may have to work together for months before reaching the first significant milestone. How can a manager outside the team tell if the team is working well in the meantime? Managers have ways to do this, even though they may be inexact.

One obvious way is to monitor team meetings. Do the team members understand each other? Or do the different functional groups on the team seem to be talking past each other? Looking at how the team is managing itself can also be very revealing. Have they worked out methods of managing and tracking the project that they all understand? Do their management methods assure that they will achieve the goals and take account of the concerns of each functional group? Finally, do the people from different functions associate voluntarily with each other? Are their meetings a pleasure or a chore? Do they talk freely and enthusiastically in the corridors? Or must they be forced to communicate?

One 3M manager told me that he had several simple ways of measuring how close a new cross-functional team was to 'gelling'. Did they talk to each other informally? Did they talk to each other on the phone when one of them was away from the office? And did they socialize with each other at weekends? When it came to the point that the team's members were socializing with each other rather than with their functional colleagues, he could say that the team had truly gelled. While he was not a Texan, he referred to this as the 'barbecue' test. When it came to the point that the team was having barbecues together on Saturdays, he would be confident that the team was working as an integrated unit.

While the barbecue test is a useful one, a manager should not use it in isolation from other signals. Managers in MGE's Lawn & Garden division all knew each other well. They all worked at the same site, lived in the same towns, and sent their children to the same schools. They socialized together extensively at weekends. But they did not work together effectively.

What the Lawn & Garden managers talked about when they socialized is revealing. They talked about their families, their friends, the personalities and preferences of senior managers, sports, local and national politics, film and theater, food and wine, in short, anything but the business problems that divided them. There was no point in bringing up a difficult cross-functional coordination problem at a dinner party. That would bring tension to the party. Everyone knew the rules. No one broke them. While people knew each other and even liked each other, that didn't mean they worked together effectively. In fact, they left business problems unresolved when there was no clear way to solve them within the normal functional framework.

The 3M manager who used the barbecue test used other tests as well. The Lawn & Garden situation would not have fooled him. He would have seen the lack of cooperation, the lack of communication, at work. He would have realized that cross-functional cooperation was not working well at Lawn & Garden. Nonetheless, the insight behind the barbecue test is useful. Free communication is a prerequisite for effective team cooperation. Spontaneous social contact is an indication that communication is working well. But is communication about essential business issues occurring? Are problems getting solved? This can be determined by observing the content of communication, not just its frequency.

Company and industry differences Companies vary enormously in their level of skill at cross-functional coordination. Some companies still operate in functional silos. Others are beginners at cross-functional cooperation, having moved within the last two decades from silos to project-based organizations. A few others are old hands at it, having established cross-functional teams as the key organizational unit decades ago.

There appear to be systematic variations across companies on this dimension. Diversified companies with lots of business units (for example, 3M) often have lots of cross-functional teams. If small, cross-functional teams can do the most important pieces of a company's work (this is the case at 3M and ConsumerCo), then the company will most likely have many small, cross-functional teams. If, on the other hand, what the company does is so complex that small, cross-functional teams are not enough, then other forms of organization will be used. I will discuss several obvious examples.

Complex assembled products cannot be developed by small, cross-functional teams. A small team can come up with a new concept for a car, but a team of several hundred people will be needed to complete the design. There are normally too many ideas to be developed, too many parts to be redesigned and fitted, too many safety checks to be made, and too much overall evaluation work to be done, for a small team to be able to do it all. Many people are needed to do the work. Since there may be three hundred people involved in the design, there will be a temptation to organize them into functional subteams. Or, in the silo system, they may not be organized into a team at all, but remain in separate functional units.

Similarly, a small cross-functional team will not be able to develop a pharmaceutical product. There are simply too many tests to be performed. Several hundred people will be needed to perform all the tests. Since a high level of technical specialization and competence is needed to perform the tests, lots of functional specialists are needed. To assure that they maintain a high level of competence and they stay at the forefront of their field, their work will have to be supervised by a senior specialist in their field.

This leads to a natural tendency to organize pharmaceutical development units around functional specialties. In fact, until competition and time pressure forced change, this was the normal way of organizing pharmaceutical development. Today, pharmaceutical companies face the challenge of doing two things at once. They must work at a speed that they can only achieve through extensive cross-functional cooperation. At the same time, they must maintain the functional expertise that is most easy to maintain when people work extensively with others in their own field and are supervised by a senior specialist in their field.

It is not an accident that many pharmaceutical companies maintain elements of a matrix. In the last fifteen years, project managers have become much more powerful. They are the ones who must push drugs through development quickly. But senior functional specialists still have important roles in training, monitoring work quality, and generally assuring functional excellence.

The differences between the pharmaceutical industry and the non-pharmaceutical industries that 3M plays in are several. Pharmaceuticals are heavily regulated, while many industrial and consumer products industries are hardly regulated at all. Innovations in pharmaceuticals involve discovering and testing the impacts of new compounds on very complex organisms. The tests involved are complex, and many potential side effects and interactions must be monitored. By contrast, innovations that impact neither the human body nor the environment are simpler and involve fewer tests of complex reactions and interactions. As a result, at 3M (excluding 3M pharmaceuticals), a small team can normally handle virtually all of the problems posed by an innovation. This is inconceivable at the pharmaceutical company, where small armies of scientists must be employed to perform and monitor all of the necessary development steps.

The impact of this difference on cross-functional team management is the following. 3M is quite expert at managing cross-functional teams. It knows how to prepare people to join them. It knows how to form them. It knows how to monitor them. It knows how to link them to business units. It knows how to develop them into independent business units capable of standing on their own. It has a track record of success in managing cross-functional teams which extends across all its business units and back many years. It has an impressive number of managers who are experienced with cross-functional team management.

Little of this is true of the average automobile or pharmaceutical company. Many companies in the latter industries are still having teething problems in getting cross-functional teams to work. Their people may have worked with one or two cross-functional projects. Their managers may, at best, have managed two of them. At 3M, equally experienced people will have worked on or managed dozens of cross-functional projects. Cross-functional projects at automobile and pharmaceutical companies are often far from smooth. Meanwhile, teams at 3M execute hundreds of cross-functional projects quite smoothly each year.

Why is there such an apparent difference in management experience and effectiveness?

There are three core reasons for the difference. One is the sheer size and complexity of pharmaceutical and automobile projects, compared to the smallness and relative simplicity of the average project at 3M. The problem of coordinating a team of two hundred people is a far larger and more complex one than the problem of coordinating a team of fifteen. As a result, the large automobile and pharmaceutical projects have problems in coordination and execution that are rarely seen at 3M.

The second reason for the difference in management experience is the relative duration of projects. When projects in automobiles and pharmaceuticals last half a decade or more, no one is going to manage very many of them. At 3M, the life of some projects is measured in days or weeks, not even months, and projects that take years are rare. As a result, 3M people can build up experience by managing many projects. They have the luxury of trying many different management techniques and seeing what works.

The third reason is the fact that it is fundamentally harder to ensure the quality of functional work at a pharmaceutical company than it is in most disciplines at 3M. Hundreds of laboratories throughout the world work on medical problems. There are hundreds of pharmaceutical company laboratories, but this is only the tip of the iceberg. There are also university laboratories, government laboratories, hospital laboratories, and other publicly funded and independent laboratories. In addition there are laboratories in companies in related industries which perform research that may have an impact on pharmaceuticals. To make things more difficult, the pharmaceutical industry sits at the intersection of a whole variety of scientific disciplines. Advances in biology, chemistry, biochemistry, molecular biology, biogenetics, pharmacology and other specialties all impact pharmaceutical research.

Scientists at pharmaceutical companies, like scientists at 3M, need to stay at or near the leading edge of their field. But to do so, they need to keep track of developments in hundreds of laboratories and in a dozen different disciplines. This makes the problem of maintaining contact with other functional specialists particularly acute. People cannot be simply detached to project teams and left to do the work. They must stay in active, often weekly contact with others in their discipline to stay near the leading edge. The management problem of assuring that this contact occurs effectively is quite large. With the explosion that has occurred in chemical and biological research in the past decade, the problem is becoming more, not less, complex. The functional side of the matrix stays in place to assure that this contact occurs. Project management becomes more messy because of the difficult problem of keeping scientists in contact with the latest advancements in their fields.

By contrast, 3M contains many people who are doing unique work in fields such as adhesives and coatings. They are, by definition, leaders in specialties that relatively few people work on. Ensuring that their skills are at the leading edge is simpler when there are only a handful of laboratories in the entire world that are doing similar work. Other 3M technical people can, through contacts with key specialists, assure that they are at or near the leading edge of their field.

Ensuring that project team members maintain leading edge expertise in their technological specialties is an issue for many companies. Whether this is easy or difficult to do is a key issue that impacts how companies organize their innovation teams. In a pioneering study, Katz and Allen (1982) explored the question of how to organize such teams. They noted that innovations can be developed either by co-located cross-functional teams or by functional specialists who continue to be located in functional departments. What should drive the choice, they say, is two things: how fast the functional specialties are changing, and the level of need for cross-functional cooperation.

If the science behind the functions is changing quickly, the functional specialists will need to stay in close touch with their colleagues, and should perhaps remain co-located with them. If, on the other hand, a high level of functional cooperation is needed, then the functional specialists should be co-located with their teams so they can communicate extensively with specialists from other functions on the teams. What the Katz and Allen framework does not solve is the problem of what to do when the science is moving quickly *and* a high level of cross-functional cooperation is necessary. Pharmaceutical companies face this problem and have not yet come to a conclusion on how to solve it.

Katz and Allen's (1982) work helps identify how project team structures vary across industries. Other dimensions of company's innovation systems vary across industries as well. I discussed industry differences and their impact on innovation management in much more detail in my previous book (Christiansen, 2000).

Links between project teams and the rest of the company

Project teams are not islands unto themselves. They frequently have contacts with other units within their own company. If a company has *specialized centers of technical expertise* within its laboratories, the team may need to consult them. If certain business units have expertise in *marketing* to potential customers, the team would do well to draw on this expertise as well. The company may also possess *libraries* or other repositories of documents and records of past work in relevant areas. Finally, the company will be very likely to have people with experience in managing innovation projects in similar areas, people who could help *coach* the team and its leaders in managing the new project.

Some of Allen's (1977) early work addressed the issue of project teams' connections with other units within their own company. In a sample of dozens of innovation teams, Allen traced communications between team members and other units within their organizations. He found that members of more successful teams communicated more frequently with other units within their companies than members of less successful teams. They saved time by not having to re-invent things, and they achieved better quality solutions by having a wider set of inputs and a wider range of critics.

Unexpectedly, perhaps, Allen also found that many members of innovation teams were reluctant to ask for help from members of their own companies. They did not want to 'lose status' by revealing the limitations of their own knowledge. This suggests that companies and teams will do better if they fight against this tendency by making it clear to team members that it is OK, even desirable, to ask for help.

3M, Eastman Chemical, and ConsumerCo did not have explicit policies to encourage people to ask for help. But asking for help and trading technical information was so common in these companies that one could say that it was built into the culture. Managers showed their approval of such behavior by regularly telling stories that involve people asking for help and succeeding because of the help.

In the typical story at 3M, the protagonist discovers a consumer need and needs help figuring out how to fill it. He consults with people in several laboratories, and perhaps sets up long-term links with some of them. 3M managers constantly repeat stories that follow this pattern. No one who hears the stories can miss the implication that asking for help is both approved and highly useful.

Links with the outside world

Whom to communicate with and frequency of communication Project teams do not just have links with other units within their company. They also, often, have links with the outside world. The most common links are with potential customers and suppliers. But teams may have links with university researchers, commercial laboratories or other research organizations, with customer or industry trade groups, with partners, or even with competitors. All these links may contribute to the success of the project by saving time and improving the solutions the project team develops.

Allen (1977), in the research discussed above, looked at project team's links with the outside world. He found that successful project teams had more contact with the outside world.

Patterns in project team communication over time Given the results presented in the two previous sections, the reader may wonder if there is any limit to the amount of communication a project team should have with other units of their company and with the outside world. In fact, Allen's (1977) work revealed a pattern of communication that suggests that there is a limit.

Allen found that successful project teams showed a specific pattern of communication over time. They communicated a lot with other units and the outside world in the early stages of their projects. During these early stages, they looked for information and ideas on how to pursue the project. Once key decisions on how to structure the project were made, the successful teams tended to reduce their level of communication with the outside, focusing instead on getting their work done. But then, near the end, they began again to communicate more frequently with the outside. But now, rather than looking for ideas, they were testing the solutions they had found and modifying them in response to feedback.

Less successful project teams showed a different pattern of communication. They communicated less at the beginning and during the middle of a project. In other words, they were not as aggressive in seeking out ideas and information early in the project. By contrast, toward the end they increased their level of communication greatly, sometimes communicating even more than the successful teams. But the content of their communication during the latter stages was quite different. Rather than testing and modifying a largely successful solution, they were, sometimes desperately, still trying to find a solution that met the basic requirements of the project. In short, they were often forced to look for help to fix a solution that was not meeting expectations.

The obvious implication is that companies should encourage innovation teams to seek help in defining the overall architecture of their solution early. They should test assumptions against as wide a range of information and opinion as possible, early in the course of the project. They should also cast a wide net for ideas.

Nature of links with the outside: the supplier example Companies' links with the outside vary in frequency. But they also vary along other dimensions as well. Using suppliers as an example, I will discuss the dimensions of level of involvement, the types of technology shared, and industry differences in levels of secrecy.

Level of supplier involvement Some companies do not involve their suppliers at all in the research and development phase. Rather, they present their suppliers with fully developed product and parts designs. In such a system, suppliers are not asked to make any creative input in the product development process at all. The *buying company does all design work.* Until the 1980s, American automobile companies were famous for following this system. They presented their suppliers with complete product designs, leaving no room for input on the suppliers' part. All but GM moved away from this system in the late 1980s and 90s.

The next level of involvement is to *accept ideas from suppliers* when the suppliers take the initiative to present them, without ever taking the initiative to solicit suppliers' ideas. Most companies will accept suppliers' ideas on an exceptional basis. If an idea is good enough, it will overcome inertia in all but the most rigid companies.

But some companies go further. Some companies actively *seek ideas from suppliers on a regular and systematic basis*. They may, suppliers willing, keep as careful track of what is going on in their suppliers' laboratories as they do in their own laboratories. EurAuto began carefully searching suppliers' laboratories for new ideas in the late 1980s. Prior to that, EurAuto had done all parts design work itself.

After reforming its links with suppliers, EurAuto did not just look for ideas. Increasingly, it began *spinning out some of the design work to suppliers' own laboratories*. Car designs at EurAuto became more and more modularized. Suppliers were given responsibility for the design of a number of modules. EurAuto remained responsible for the design of certain key modules, as well as for the integration of the overall design.

The amount of control suppliers had over modules varied. Suppliers were given complete control of the design of some modules. But, in other areas, EurAuto brought supplier personnel into the design process, while keeping overall control of the module in house.

Types of technology shared (or not shared) with suppliers EurAuto made clear distinctions between which design problems it shared with its suppliers and which it took care of itself. EurAuto *retained technologies that it considered core skills* for an automobile assembler. It designed its own engines and chassis, for instance, while allowing suppliers to design most accessories, trim and other nonkey systems. EurAuto also *retained certain design decisions that it considered key to the competitive saleability* of the car. It designed its own dashboards and the look of its interiors because it believed that the look of these components was key to the customers' impressions of the car. It also designed its automobiles' exteriors for the same reasons.

Levels of secrecy by industry Some industries are very secretive. Relatively little information is shared between suppliers and customers in consumer products industries, for example. A manager at

Eastman Chemical described to me some of that company's contacts with one of its major customers, a consumer products giant called GemCo (a pseudonym). Periodically GemCo representatives would come and ask many questions about chemicals Eastman had under development. But the GemCo representatives would often not reveal what they were looking for. Eastman representatives would offer to set up projects to develop custom chemicals for GemCo, if only GemCo would tell them what it was looking for. But GemCo wouldn't do it. The GemCo buyers did not want to reveal what GemCo had in mind, since they did not want competitors to find out what the consumer products giant was planning. Eastman was left with no information about how it could help GemCo in its search.

The automobile industry provides a contrasting example. Many universities and independent laboratories do research on motor vehicle related topics. The results of much of this research goes into the public domain. Research performed within automobile companies is shared less freely, but is often written about in industry trade journals or discussed at trade shows or in other industry forums. As a result, more information and ideas are shared among suppliers and customers in the automobile industry than in many consumer products industries.

While I am not aware of any detailed study of secrecy in technology sharing and how it varies across industries, a few preliminary conclusions can be formed from these examples. There is little public research in consumer products areas, while there is much public (university and government laboratory) research relating to motor vehicles. Thus, information on motor vehicle technology is available from public laboratories, while information on consumer products technology is rarely available from public laboratories. The availability of information from public laboratories helps 'prime the pump' for a relatively open sharing of information.

As an aside, I note that the high level of public interest in motor vehicles is due to at least two reasons. The first is the link to important and controversial issues, such as pollution control and energy consumption and conservation. The second is the size of the industry and the size of related industries, such as the petroleum industry. These industries jointly form one of the largest sectors in a modern economy. The consumer products sector as a whole is also quite large. But while the motor vehicle industry is focused around one core product, motor vehicles powered by internal combustion engines, the consumer products industry has no such focus. The latter is fragmented into many micro-industries, no one of which is nearly as large or as important as motor vehicles.

The second reason is linked to the first, since both are driven by industry size. Many players in the motor vehicles and petroleum industries have laboratories that do research work on internal combustion engines and other aspects of motor vehicle technology. Each laboratory has an incentive to stay at or close to the 'leading edge of technology'. To do this, they must keep informed of what is happening at other laboratories. But to find out what is happening in other laboratories, they must share what is happening in their laboratory (Von Hippel, 1987). This gives them an incentive to share information about what they are doing. While laboratories are unlikely to share information that is viewed as key to their company's competitive position, they are likely to be much more free to share information viewed as inessential, or easily available to other players at an equivalent position in the industry (Von Hippel, 1987).

Laboratories in consumer products and other niche industries are in a very different position. For such laboratories there is no large international network of dozens of laboratories, all working on related technologies. Rather, there may only be five or six laboratories in the entire world that are doing work in their area. The other laboratories may all be owned by competitors, making it problematic to share information.

Competing laboratories may share information when both see benefit in doing so (for example, joint development ventures, or other joint research programs). But such sharing will be rare when laboratories are doing research viewed as key to a company's future competitiveness (Von Hippel, 1987).

Project supervision

Number of different people a project reports to Project supervisors form part of the organization structure around any project team. One key structural issue is whether projects report to one supervisor or several. Most projects at Eastman Chemical report to several supervisors. Projects at Eastman have a direct supervisor who handles normal monitoring and other normal supervisory issues. But most projects also have a formal relationship with someone at a higher level.

Level of highest report The second structural issue is what level the project reports to. At Eastman and elsewhere, a higher level project sponsor has two key roles. First, he helps manage the project's internal relations. When the project runs into an organizational road-block, such as a refusal by some other unit to give timely aid to the project, he steps in to help dissolve the roadblock. He is also there to give 'reinforcement and support' to the project team, to show them how much the company as a whole appreciates and needs the work they are doing.

At many other companies, projects have a formal reporting rela-tionship with only one person. This supervisor will handle all normal supervisory work. In addition, she or he will do as much as possible to break roadblocks and to show the team how much their work is needed and appreciated by the company. Typically, the supervisor will also look for help from higher level people on an *ad hoc* basis. When the project runs into a serious roadblock, the team's direct supervisor may ask for help from his or her supervisor, or from someone higher up who has taken a direct interest in the team's work. Similarly, when the team needs to be reminded of the importance of their work, the supervisor may recruit someone from higher up to reinforce the message. Thus, while at Eastman, projects typically have a perma-nent, formal relationship with someone senior to the team's direct supervisor, project teams at other companies often develop such rela-tionships on an *ad hoc* basis.

As I have indicated, supervisors play important roles in breaking roadblocks and in giving support to team members. Supervisors at several levels are often involved in performing these roles. But higher level managers may play other roles as well. They may help monitor a project's progress, they may make and influence project funding deci-sions, they may act as a consultants to project teams on specific prob-lems, they may mentor project leaders on project management, and they may contribute ideas or otherwise participate in project problem solving. I will discuss these roles, and others, in more detail in the chapter on management of individual projects. (See Table 6.8 for a summary of key issues in the area of project structure.)

Table 6.8   Variations in project structure and their impact

Aspect of structure	Tool or variable . . . . Impact	
Where projects fit into the company's structure	▪ Project chief's power	▪ Increased power means projects will have better access to resources
	▪ Whom projects report to	▪ Higher level report gives better access to resources
	▪ Permanent versus non-permanent project teams	▪ Permanent teams facilitate continuous innovation and transfer/retention of learning, limit need to build teams
Structure of project teams	▪ Requirements for cross-functional (CF) cooperation: – Common language – Understanding of other functions' values and concerns – Common methods of planning and coordinating work	▪ All help facilitate cross-functional (CF) cooperation: some common language, common understandings and common methods are necessary even for a minimum of cooperation
	▪ Methods of building CF capacity: – 'Tiger team' – Co-location – Work on common problem – CF teams as primary organizational unit – Special-purpose links between functions – Off-site networking through exec education – Strong project leaders – CF coordinating groups within large teams	▪ All help increase CF work capacity: – Tiger team includes most other techniques, but usually involves separating team from rest of organization, impacts only the team – Other techniques are less powerful but can be used beyond the bounds of one team, are also less disruptive of existing organization
	▪ Adapting personnel to CF teamwork	▪ Difficult for older functional experts who have much to lose, easier for young people with little to lose

(cont'd)

Table 6.8 (cont'd)

Aspect of structure	Tool or variable . . . . . Impact	
	■ Measuring the effectiveness of CF cooperation: – Outcome measures – Process measures	■ Both outcome and process measures useful
Links between project teams and the rest of the company	■ Links between teams and other teams, business units, centralized centers of competence, libraries, and so on	■ Links with all these areas improve information flow to team
Links with the outside world	■ Number of links and frequency of communication with outside world ■ Pattern of communication over time ■ Level of involvement with suppliers ■ Types of technology shared with suppliers	■ More links and more frequent communication both help team keep pace with developments elsewhere ■ Success more probable if team communicates widely early (while structuring project) ■ Sharing work widens range of skills applied to problem ■ Retaining core skills guards competitive advantage; sharing out less key work retains resources for key areas
Project supervision	■ Number of different people project reports to ■ Level of highest report	■ More reports gives more links, leverage ■ Higher report gives more leverage over resources

Project management methods

As I noted in the introduction, many books have been written about managing innovation projects. I will not try to duplicate the contents of these books here. The focus of this book is on the way the management of an entire company impacts its ability to innovate. Project management methods are a part of that. But since project management methods have been covered in great detail elsewhere, I will not discuss them in the same detail that I have discussed more global things such as communications, funding, strategy and goals, and so on.

I will focus my attention here on aspects of project management that go beyond the project team, particularly those where senior management needs to be involved. Senior management should be involved in selecting and training project management. They will also, very likely, be involved in determining whether projects are managed in a highly formalized, rationalized way, or in a more *ad hoc*, 'responsive to events' way. In addition, some senior managements are involved in managing cross-functional coordination within teams and across the company as a whole. They may also be involved in developing specialized skills needed across several projects, particularly skills that involve coordinating people within different units. I will discuss each of these four aspects of project management below.

There is one project management method that I will not discuss here. Senior management teams often set goals for development projects. Since at times such goals affect business units (as when business units manage projects), I discussed them with other business management methods in Chapter 3. When such goals impact only development projects and not business units, they would more properly be classified as project management interventions.

Finally, there are two special situations in the history of a project team where senior management involvement in particularly useful. One is when a key technical decision has to be made. The second is when the product is ready for launch. I will discuss senior management involvement on these special occasions after discussing the more global management issues. (See Table 6.9 for a list of key questions in the area of project management methods.)

For the reader who wants a more detailed discussion of how innovation projects can most effectively be managed, I would recommend a recent book on the subject, such as *Project Management* (Meredith and Mantel, 1995).

Table 6.9   Questions to ask about project management methods

Managing project managers
■ Do we understand what project managers need to know and need to be able to do?
■ Do we select project managers effectively?
■ Do we train project managers effectively?
■ How much experience do project managers have before becoming project managers?

Mentoring
■ Do we have people who can guide (mentor) project managers?
■ Do experienced people accept to do mentoring?

Formalization
■ Do we have an appropriate level of formalization in our project management system?
■ Do we formalize and rationalize the management of repeated procedures?

Uncertainty
■ Do we understand the impact that the level of uncertainty has on project management?
■ Do we train project managers to identify and deal with uncertainty?
■ Do we effectively adapt our project management methods to the level of uncertainty present in the project?

Cross-functional and cross-unit coordination
■ Do we coordinate the activities of different functions effectively?
■ Do we coordinate development activity across different units (for example, with operating units) when appropriate?

Key decisions
■ Do we identify key technical decisions and make these decisions appropriately?
■ Do we have an appropriate quality and reliability level at launch?

Selecting and training project managers

Companies vary widely in their methods of selecting and training project managers. Briefly, selection methods varied from very *ad hoc*, 'he happened to be available', to very systematic. Training varied from none to very extensive. The more innovative companies were more systematic both in their selection methods and in their training methods.

Selecting project managers To be more specific, companies had three methods of selecting project managers. Phil Lang was assigned to lead the Med-X project at Northern Pharmaceuticals for no other reason than the fact that he was available. There were a limited number of people at Northern who were considered to be competent project managers, and Lang was one of them. Since he was available, he got the project. There was no skill matching or evaluation beyond that.

At Industrial Chemicals, George Marsh was given the task of finding uses for co-products because 'he happened to be available and he needed something to do'. Again, there was no skill matching beyond the fact that he was a competent chemist with some sales and marketing experience who could be trusted to do the job.

In these two cases, there were two criteria for selecting the project manager. The first was passing a minimum hurdle of competence. The second was availability. The first available person who passed the minimum hurdle of competence was chosen for the job. I would refer to this as a *whoever is available* selection system.

In some cases, people got jobs as project managers because it was they who had the idea for the project in the first place. Once Marsh proposed that Industrial Chemicals look seriously into the Chemical Residues idea, it became his project because it was his idea. It remained his project even when the budget was increased to several million dollars per year, even though he had no experience running a comparable project. This is a case of a *whoever has the idea* selection system.

Industrial Chemicals management became more sophisticated in selecting project managers as time went on. When it became obvious that George Marsh had limitations as a project manager, division management decided to select a new project manager using a more systematic methodology. First, they carefully analyzed the project to determine what kind of skills the manager needed. Then they constructed a profile of the ideal project manager. Then they looked for a person who fit the profile. Since no one in Industrial Chemicals fit the profile, they looked outside Industrial Chemicals. No one in the parent company, MGE, fit the profile either, so they looked outside MGE. Finally, with the help of a headhunter, they hired Ken Peters, then employed at a European regulatory agency, to lead the organization.

It is instructive to look at the type of skills the new project manager had. He had spent much of his career working in government. From this experience, he knew European regulatory bodies intimately. He also had experience managing projects. While he was not familiar with the Chemical Residues technology, nor with its market, Industrial Chemicals management believed that he could easily be brought up to speed on these issues. Other team members were already skilled in these areas. What the team needed, in management's view, was a leader who was skilled at project management and knowledgeable about the European regulatory environment. Obtaining appropriate regulations and guiding the project through regulatory hurdles was viewed as a key task for the new project manager.

Ken Peters was not 'available' when Chemical Residues needed a new project manager. Nor was he the person who had the idea. Rather, his skills were a good match with the skills the project needed. Selection on this basis can be called *skill matching*.

3M, Eastman Chemical and ConsumerCo all practiced variations in skill matching. While these three more innovative organizations rarely hired people from the outside to lead projects, they did carefully study what skills project managers needed. It is unlikely that any of these organizations would have let George Marsh run a project for any length of time. While he was a competent chemist, Marsh simply did not have any skills or experience at project management. The fact that he was available, and later that he pushed the idea for Chemical Residues, would not have been enough to give him the job of project manager. He would doubtless have been given responsibility for technical development of the project (his job under Ken Peters), but someone else would have been given responsibility for organizing and managing the project on a daily basis. This is the system Industrial Chemicals moved towards after its search for a new project manager for Chemical Residues.

Project managers in all projects need to have some skill at project management. That is their core job. It is useful if they also have some skill and/or experience in the technical issues that are key concerns for the project. In the case of new product development, some skill/experience in the product's prospective market is useful as well. In heavily regulated industries, skill at navigating the regulatory environment is useful. Beyond these four core areas, other skills, such as managing a company's internal environment, may be key in specific cases. If the project manager is not strong in all areas, he will have to be assisted by senior team members who are strong in the areas where he is weak.

Training project managers The extent to which companies trained project managers varied greatly. Several MGE divisions had no formal training whatsoever in the 1980s. But once Industrial Chemicals management discovered how important it was to have a project manager with the right skills, the division set up a formal training program, lasting several weeks, which all project managers were required to go through. The formal training covered many key topics, from project planning to personnel management to marketing and technical topics. The curriculum matched the areas identified above as key skills for project managers.

Project manager training at ConsumerCo and 3M was actually less formal than the system Industrial Chemicals set up in the 1990s. But both of these innovative companies had many people who were experienced at managing innovation projects. As a result, much learning took place in the form of apprenticeship. Senior team members could learn project management skills from their own project manager. After working on several projects, perhaps with some experience managing part of a project, they could be given responsibility for a project of their own.

These companies also had active mentoring systems. Senior managers with project management experience served as mentors for more junior project managers, coaching and guiding them through the in's and out's of managing a project. This informal, one on one, training system worked as well as the more formal systems that existed at other companies. I discussed with MGE the advantages of a more formal mentoring system. But it was clear that the company simply did not have a sufficient number of experienced project managers who could function as mentors.

3M is particularly conscious of the fact that the manager of a new product development project is often, in effect, a new business unit manager. When the new product is an extension or variation of an existing product line, then the infrastructure of the existing business unit can be used to house the project. But when the new product is truly new (that is, neither an extension nor a variation of the existing business), then a new business unit will have to be developed to house it.

3M deals with this by pairing new projects with existing business units. The administrative infrastructure of the old unit will administer both the old business and the new business until the new business can be self-supporting. The project leader will not be completely on his own. Rather, he will be able to turn to the head of the existing business unit as his mentor. In effect, he is training as an apprentice to the existing business unit head, and learning business unit management skills in the process.

Formalization and rationalization of project management

A problem arose in MGE's Industrial Chemicals division in the mid-1990s when Mark Green, a senior manager from Northern Pharmaceuticals, took over leadership of Industrial Chemicals. Green had helped establish a very formal, rationalized project management system at Northern. Projects were planned months, even years in advance. The project manager could plan what each member of the team would have to do many weeks in advance. Senior managers monitored projects by checking whether they were meeting milestones. The milestones were common to all projects, and formed part of a generic project plan that all project teams were expected to follow.

When he arrived at Industrial Chemicals, Green found that very little of this planning infrastructure existed. Some projects had milestones but others didn't. Projects that had milestones didn't have the same milestones. Project planning was far less developed than in Northern. Some project managers had plans that extended for a few months into the future. But no one had the extensive, detailed plans, with target completion dates, that Green was used to seeing in Northern. This disturbed Green greatly. As a result, he asked his project managers to match the level of detailed planning achieved in Northern.

Many project managers protested that this level of detail was not appropriate for their projects. Ken Peters, for instance, said that it was hard to plan very far in advance when he didn't even know what the regulatory environment would be six months in advance. The uncertainties around the development of the technology and the market's response to it made it even more difficult to plan. Whatever plans he made would have to be revised whenever one of the following occurred:

- An unexpected change in the regulatory environment
- An unexpected change in the market
- An unexpected result in a test of the technology.

When I visited companies like 3M and ConsumerCo, I found that their project planning systems were as informal as those at Industrial Chemicals. A few milestones were charted out. Tasks were planned for a few months or weeks into the future. But there was no sign of the sort of detailed, long range planning present in the pharmaceutical industry. By contrast, in the motor vehicle industry, project planning was rampant. Plans as detailed as those in pharmaceuticals were not just common but essential.

Projects facing high uncertainty versus projects facing low uncertainty In comparing across industries, it is clear that different levels of formalization are appropriate in different circumstances. In projects where there are high amounts of uncertainty, where one knows little about what the environment will be like several years hence, detailed long-range planning serves little purpose. In other industries where the regulatory environment is already in place (pharmaceuticals), or where a complicated product architecture dictates a long, carefully-planned development process, then detailed long-range plans are useful, even essential.

This difference in the need for and utility of long range planning is one difference between industries that I discussed in a previous book (Christiansen, 2000). But even within a single industry, one project may face far more uncertainty than another. Managers should be aware of the fact that some projects can benefit from detailed, long-term planning while others can't. When the tasks that must be performed can be foreseen many months in advance, then long-term planning is useful. But when the environment or the technology are highly uncertain, it may be impossible to foresee which tasks will have to be performed more than a few months or weeks in advance. In such situations, detailed, long-term planning may be useless. Identifying contingencies and planning several scenarios may be useful. But there is a danger that the attention devoted to detailed planning may distract project leadership from more important and pressing issues.

Training managers to deal with low and high uncertainty projects
In low uncertainty situations, the tasks the project team will have to perform can be foreseen many months, even years, in advance. In these situations, project managers can usefully plan out tasks far in advance. The project plan can then be rationalized, reengineered, or otherwise improved to produce a better product faster and cheaper. Senior managers can monitor low uncertainty projects by making sure that the project plan is in place, by identifying key milestones the team must reach, and by monitoring progress toward the milestones. They will judge the project manager's performance by whether he was able to deliver against the plan.

In high uncertainty situations, the picture, and managers' role in it, is quite different. The tasks the project team will have to perform cannot be foreseen more than a few weeks in advance. Therefore, detailed, long-term project planning is virtually useless. Some scenario planning may occur, but detailed plans stretching out more than a few months may not exist. In the absence of a reliable, detailed plan, reengineering efforts are useless.

Similarly, senior managers cannot necessarily monitor high uncertainty projects according to milestones fixed long in advance. Events may force the company to alter the milestones. In addition, there may not be any way to foresee how long it will take to reach key milestones. In such a situation, senior managers cannot judge the project manager's performance on the basis of the time needed to meet milestones, since they cannot foresee what kinds of problems or changes in plan will arrive before the milestone is met.

As a result, management of a high uncertainty project is very different from management of a low uncertainty project. It revolves much less around adhering to a plan and much more around identifying, monitoring and managing areas of uncertainty. Project managers need to identify which aspects of the project (technologies, aspects of the regulatory environment, customers, and so on) could provoke unexpected or unpredictable changes. They need to monitor these areas carefully. And when something changes they need to take the appropriate decisions. Rather than managing to a plan, they need to react intelligently to the unexpected.

Senior managers need to monitor high uncertainty projects by making sure that project management has identified key areas of uncertainty and is monitoring them appropriately. They should also evaluate project managers on the basis of how well they react when changes or other unexpected events occur. Monitoring adherence to plan is not so important as understanding why the plan was adhered to or changed. In uncertain situations, quickness is reacting to change is important. Adhering to a plan, when the circumstances the plan was written for have changed, would be a mistake, not something to be rewarded (see Muzyka, 1989).

Formalizing repeated procedures, retaining other knowledge At a lower level, there are circumstances where formalization is almost always an advantage. Until the mid-1980s, EurAuto had very few written procedures. Tests of automobile components were performed very regularly. Some tests were performed several times on each model and repeated from model to model. But no written procedures for these tests existed. Methods of performing the tests, and standards for the results, were simply passed from one person to the next orally.

In the mid-1980s, EurAuto's management team decided that oral memory was no longer enough. It mandated that the procedures for repeated technical tests be written down and codified. This was a way of assuring that tests were performed consistently over time and from model to model. It was also a way of assuring that the methods for performing the tests would not be lost in the case of loss of key people.

This example illustrates the advantage of formalizing repeated procedures. Writing things down improves consistency and guards against the loss of the technology. It also allows projects to benefit from technology developed by earlier projects.

Of the companies in this sample, Eastman Chemical had the most formal system for writing things down. During and at the end of innovation projects, project team members are expected to write down things they have learned. These 'learnings' are preserved, cataloged via an indexing system, and made available to later projects.

Cross-functional coordination

Companies vary in the extent to which they try to achieve cross-functional coordination within project teams. The subject rarely came up in my discussions with managers in MGE's chemical divisions. But it was on everyone's lips at 3M, Eastman and ConsumerCo. While programs and procedures existed at these companies to encourage cross-functional coordination in all project teams at these more innovative companies, few such programs existed in MGE's chemical divisions. By contrast, cross-functional coordination was a big concern at MGE's Northern Pharmaceuticals division.

Detailed, inter-functional project planning/tracking systems Northern Pharmaceuticals actually had the most extensive program for encouraging cross-functional cooperation. In the early 1990s, Northern developed detailed, inter-functional project planning and tracking systems. These systems were designed to facilitate coordination between the dozen different functions involved in pharmaceutical development. Systems developed for one project were then exported and used for later projects. These systems proved highly useful for coordinating the actions of several functions across the multiyear life of the typical pharmaceutical project.

Leaving the problem to the project manager By contrast, projects in the chemical divisions did not have common systems. Coordination across functions was an issue within each project, but was not viewed as an issue for the division as a whole. Since each project had different problems, and often a different mix of functions, each project leader was expected to work out his problems on his own.

Ensuring coordination, project by project Projects differed at 3M as well. But nonetheless, senior managers were concerned with the development of cross-functional coordination within each project. Effective cross-functional coordination is viewed as one of the keys to the company's success at innovation and a key competitive advantage. So young people are brought into cross-functional projects early to assure that they have cross-functional experience. General managers monitor each project to assure that cross-functional coordination actually happens. As they gain experience, 3M people learn to coordinate their work with that of other functions as a normal part of their work.

Increased interest in cross-functional coordination over time Companies that, in the 1980s, were not concerned with cross-functional coordination have tended to become more concerned with it. In the early 1980s EurAuto paid little attention to cross-functional coordination. Different functions happily worked in their own silos. But by the late 1980s EurAuto managers were all concerned about building effective cross-functional coordination. The story at USAuto was similar. Shocks in the early 1980s led that company to begin breaking down its functional silos.

Evolution has occurred even at Industrial Chemicals. In the 1980s, at best a small minority of Industrial Chemicals' managers were concerned with improving cross-functional coordination. By the mid-1990s, that changed. Project and business unit managers more commonly talked about the challenges they faced in coordinating multiple functions. The company set up several executive education programs designed to familiarize its management team with the concerns and methods of different functions.

Other methods of encouraging cross-functional coordination I've discussed more global methods of encouraging cross-functional coordination in the section on project structure. The reader should refer to that section for a more detailed discussion of methods different companies used to encourage cross-functional coordination.

Balance of power between functions In most companies, different functions do not have the same weight. In companies producing fast moving consumer goods, it is typically the marketing function that has most weight in decision making. In consumer durables, technical functions may have more weight. In industrial products companies, technical functions may predominate. But such balances of power are not always stable.

A ConsumerCo manager said that the balance between technical and marketing functions had changed slowly but perceptibly over ten years. In the 1980s, technical concerns usually had a higher weight in discussions of how to develop a new product. But by the 1990s, marketing concerns were beginning to predominate over technical concerns.

Marketing concerns also grew in importance at EurAuto. The company admitted to having made whatever vehicle its engineers wanted through the 1960s and 70s. In the 1980s, this strategy was no longer possible, and the company had to learn to take market considerations, and marketers, much more seriously.

Managers in MGE's chemical divisions talked about a similar evolution, but one that didn't go as far. One manager said that there had been several attempts to bring professional marketers into Industrial Chemicals. But these attempts had failed. Industrial Chemicals management is dominated by people with technical training, and marketers have simply never succeeded at the top levels. The story in Lawn & Garden is different however. There the representatives of the regional sales divisions were given representation on new product development committees for the first time in the mid-1990s. The weight given to marketing concerns in Lawn & Garden was clearly increasing.

Coordination across units

In a global industry, a project team may have to obtain help from people throughout the world at key points in the project's life. It may be necessary to obtain input from many different sales and marketing units to develop realistic sales targets. It will be necessary to get cooperation from sales and distribution units throughout the world to manage a successful worldwide launch.

The team cannot assure cooperation from all these units by itself. In most companies, a team would need help from senior management to assure that far-flung units supply needed information and cooperate with the launch.

Senior management actually has two roles in assuring effective coordination of far-flung units. The first is setting priorities, that is, using its hierarchical force to assure that the units do the necessary work. The second is ensuring that any needed common language and common working practices are in place.

The importance of ensuring common language and common working practices are often overlooked. This may be because in many multinational companies, both are already in place. But many multinational companies do not actually have the capability to act in a coordinated fashion across many countries. Each local unit may be used to acting independently, organizing its own work in the way that it finds most effective. A company in this situation may find it quite difficult to manage a multinational effort, such as a global launch. Senior management intervention will be needed in several areas.

First, obviously, senior management may have to use its hierarchical weight to ensure cooperation. Local units working according to their own priorities may only reluctantly release resources for a global launch. But second, some effort may be required to be sure that different units are able to coordinate their efforts. Some common language and common working practices will be needed to achieve effective coordination.

The importance of common language and common working practices is best illustrated by showing what happens in their absence. Phil Lang, head of the Med-X project, described to me what happened when he began working with Northern's country-level distribution units to manage a worldwide launch. He first outlined what each unit would have to do. Then he sent a questionnaire to each unit asking them how much time they would need to complete each task. Lang thought the questions were simple and straightforward. But the responses he got surprised him.

One question involved the time needed to develop local marketing materials for the new product. The answers varied from *one* week to *fifty-two* weeks. Lang himself saw no reason why it would take more than four to six weeks to complete this task. But several units had said it would take them half a year or more. Lang thought that perhaps these units were imagining that 'developing local marketing materials' would involve a far more elaborate piece of work than Lang intended. An alternative explanation was that some units had no procedures for developing local marketing materials and had no real idea of how long it would take.

Variations on other tasks were not this wide. But they still varied widely. Lang concluded from this initial inquiry that the local units did not really have common definitions of what 'developing marketing materials' meant. Other tasks, like identifying key opinion leaders, were also understood differently by different units.

Lang was surprised. But since he was managing Northern's first global launch, he was not too surprised. For years the countries had worked independently and developed their own definitions and procedures. No one had ever before tried to coordinate the actions of so many units. He was exploring unknown territory and had to build the coordination capability up from the bottom. He planned to run a number of inter-country meetings to sort out what each country management team would do to finish each of the marketing tasks. The meetings would also help the country teams develop a common language to describe common tasks.

Companies like 3M and ConsumerCo avoid this problem by facilitating much cross-border contact. 3M seconds technical people from one laboratory to another quite frequently. In addition, it has frequent technology fairs that bring technical people into contact. 3M marketers have managed sales on a global basis for many years, leading to much contact between marketers in different countries.

ConsumerCo rotates people across borders frequently. In addition, all ConsumerCo managers spend time in training programs that bring them into contact with ConsumerCo people from different countries and different functions. Both these techniques help maintain a common language and common procedures.

Key technical decisions

At times, it is useful for senior managers to be involved in key technical decisions. This is particularly true when the project team has the choice of following one of several technical paths. Which path to choose may determine the fate of the project. One path may work while the other does not. Or perhaps the team should follow both paths to see which works best. But this may demand additional resources, which will have to be provided by senior management.

Senior management should encourage the team to identify such key decision points. It should encourage the team to look at the costs and benefits of selecting either path, or of following several paths. Sometimes, decisions should be postponed until the team can generate more information on which path will work best. But exploring several paths may cost significantly more. Since budget issues are involved, the cost of choosing several paths versus one should be evaluated carefully.

Issues to look at include the following. First, how late can the decision be made? In some cases, there may be no cost to delaying the decision. In others, there may be a high cost, meaning that the decision must be made quickly on the basis of the evidence available. In the first case, senior management should encourage the team to wait. In the second case, senior management should assure that the decision is made with the maximum of evidence.

The second issue involves whether the decision is reversible or not. How easily can the decision to choose one path be altered if the path does not work out? Some industrial and consumer products can be constantly adapted. If there is little cost to changing the technology later, then there is little risk involved in choosing one path. In this case, the project team should just choose one path and go with it until it succeeds or fails.

On the other hand, key technologies in complex assembled products can only be changed with difficulty. If an automobile development team has to choose between two possible solutions for a technical problem, there may be no going back on the decision. Many other parts of the car may be fitted to the new technology once the decision is made, making it extremely costly to go back on the decision.

Senior management should make sure the team has identified key technical decision points, that it does not make decisions prematurely, and that it understands whether the decisions are easily reversible or not. If the decision is not reversible, senior management should make sure that the team explores the options as fully as possible before deciding. This may involve allocating enough resources to allow the team to follow several paths until it determines which one is superior.

Another aspect of key technical decisions is their implications for other projects. Innovation teams do not just develop new products and processes. They also develop new technologies. These new technologies may be useful for later innovations in ways the team cannot foresee.

Senior management is likely to have a broader perspective on whether new technologies the team is developing will be useful elsewhere. This should be taken into account when the team must choose between two or more potential development paths. If both branches of a path are potentially useful to other teams, perhaps senior management will fund development of both branches. If only one shows any sign of being widely useful, then perhaps that path should be chosen so that the company will be able to exploit the potential spin-offs.

The launch decision

Quality level at launch Since product launch can link the reputation of the whole company to a new product, senior managers should be involved in launch decisions. The product's quality, in particular, will have an impact on the company's quality reputation. So 'achieving a specified level of quality' should be a key criteria by which the product is evaluated before launch.

Some companies routinely launch products that are not finished. Some software companies are famous for releasing product that still has bugs. The bugs will be worked out and the product perfected in cooperation with the first users. While the company's reputation for quality may suffer, its reputation for getting the product out 'on time' or 'when promised' may be enhanced. In addition, it may be able to pre-emptively take a market before more careful rivals perfect their products and enter.

Other companies wait until products are in 'defect free' condition before launching them. This may be costly, in that the product may be delayed and revenue foregone. But it will enhance the company's reputation for producing reliable products.

Senior managers can and should carefully weigh their positions on what quality level products should achieve before launch. Generally quality should be consistent with the company's overall quality position. But some launches may be made at a lower quality level as long as they are clearly labeled as 'test launches' or 'experimental products'.

Amount of testing before launch Another issue in managing launches is how much testing to do before launch. Some companies do enough consumer testing that they are fairly sure how much the product will sell. Others do little and are surprised. Technology testing is also useful, as it reduces the risk that the product will perform differently in the field than in the laboratory.

In general, the higher the risk and the more resources the company is putting into a product, the more testing it should do. But at times, time constraints, in the form of a need to get the product into the marketplace quickly, may force a reduction in testing. The automobile industry, for example, makes fewer prototypes and does fewer crash tests than it did in the past. It can do this because it has developed methods to simulate tests, often through the use of computer models. In effect, it gets more information out of fewer tests.

Consumer products companies similarly conduct targeted tests, where products are tested in carefully selected samples of consumers. In effect, these companies have devised ways of collecting large amounts of useful information from a small number of people.

There are two mandates for general managers from these examples. One is to determine how much testing is needed. They should judge this on the basis of the amount of risk involved and the cost of any delays involved in further testing. The second mandate is to push teams to develop ways to maximize the amount of information they obtain from whatever testing is done.

Managing product complexity at launch The third issue at launch which may concern senior managers is how much newness to allow in the product and the production process that accompanies it. This is an issue mainly in the case of complex assembled products. An example will illustrate.

An automobile is a complex assembled product that includes dozens of subassemblies and several thousand parts. Changes in parts and subassemblies can make for difficult adaptation problems in the factory. If each part is new, the subassemblies are new, and, for good measure, the process by which it is assembled is new, then the company's factories are unlikely to be able to launch the car on time at a reasonable level of quality. They may drown in the complexity of managing all the changes involved in the new car model.

As a result, some companies, including EurAuto, have established rules governing the amount of change allowed at any given time. At EurAuto, the rule is 'Change the car, change the engine, or change the assembly process, but never more than one of these at once'. In other words, when EurAuto introduces a new model car, it will put an older and well-tested engine into the car. It will build the car using an assembly process that is equally well tested. In this way, it can identify and work out any problems in the car's design without having to worry about the engine or the assembly process.

Similarly, when EurAuto introduces a new engine, it will introduce it in a car model that has already been in production for several years. It will not change the assembly process when it introduces the new engine. Rather, it will focus on working the bugs out of the engine design before changing the car or anything else.

A new assembly process, which may involve more extensive use of robots or a radical change in factory layout, will only be introduced in an established car model with an established, reliable engine. That way the factory's engineers can concentrate on optimizing the assembly process, while not having to worry much about the car or the engine.

The difficulty of implementing a new car model is also driven by the number of parts changed. A manufacturing manager at USAuto told me that the new models the company introduced could have anywhere from 400 to 1500 new parts. He was counting changes in the car's body, chassis and interior, excluding the engine and drive train. The job of implementing the production process for a car with 1500 new parts was vastly more difficult than for a car with only 400 new parts. He argued that automobile quality would increase if engineers limited the number of changes made in new car models. More parts changes made manufacturing's job more difficult and led to lower quality in assembly. If new car designs had only 400–600 new parts, he could minimize defects in assembly much more quickly and reliably, he said. (See Table 6.10 for a summary of key issues in the area of project management methods.)

This ends my discussion of the ways general managers impact overall project management systems. In the next chapter, I will look at ways they interact with individual projects, and at how their behavior affects the success of the projects they work with.

Table 6.10 Variations in project management methods and their impact

Method	Tool or variable . . . . . Impact	

Selecting and training project managers	■ Criteria for selecting project managers:
	  – Availability
	  – Whoever had idea
	  – Match with skills needed to run project
		■ Selection on basis of skill match gives better chance of success

	■ Extent of training for project managers	■ More training and experience mean more effective project management
Formalization, rationalization of project management	■ Level of formalization	■ More formalization useful in low uncertainty projects, less useful in projects dealing with high uncertainty

	■ Training managers to deal with low and high uncertainty:
	  – Detailed planning, rationalization in low uncertainty projects
	  – Methods of monitoring and dealing with uncertainty in high uncertainty projects
		■ Training should be appropriate to the type of project they will manage

	■ Formalizing repeated procedures	■ Aids in transmission of knowledge and method
Cross-functional coordination (see also section on project structure)	■ Establish detailed, cross-functional (CF) project planning/tracking system	■ Useful/essential for large projects, particularly projects with low uncertainty
	■ Give project manager enough power to enforce cooperation	■ Useful in all projects, may be essential high uncertainty projects which are difficult to plan

(cont'd)

Table 6.10 (cont'd)

Method	Tool or variable . . . . . . Impact	
	■ Monitor CF cooperation in each project ■ Manage the balance of power between functions to ensure that each has a voice	■ Useful if supervisors are close enough to team to do it ■ Essential in companies historically dominated by one function
Coordination across units, specialized skills	■ Senior management support for coordination ■ Establish common language and working practices	■ Useful to bring uncooperative units into line ■ Essential for routine coordination
Key technical decisions	■ Delay decisions that will make or break project until maximum information available ■ Senior management involvement to assure team manages these decisions effectively	■ Can avoid premature commitment to a path that leads nowhere ■ Can help avoid premature decisions, 'rush to judgement'
Launch decisions	■ Quality level at launch ■ Amount of testing before launch, amount of information from each test ■ Complexity of launch, don't change too much of product and process at once	■ Affects company's image ■ Tests limit risks, getting maximum of information from each test limits cost ■ Limiting complexity of changes limits risk of failure, low quality result

Ways General Managers Can Influence Individual Projects

General managers often have links with individual projects. They may supervise them, participate in them, or otherwise have an impact on them. In this chapter we will discuss the variety of ways they impact individual projects.

We will first look at how general managers impact projects during project set up. Decisions made by general managers at this stage can have an impact on a project throughout its life. Second, we will look at the numerous processes involved in routine supervision. Third, we will look at the ways general managers can contribute to projects by acting like members of the project team. Fourth, we will discuss general managers' role as consultants, or mentors, to project teams. Finally, we will discuss cases where general managers take control of a project and make operational decisions for the team.

Project set-up

General managers are often involved in setting up projects. Decisions made at this stage can have an impact on the project that lasts well beyond the initial stages. Errors made at this stage can impact the company as a whole as well. Familiarity with the ins and outs of project set-up may help a general manager to avoid errors and give projects the best possible chance to succeed.

Some decisions that seem simple and obvious actually have more meaning than is commonly realized. One such decision is the decision to give an initiative formal project status. Quite apart from the decision to fund a project, the decision to give formal project status often has an impact on what the people involved in the initiative can do. As a result, the first type of intervention we will discuss will be giving a project formal status.

The second topic in this section will be the funding decision. Here we will not be looking at the funding system overall. This was discussed in an earlier chapter. Rather, we will look at how general managers impact individual projects as a result of funding decisions they make for those projects.

The third topic will be reporting structure. The section covering this topic will focus on the implications of the reporting relationships set up for the project. The fourth and last topic will be the selection of initial personnel. (See Table 7.1 for a list of key questions in the area of project set-up.)

Table 7.1   Questions to ask about project set-up

Project status
■ Do we understand the effects of giving an initiative formal project status?
■ Do we use this status appropriately?

Initial funding
■ Do we make appropriate initial funding decisions?
■ How often do we give funding to projects that shouldn't be funded? Why? What can we do to avoid this?
■ How often do we not give funding to projects that deserve funding? Why? What can we do to avoid this?

Supervision
■ How do we determine who new projects report to?
■ Are the resulting reporting relationships appropriate?

Personnel selection
■ How do we select initial personnel for a project, in particular the project chief?
■ Do initial personnel choices work out? Why or why not?
■ What can we do to improve selection of initial personnel?

Giving an initiative formal project status

In some organizations, giving an initiative formal project status can have an impact on the initiative's chances of achieving success. In the first place, formal project status gives the initiative a legitimacy that it may lack without it. The formal project designation means that senior management approves of the work and recognizes its importance. Lack of formal project status may mean the opposite. More concretely, formal project status may give team members the right to ask for and receive a budget; the right to allocate time officially to the project, rather than working on it on their spare time; and the right to ask for help from other parts of the organization. In an organization where such 'official status' is important, all these things may be crucial in helping the team advance the project.

This being said, there are circumstances where a team would prefer to avoid having official status for a while. If a team or an individual is working on a project that they know senior management would kill if they knew about it, it is to their advantage to continue hiding the project. If they believe the project will be valuable to the company in the long run, they should hide the project until they have developed it enough to be able to show its value clearly and convincingly to senior management. By hiding the project, they sacrifice the possibility of getting official help or senior management support. But if such support would not be forthcoming anyway, then there may be no cost, and considerable advantage, to hiding the project.

The advantage of official project status is that the project will get formal recognition, more access and, very likely, more resources. But with this comes more supervision and higher expectations for performance. If the project is not ready to meet these higher expectations, the team may be better off continuing to work in a nonofficial way on the project.

Funding decisions

In an earlier chapter, I discussed how general managers can improve a project funding system. But besides setting up the system overall, they are also involved in making funding decision for individual projects. Whether they give the right amount of funds, too little, or too much will have a major impact on the project's chances of success.

Funding errors when projects deserve funding Several kinds of errors are possible in funding decisions. Given that a project is worthy of being funded (that is, it is very likely that it will produce something valuable for the company), then three outcomes are possible. The project may be given the right amount of funds, it may be given too little, or it may be given too much. The error of giving too little funding has one obvious impact. The project will not produce what it could for the company. Or it may produce it too late to be of much use.

The error of giving too much funding (in other words, more than the project team can constructively use) creates two problems. The first is that the company is wasting money. Some of the money it is spending on the project would be better used elsewhere. The second is that the project team itself is likely to lose discipline. When resources are too abundant, the team may go in multiple directions and try to do everything, rather than thinking carefully through what needs to be done to advance the project.

Ken Peters, the second head of the Chemical Residues project, said that this had happened with Chemical Residues. When senior management discovered the project and increased the budget by a factor of five, the project team wasn't able to effectively manage the money. There was no coherent plan for spending so much money. So the money was simply used to fund whatever activities the team could think of to advance the project.

Determining the optimum level of funding So how can general managers determine what the optimum level of funding is? It is hard to make a general rule, but one thing is clear. An intimate knowledge of the project and of what is required to advance the project helps. If the general management team doesn't have the time to acquire such knowledge, they should make sure that the project team has thought through these issues thoroughly.

The usual method of managing budget requests is to require teams to document what needs to be done and how much it will cost. But this kind of simple process can lead to game playing, particularly if the company has more projects than it has the money to fund. In such organizations, teams may learn that the way to get what they want is to exaggerate what they need. They present inflated budget requests and then reduce their request under senior management pressure, finally arriving at a number which covers what they originally needed. In the process, senior management learns little about what projects really need and has difficulty making trade-offs among different projects.

Some companies, to limit game playing, ask their project teams to present multiple budgets. What is the minimum the team would need to keep the project going at all? What would it do with this minimal amount of money? How would it shut down the project if it had to, salvaging the learning achieved? What is the maximum budget it could constructively use and how would it use it? And, finally, what is the most reasonable mid-level request and how would this be spent? (Sharpe and Keelin, 1998.) By asking the team to present multiple scenarios, management forces the team to think through what is really needed. The documentation behind the request will help senior management understand what the team really needs. This helps managers make decisions on the basis of real need, rather than politics.

Funding errors when projects don't deserve to be funded Innovation projects often do not work out as planned. They don't produce the successful new products they were supposed to produce. Or they don't produce the process cost reductions that were expected. Such products are sometimes defined as failures. But often these 'failed' products produce technical or other learning that proves valuable to the company in other areas (Leonard-Barton, 1995).

But what if a project finishes without producing anything valuable for the company: no viable new products, no cost reductions, no useful learning? Is this a sign that the funding system failed? Perhaps.

One way to look at projects that produce nothing of value is that they are a waste of money. But did the funding committee have any way to foresee that the project would produce nothing? Often the answer is no. In that case, the money spent on the project was simply part of the cost of innovation. But sometimes the funding committee could have foreseen that the project would not work. Then an error has occurred and the waste could have been avoided. By analyzing the reasons for the error, management may be able to find a way to improve its funding system. An example will illustrate.

Lawn & Garden funded the LawnCare49 project for several years in the face of evidence that the product was not going to come close to working as planned. Why? Because management ignored the evidence of likely failure. Too many of their hopes for the future of the division were tied up with the project. They did not want to face the fact that the product might not live up to their hopes.

To avoid further errors of this kind, division management altered Lawn & Garden's funding system in two ways. First, market information was given much greater weight in early funding decisions. And second, marketing people would be represented in all funding decisions. Senior management increased the weight given to market information because it was marketers and regional sales people who had presented most of the evidence that LC49 would not work. Their evidence had been ignored. Nothing obliged the funding committee to give weight to market evidence in its funding decisions. Management thought it could avoid this problem in the future by obligating funding committees to look at market information and by putting representatives of the regional markets on the funding board.

LC49 was not a total failure. Some sales were achieved and much was learned. But the product was far from meeting expectations. Management later judged that they had expected too much from the project and spent far too much on it. By analyzing what went wrong, management was able to identify and correct flaws in its project funding system.

Reporting structure

Where a project should report is an issue that looks simple but has complex implications behind it. Companies can benefit from thinking carefully about some of the complexities when they assign reporting relationships to projects.

Options for reporting Reporting has both a vertical and a horizontal dimension. The vertical dimension is hierarchical. At what level should a project team report to: to a functional manager? to a business unit manager? to a division manager? or higher? The other dimension is horizontal. If the project reports to a business unit manager, then which one should it report to? The company may have dozens of business units. To which one should the project be assigned?

In some cases, the question of where a project should report hardly seems important. The answer appears obvious. But even in these cases, the question may be more complicated than at first sight. An example will illustrate.

Suppose someone in the office products business unit of a manufacturing company develops an idea for a new office product. The business unit can fund development and has the right resources to support the project. The business unit head is interested in the project. So, obviously, the project will report to someone in the business unit, probably the business unit head. But is the business unit head really the right person to oversee the project? He or she will have many other responsibilities and may not be able to devote enough time to supervise the project adequately.

There are actually a number of other people the project could logically report to. If technological problems and the availability of technology resources are key to the project, then it might be best if it reports to the technology or manufacturing head. On the other hand, if finding the right market niche is the real issue, then the head of marketing might be the most logical supervisor for the project. Then again, perhaps the project will need support from outside the business unit to be able to exploit its potential fully. Or the results of the project might be of benefit to other business units. In these cases, it might be logical to have the project report to someone above the business unit head.

Choosing among alternatives How should a management team choose among these alternatives? The first point to be made is that the team may need to report to more than one supervisor. For instance, if most of the resources needed to support the team are in the business unit, but the teams work will have major implications for other business units, it would be logical for the team to have two supervisors. Someone within the business unit would monitor the team's ongoing activity, while someone at a higher level would monitor the interface with other business units.

The second point to be made is that, in general, the project's supervisor should be knowledgeable about the issues that will be key to the team. If the key issue is marketing, then a marketing person would be best placed to supervise the team. But if the key issue is technical, it would be best to have a technical person supervise the team. If, on the other hand, both of these issues matter, then it may be best to have a general manager, such as the business unit head or one of his or her close lieutenants, supervise the team.

The third point is that the supervisor should be in a position to influence or control the resources that will be key to the team. This is one thing that determines how high in the hierarchy the team should report. If resources from several different business units will be needed, then at least one of the team's supervisors should in a position to influence each of these business units.

Reporting to a high level of the organization has both an upside and a downside. If a team reports to a group head, not just a business unit head, resources will come more freely. But there may also be much higher pressures for performance. Any success will be more visible within the organization. But so will any failure. The group head's aid may greatly help the project to succeed. But interference from the group heads, if they have their own ideas about how the project should be run, may be a serious handicap. Such issues and the personalities involved should be carefully considered before reporting relationships are set up for an important project.

How reporting works in overly political organizations The points I raised in the last few paragraphs had a common starting point. They focused on the issue of what was good for the project. The project might need several reports. It needs to report to people who know the issues that are key to the project. And it needs to report to people who can influence the resources that are key to the project. But the business unit heads and others who are the project's potential supervisors might have a quite different perspective. They might look at the question of where the project should report from the perspective of what is good for them, not what is good for the project.

The way this works out in practice is the following. If the project is expected to be successful, people will fight over it. Every business unit and group head with any potential claim on the project will want to supervise it, because they will expect to benefit personally from its success. They will want credit for its success and they will want to enjoy the revenues and profits they expect the project will produce.

By contrast, if the project is viewed as highly risky or a likely failure, no one will want to touch it. They will not want the possible failure to be part of their record. Much better that one of their rivals have his or her record tarnished by supervising the project.

Variations of this occur when a project brings CEO-level attention or a large amount of outside resources (for example, grants, corporate money, and so on). Everyone will want the attention and use of the resources. On the other hand, if the project is starving for funds and needs large infusions of cash, no one will want it on his books. Such a project might cause corporate to cut annual bonuses, after all.

Lawn & Garden's LC49 project actually went through both of these extremes. In the early 1990s, corporate management took a strong interest in the project and division management viewed it as a cornerstone of the future of the company. At that point, everyone wanted to supervise the project. Every business unit or corporate manager with any claim to the project wanted a piece of it. The situation reversed dramatically in the mid-1990s when it became obvious that the product was failing to meet expectations. Then suddenly no one wanted to have anything to do with it. Some managers even argued that the project should be killed.

Senior managers can limit such political behavior by three means:

1. They can rigorously insist that the criteria of 'what is good for the project' be used in determining to whom the project should report. Eastman Chemical and others have been quite successful in implementing such criteria.

2. They should do whatever they can to reduce the stigma attached to working with 'failed' projects. This will reduce the tendency to treat risky projects as 'hot potatoes' that everyone tries to pass on to someone else. In part this stigma can be reduced by the way senior management deals with failure. Eastman, for example, never has failed projects. It does have projects that were appropriately terminated, but that doesn't mean they failed. The project teams did what they were supposed to do: they found out whether the path being explored would work. In the Eastman world, this should be rewarded, not penalized. Another thing that reduces the stigma of failure is lots of experimentation. When everyone has tried often enough that they have failed at least once, as at 3M, then no one will be in a position to stigmatize other people's failures.

3. To the greatest possible extent, senior management should spread credit for successes as widely as they can. In particular, no one person should be given the lion's share of the credit. While a project's supervisor may claim credit for the project's success, actually many people contributed to the success, including the project team, the supervisor, and many others in the organization. No one should be allowed to claim more than a small share of the credit. This is another problem that tends to diminish if the company tries enough innovations. If the company tries enough new things, then everyone will participate in some successes and will be appropriately recognized.

Selecting initial personnel

Sometimes companies assign people to project teams 'because they are available'. This is rarely, by itself, a good enough reason to assign someone to an innovation project. The key issue should be skill matching. A careful analysis of the skills needed to make the project succeed should be done. This skill analysis should cover not only technical and marketing skills, but also project management skills and skills at gaining the cooperation of others outside the project team. The latter skills might involve gaining the cooperation of others within the company, customers, suppliers, other industrial partners, or regulators. To give the project its best chance of success, people should be assigned so that someone on the team can cover each needed skill area. This may involve hiring people who are not formally 'available.'

Besides skills, enthusiasm, interest in the project, and commitment to its success are important. Enthusiasm and commitment bring with them an increased ability to engage the cooperation of others.

The main distinguishing feature of successful general management intervention at this stage is the willingness of the general management team to look carefully at the skills required by each project. Industrial Chemicals' management first chose whoever was available to staff the Chemical Residues team. But when this proved inadequate, they took the time to construct a profile of what they needed in a project manager. They then went outside the company to hire such a person (there was no such person 'available' within the company). But the results, in terms of improved performance of the team, were well worth the effort. (See Table 7.2 for a summary of key issues in the area of project set-up.)

Routine supervision

Many types of behavior are involved in the routine supervision of an innovation project. In talking with general managers and observing how they deal with projects, we have identified twelve types of behavior that we have classified under routine supervision. These twelve types can be gathered into four clusters.

Routine communication, identification of critical issues, and ongoing funding decisions all relate to project maintenance. Managing contacts inside the company, managing goal conflicts, and managing contacts outside the company all involve the project team's contacts with the rest of the world. Setting performance expectations, evaluating team performance, recognition and protection all relate to performance

Table 7.2   Aspects of project set-up and their impact

Aspect of project set-up	Tool or variable . . . . Impact	
Formal project status	■ Give a project formal project status	■ Easier to obtain resources, cooperation (in most companies)
Funding decisions	■ Give optimum funding, not too much, not too little	■ Assures team will focus on essential items and finish them (no waste)
Reporting structure	■ Set level of highest vertical report ■ Set where in organization project will report, match project need with local competences	■ Gives a signal of the project's importance ■ Good fit of competences needed with competences available helps success
Selecting initial personnel	■ Assess skills needed (including project management skills, ability to gain cooperation from others outside the team); find people with skills needed	■ Increases chance of success

management. Finally, detecting mistakes and changing personnel relate to correcting problems.

The reader may be surprised that I omit mentoring and coaching from this list. Actually we view mentoring and coaching as important enough to deserve a separate section. The mentoring/coaching/consulting section appears just after the close of this section. (See Table 7.3 for a list of key questions in the area of routine supervision.)

Project maintenance

Routine vertical communication I will examine three aspects of routine communication in this section: top-down communication, bottom-up communication, and whether or not communication is managed in a systematic way.

Table 7.3   Questions to ask about routine supervision

Communication

- Are the appropriate levels of management continuously aware of key issues and progress in innovation projects?

- How do we determine which level(s) of management should supervise each project? Or should be informed of each project?

- Does management effectively help teams create and maintain contact with key outsiders?

Conflict management

- Does management effectively identify and resolve conflicts between innovation teams and other units within the company?

Performance management

- Are performance expectations set at an appropriate level? At a level which will stretch and inspire the team without discouraging them?

- Do evaluations of team performance take account of the full range of the team's contribution to the company, not just financial results?

Recognition and protection

- Do teams receive appropriate recognition, even in the case of terminated projects?

- Are teams protected from unconstructive interference from senior managers?

Error identification and correction

- Are mistakes (including poor personnel selection) identified and corrected quickly?

1. *Top-down communication.* Innovation ideas and projects can benefit from several types of communication from top management. First, when top managers make it clear that they want junior people to present innovative ideas, this will make it more likely that junior people will present their ideas to senior people and pursue them. A manager at EuroChem said that junior people were prone to 'hide their ideas in a drawer' at his company. A few clear expressions of interest from managers at several levels might have done much to alleviate that problem. Second, when top managers express interest in projects, their words will stimulate other

people, including mid-level managers, to support the projects in question. Top management interest will stimulate management interest right down the chain of command. Third, requests for information about specific projects will stimulate the interest of mid-level managers in those projects. This can also help senior managers get information about key projects that is not coming through normal channels. Such questions can also force mid-level managers to work on problems (such as roadblocks delaying projects) that they would not otherwise work on.

2. *Bottom-up communication.* To give assistance to projects, senior managers must hear about them. Direct reporting links, which bring information about key projects to senior managers, are helpful. But informal means of stimulating bottom-up communication are useful as well. Top managers can ask questions in conversations, or they can find other ways to contact project managers informally. MGE's executive committee heard about the Chemical Residues project through the local newspaper. Paul Thomas, an executive committee member, read about the project in his local daily. The fact that he learned about the project only through such a channel indicates that little bottom-up communication about innovation projects occurred at MGE. After this incident, the executive committee and division management set up formal systems of communication that would ensure that top managers got sufficient information about innovation projects.

3. *Systematic or unsystematic communication.* Communication between general managers and innovation projects was not systematically organized at MGE. Business unit and project managers resented the fact that top managers communicated with some project teams and not others. They believed that some projects were given top management reports on the basis of 'personal favoritism'. The reasons why some projects had such high level reports and others didn't was never effectively explained. The contrast with Eastman Chemical was quite sharp. Of Eastman's 500 projects, about fifty have dotted line reports to senior management. Five report directly to the CEO. Yet we found no evidence that this caused resentment on the part of the less favored projects. The reason for the lack of resentment at Eastman was that Eastman had systematic and transparent means for

selecting the projects that had high level reports. Those projects that were viewed as most key to the future of the company reported to the top. The next most important tier of projects reported one level down. The fifty projects viewed as most important all had dotted line reports to senior levels. Everyone knew how the projects were selected. Everyone knew the results. While some could argue with the details of the choices, the overall process was structured to be fair. And no one disagreed with the principle behind it.

Identifying critical issues Identifying critical issues, those that will have a significant impact on the project's success, is a key task for the project team. Critical issues should be identified early in a project's life, even before significant funding has been received. Once the team knows what the critical issues are, it should address them and resolve them as soon as possible in order to get a better idea of whether the project has a chance of success or not. If they cannot be resolved quickly, then the team should monitor them closely until they are resolved.

Early identification and, when possible, resolution of critical issues helps the project team's work in several ways. First, it helps them prioritize what to work on first. Second, it may enable them to save money. When work on critical issues can be done first, spending on other, less critical parts of the project can often wait until the critical issues are resolved. If major spending can be delayed until it is more clear whether the project will succeed or fail, then the team will be able to avoid spending a lot of money if the critical issues cannot be worked out.

Given the usefulness of identifying critical issues early, general managers should ensure that each project team performs this task. Increasingly companies in the sample were requiring teams to identify critical issues as part of their requests for funding.

The importance of critical issue identification, and the problems that occur when senior management does not effectively require it, can be illustrated with an example. George Marsh, the first head of the Chemical Residues project, was never trained as a project manager, and he mishandled several critical issues. Two were particularly important. First, he failed to identify North America as the key leading market. As a result, too much of the team's development effort was focused on European customers and regulators. The team did not have a product ready for American customers in the early 1990s. Their failure in this respect allowed others to capture the market. No one on the team realized the importance of the American market until Ken Peters took over the project in 1992.

Second, while Marsh's team conducted many tests of the Chemical Residues technology, they failed to document these tests sufficiently well to use them in regulatory applications. Necessary records were simply not there. Again, no one discovered this failure until Ken Peters took over the project.

It is obvious that George Marsh did not deal adequately with these two critical issues. What is less obvious is Industrial Chemicals' management's role in this failure. While Industrial Chemicals' management was not willing or able to talk in detail about their role during this period, I was able to find some things out. It appears that no Industrial Chemicals senior manager paid enough attention to the project in this period to be sure that George Marsh was adequately dealing with critical issues. Industrial Chemicals imposed no formal requirement to identify critical issues at that time. There is no sign that Marsh ever did identify them. And no one on the management team was there to force him to do so.

But of course, identifying critical issues is not enough. Project teams must deal with them adequately as well. Even managements that force teams to identify critical issues cannot always be sure that the teams are dealing adequately with these issues.

As an illustration, let's suppose that Industrial Chemicals' management had asked Marsh to identify the key issues in Chemical Residues. Suppose further that Marsh had told them that the two key issues were:

- Developing a formula that will sell to the key customers in the key market, Europe
- Convincing regulators that regulations favorable to the Chemical Residues solution were needed.

Would Industrial Chemicals' managers have noticed that the key lead market was not Europe, but the US? And would they have noticed that Marsh was not documenting his work adequately enough to meet the regulators' standards of documentation? The answer in both cases is, 'Probably not'. Industrial Chemicals' managers were simply not close enough to the project to catch the fact that Marsh was not dealing adequately with the critical issues.

But failing to deal with critical issues already identified is really another issue. Managers cannot always be close enough to a project to evaluate everything the project manager is doing. The fact that Marsh did not identify the critical issues, and that no one in Industrial Chemicals' management forced him to, is one thing. The fact that he made mistakes in trying to deal with the critical issues is another.

I will deal with the issue of catching mistakes in a later section, entitled 'Detecting mistakes'. The point of this section is that senior managers should force project managers to identify critical issues and develop plans to deal with them. This is something Industrial Chemicals' management did not do in Marsh's case. To their credit, once they recognized their mistake, they built critical issue identification into the funding screen so that future project managers would have to think through what the critical issues facing their projects were.

Ongoing funding decisions Once a project has received its initial funding allocation, the battle for funding is not over. Teams managing projects of any size will, in most cases, be obligated to return to the funding source for more funds before the project is over. Project supervisors normally have a major role in these ongoing funding decisions.

Three questions to be asked in giving a project more funds are:

■ Is the project making progress?
■ Is the project likely to succeed, that is, to bring something of benefit to the company?
■ Is the cost worth the likely benefit?

Supervisors should know the answers to the first two questions. The answers should come out of their normal monitoring of the project. They should, in addition, have a clear and defensible position on the third question.

In effect, in making the initial allocation of funds, the funding committee made the judgement that the project's benefits would be worth the cost. The question that should be considered in an ongoing funding decision is, 'What has changed?' If the project is achieving something, new information will be available. Does the new information confirm that the benefits will be worth the cost? Or does it show that the project may not be worth the price? The project supervisor should conduct his or her monitoring in a way that gives the answers to these questions.

Managing the team's contacts with others

Managing contacts inside the company Project teams often need access to resources controlled by other units within the company. They may need technical, marketing, manufacturing or other resources that are controlled by people who have no direct link with the project. Part of the project supervisor's job is to assure that the team obtains access to these needed resources.

In effect, this is a situation where the supervisor's hierarchical position matters, and where reports to top management levels may play a key role. Supervisors normally have more power than the project teams they supervise. They also have more extensive and more senior networks of contacts within the company. They are in a better position to get the attention of those who control needed resources. They are also in a better position to influence and bargain with those who control needed resources. This is one reason why companies like Eastman Chemical make sure that very important projects report to very high level people. A project defined as very important to the future of the company will report to the CEO because the CEO can command anyone's attention and assure that the project has whatever resources it needs.

Supervisors can also help to facilitate communication across functional or language barriers. When a small, technically oriented project team is staffed with junior people, there may not be anyone on the team who has experience dealing with people from marketing. In a case like this, the supervisor may have to step in to facilitate links with marketing, or to appoint someone with marketing experience to the team.

Managing goal conflicts Sometimes simple negotiation or request is not enough to obtain needed resources. Sometimes the units controlling the resources have goals or obligations that are fundamentally in conflict with the needs of the innovation project. An example of this occurred at MGE.

A team in the Advanced Plastics business unit of the New Materials division was developing a new set of materials for use in safety shields and other safety equipment. The project was called the Safety Materials (SM) project.

Once the SM team had developed a preliminary product design, they needed a steady supply of Q, a key raw material. Q was needed for internal tests and development work, as well as for sale to customers interested in testing the products themselves. The only place to obtain Q within the company was from a factory owned by another business unit.

The problem was the factory didn't want to sell Q to the SM team. The factory had its own goals. It sold high volumes of Q to industrial customers. The factory was running at full capacity and prices were quite high. There was, in fact, a large order backlog. Handling the small quantities the SM team wanted would disrupt the smooth operations of the factory, and diminish the factory's ability to serve its core customers.

Frank Kelly, the head of the Advanced Plastics business unit and the supervisor of the SM project, tried to resolve the issue by speaking with the factory manager. But he couldn't resolve it at that level. The factory's goals, which it had negotiated with the division head, were simply in conflict with the SM project's needs. To resolve the situation, Kelly had to go to division management to have the factory's goals revised. The factory's goals were revised to give priority to supporting the division's innovation projects. The factory's evaluation and bonus systems were revised so that factory management would not be penalized for accepting low volume business from innovation project teams.

This type of intervention is necessary when fundamental conflicts exist between the goals of innovation projects and those of operating units whose support the innovation projects need. There are at least four methods of resolving such goal conflicts. The first is to change the goals of the operating unit to give it an incentive to help the innovation team. This is what happened in the Safety Materials case.

The second is to allow the innovation team to seek needed support elsewhere, for example from outside the company. This works only if the following conditions obtain:

1. The needed resources are available outside the company
2. No important confidential information will be compromised
3. Using an outside supplier will not compromise the company's competitive advantage.

The third method of resolving goal conflicts is to change resource allocations to give the innovation team more bargaining power. The fourth is to impose a new overall goal that brings the goals of the innovation team and the operating unit into alignment. In most cases, the project supervisor will need the help of a general manager with responsibility for the operating unit to have these changes implemented.

Managing contacts outside the company At times innovation project teams need help in managing contacts with important people outside the company. Two examples from the history of the Safety Materials project will illustrate.

After several years of development and testing, the project team had pushed the design as far as it could on its own. It now needed to work with a manufacturer to see how its products could be applied in an actual industrial situation. The team contacted several manufacturers, but was unable to get their cooperation. It seemed that senior executives in the manufacturing companies would have to authorize such testing and experimentation, and the team was unable to get their attention.

Frank Kelly, the team's supervisor and the head of the Advanced Plastics business unit, stepped in to help. He contacted senior executives at the manufacturers and obtained their cooperation. His title and his status as a business unit head enabled him to get their attention and cooperation, something that had been impossible for the team.

Later, the team needed the help of US government regulators. The manufacturers who were the potential customers were dragging their feet. They were interpreting existing regulations in a way that did not oblige them to use the SM team's new materials. The team wanted a clarification and perhaps a strengthening of the regulations. Unfortunately, the regulators received dozens of calls from the industry each week, and the team could not get their attention.

Once again, Frank Kelly stepped in. Again, his position as a Vice-President of a well known company and as head of the Advanced Plastics business unit got him the kind of audience the team could not obtain. He brought team members along with him to a meeting with senior members of the regulatory agency. They explained the situation and the regulators promised to respond.

This type of intervention, managing contacts outside the company, works much like internal contact management. In both cases, the project supervisor has a better title, more hierarchical weight, and better contacts than the project team. He can use his weight and contacts to get audiences the team cannot get, and to break roadblocks the team cannot break.

Performance management

Setting performance expectations

This is a complex part of the supervisor's role. The supervisor must first determine what are appropriate expectations. Then he or she must determine how these expectations will be used, that is, what role they will play in the management process. Depending on how they are used, the expectations may be very specific or very general. The manager will then have a number of options of how to communicate the expectations to the team. In addition, it may be necessary to communicate the expectations to others, particularly to those whose cooperation the team needs to get its job done.

1. *Determining appropriate expectations.* In some cases, teams work without any particular expectations of performance. This may be appropriate when a team is involved in early exploration of a new area. But it is rarely appropriate for a development team that is trying to develop a specific product for a specific market. In the latter case, it is not only appropriate, but also useful, to have clear expectations of what the team will produce, for whom, and when. When unexpected problems or opportunities come up, these expectations can be altered. But in the meantime, they provide useful guidance for the team. In addition, the expectations can usually be turned into mileposts and checkpoints that senior managers can use to monitor the progress of the team.

One questions to be answered, 'Who should set expectations?' The team can set its own expectations, the project supervisor can set them, or senior management can. Or they may be set through negotiations among these three levels. Another question is, 'How high should the expectations be?' I will look at the issue of who sets expectations before going on to the question of how high they should be.

Who sets the expectations can be key in motivating the team. If the team does not have a role in setting expectations, it is possible that they will not accept the expectations, but will simply give up and fail to perform. Alternatively, it may spend needless time arguing with its supervisors about what the expectations should be. These problems are particularly likely to occur if the team believes that those imposing the expectations know little about the project. In that case, they will view the expectations as being based on the supervisor's imagination and little else.

MGE provided several stories of difficulty in creating appropriate expectations. Once it took an interest in innovation, MGE's senior management studied the business plans of many of the company's innovation projects. In three of the four projects we followed, their approach to setting expectations after the audit was the same. They insisted that the revenue and profit projections be doubled. In effect, they dramatically increased expectations for each project's performance.

The Chemical Residues team was still too early in development to care very much about long-term profit expectations. This was not the case with the other two teams. The LC49 team felt considerable pressure to perform. This added to the pressure to get the product out quickly. It may have contributed to the team's willingness to overlook signals that indicated that the product was not going to perform as well as expected. In effect, the increased performance pressure may have led the team to be less careful and cautious than it would have been otherwise.

The Safety Materials team initially bought into top management's desire to increase expectations. In effect, top management offered a carrot. It said that the team would stand a far better chance of winning an internal prize for innovation if it increased its revenue and profit projections. The team increased its projections and won the prize. But, within a few months, the team realized that its new projections were quite unrealistic. After that, the team leader lost several months arguing with top management about what the real expectations should be. This was a case where the team did not believe that senior management knew enough about the project to set appropriate expectations. Paul Thomas, an executive committee member who took an interest in the project, was inclined to punish the team leader for not being aggressive enough. Frank Kelly, the business unit head, protected the team leader for a while, but then agreed to find a new person.

With respect to the second question, 'How high should expectations be?' the answer is clear. Expectations can be either too low or too high. They are too low if the team things it will be easy to reach them. They are too high if the team views them as impossible. In between these two extremes, the expectations should be high enough to stretch the team. If they look close to impossible, that is not bad. But they should not be viewed as either impossible or easy.

2. *The role expectations play.* The expectations top management has for a project are often used to *evaluate team performance*. If the team meets management's expectations, it will be *rewarded*. If it fails to meet them, it may be *punished*. But this is not the only way to use expectations. Nor is it always desirable to link rewards and punishments so tightly to expectations.

In particular, punishing innovation teams that fail to meet expectations is counterproductive. It serves to deter people from participating in risky projects. Innovation teams almost never have 100 percent control over the outcome of their projects. Projects may fail because of factors totally beyond the team's control. Punishing a team for an uncontrollable failure is a pointless exercise that will discourage people from ever becoming involved in risky projects.

Rewarding success is less problematic. But it has several pitfalls as well. The main pitfall is that it is difficult to identify, much less reward, everyone who has contributed to a success. Those who have contributed, but who are not rewarded, may feel resentful.

Ken Peters anticipated this problem after he took over the Chemical Residues project. MGE management promised him that they would reward him highly if the Chemical Residues project succeeded. But they made no similar promise to the rest of the project team. It was clear that any rewards would be skewed heavily towards Peters, the project leader. Peters himself viewed this as unfair, since the team's contribution was as large as his, if not larger.

The problem of just rewards is recognized at 3M. When an individual does something on his own, he is rewarded. But teams sometimes refuse to be singled out for recognition because they don't want to set themselves apart from the many people outside the team who have helped them.

The lesson of these examples is that if there are rewards for meeting expectations, they should be shared by all who contributed. They should not be limited to the project leader, or even necessarily to the project team.

3. *Specific or general expectations.* Expectations at MGE were quite precise. They detailed, virtually to the dollar, how much revenue and profit each team should produce. They were stretch objectives, indeed. But the question is, 'Is this much precision necessary?' Expectations at 3M and ConsumerCo were not nearly as precise as those at MGE. A ConsumerCo manager talked to me about a conversation he had

with the CEO when he took over a business unit. The CEO gave him no specific directions. Nor did he have any specific expectations. Rather, he told him, 'Do the best you can.' He had an open-ended expectation that the manager would perform well. Exactly how well he performed, in financial terms, would depend not only on his own efforts (expected to be high), but also on circumstances such as the economy and competitive activity. ConsumerCo would take these circumstances into account when it later evaluated his performance.

The manager in question found this open-ended expectation quite liberating. He resolved to perform well, to do the best he could. And he did. There was every sign, two years later, that the CEO was satisfied with his performance.

There are three differences between MGE and ConsumerCo that involve specific versus open-ended expectations. One is that the ConsumerCo manager was a trusted member of the ConsumerCo management team. He had already proven himself as a competent manager both of innovation projects and of ongoing operations. The CEO could be confident that he would indeed do the best he could. MGE's project managers, by contrast, were untested. Senior management didn't know them. This may have been one reason why it set far more specific goals.

The second difference is that ConsumerCo management was far more habituated to the unpredictable nature of innovation projects. As one manager told me, if the revenue number in an innovation project's budget was $10 million, management knew full well that the actual result might be $2 million, $20 million, or anything in between. Management took this into account when making other plans.

For example, ConsumerCo's manufacturing operations were set up in a very flexible way. If a new product came in with a revenue of $2 million, instead of $10 million, manufacturing could deal with it. The system was flexible enough that the capacity could be used elsewhere, or left to lie fallow at little cost. If, on the other hand, the revenues were $20 million instead of $10 million, manufacturing could deal with that as well. Production could be doubled quickly and almost without cost. As a result of this flexibility, the company incurred minimal costs when an innovation project missed its budget. Little or no capital was wasted, and the cost of readapting the capacity was virtually nil.

MGE took innovation project budgets more seriously. When the LC49 project forecast revenues of $10 million, manufacturing took this projection quite seriously. At the project team's request, they built permanent capacity able to support revenues of $10 million. This proved to be a mistake. When actual revenues turned out to be much less than $10 million, the new capacity stood idle, at substantial cost to the company.

MGE could have taken a more flexible approach. Flexible manufacturing options that did not involve building any new capacity were available. But so high was the level of confidence in the revenue projections that the company went ahead and built the capacity. Having made this mistake once, management resolved not to make it again.

The third difference between ConsumerCo and MGE is the way expectations are used in evaluations. MGE rewarded and punished people according to very precise expectations. Innovation team bonuses were linked to the team's budget projections. If they didn't come close to meeting projections, they would receive no bonuses. If they beat expectations, they might receive quite high bonuses. The process was automatic, and there was no discussion. The contrast between the MGE method and the ConsumerCo method couldn't be greater. At ConsumerCo, there was nothing automatic about the link between financial performance and bonuses. Discussion was the rule of the day.

The way annual evaluations work at ConsumerCo is as follows. Supervisors are aware of the financial results a manager achieved, but whether the manager met 'targets' is not the key issue. Most managers do not so much have targets as they have flexible guidelines. The real issue during the evaluation is, 'How did the manager achieve the results he or she achieved?' The results themselves are not the end of the discussion but the start of it. The supervisor will look at how the manager treated or developed her brand, how she developed her people, and whether she built ConsumerCo's long-term assets during the course of the year or used them up. The evaluation, at its best, is used as a learning session, an occasion to explore what went well, why, and what could have gone better.

Much learning can occur during ConsumerCo's evaluations. The learning comes from the fact that the expectations are flexible and are used as something that will stimulate discussion. MGE's evaluations, by contrast, are not set up to stimulate learning.

4. *Communicating expectations to the team.* Supervisors and other senior managers communicate their expectations to team members

through two primary means. They can communicate them through written documents such as budgets, technological development plans, marketing plans, or other plans. Alternatively, they can communicate directly with team members via speeches, conversations, or other direct contacts. A key distinction here is whether the expectations are negotiated with team members or dictated to them.

If expectations are negotiated, it is very likely that team members will accept them. If expectations are dictated, immediate acceptance is less likely. But if team members can be convinced that the expectations are realistic, achievable, and otherwise appropriate, they are likely to accept them as well. If they do not view them as realistic, achievable and appropriate, then they will feel top management's communication as unwanted pressure. This is likely to make them resentful.

Of course, top management may view pressure for success as appropriate when it has given substantial resources to a team. The question here is, 'Was there an open and frank discussion between top management and the team about what was appropriate and realistic before the resources were given?'

If the answer is, 'No, top management never discussed its expectations with the team', then management has little justification for expecting the team to live up to expectations they never signed off on. If, on the other hand, the team agreed to meet top management's expectations then management has a right to expect the team to live up to them. If it later finds out that the team's agreement was driven by their desire to get the money, not on realistic evaluation of what they could do, then management has a right to be angry.

5. *Communicating expectations to others whose cooperation the team needs*. While senior managers often apply pressure on teams to meet expectations, at times it would be more appropriate for them to apply pressure elsewhere. If a team needs cooperation from other units, and the cooperation is not readily forthcoming, then managers should pressure those units to cooperate. The other units may have short-term profit goals that may not be compatible with investments in innovation. They may not invest enough unless they are under pressure from top management to do so.

People directly involved in the project, ironically, have less need for pressure. Not only is the project their primary responsibility, but also they directly experience pressure from potential customers and competitors. The customers may be asking them to produce the product as quickly as possible. The competitors will be there threatening to take the gains. With this natural business pressure in place, additional pressure from senior management is often superfluous.

For the units whose support is needed, the situation is different. These units may have no direct contact with the project's potential customers. They have no reason to worry about the project's potential competitors. In fact, the supporting unit has its own customers and competitors to worry about. To get this unit's attention and cooperation, a senior manager's intervention may be needed. If the cooperation is not forthcoming, applying pressure will be appropriate.

Evaluating team performance The easy way to evaluate team performance is to look at the financial results and to see if they meet expectations or not. As in many situations, the easy way is not the right way. Two other issues should be looked at as well. One is how the team reacted to unexpected events. The other is what the team contributed in terms of new learning.

Since many uncontrollable things can affect innovation project results, evaluating the team's performance without looking at how they dealt with unexpected events is a mistake. A key question the venture capitalist asks when evaluating a CEO is the following: 'Did he or she react appropriately to unforeseen events?' The team leader should be evaluated in a similar way. Did he deal appropriately with unexpected events that affected his project? This question will lead to a discussion that, at its best, will consider four issues:

1. What happened
2. Why it happened
3. How the team reacted to unexpected events
4. Other, perhaps better, ways it could have reacted.

Such a conversation can lead to considerable learning, for both the team leader and the supervisor.

If the project is a straightforward development project with a stable technology and a stable market, then the discussion will be less useful. If all tasks can be programmed in advance (as in the automobile case), then it is appropriate to evaluate the team leader on the basis of whether he or she met pre-set expectations. But most innovation projects are subject to unforeseen events. In this case, the team's creativeness and flexibility in responding to change and unexpected events should be given at least as much weight as meeting targets.

The second additional thing to be considered is the team's intellectual contribution. Innovation projects can be very successful even if they don't produce a dollar of revenue. They may produce technical or market learning that can be applied in other projects. Technological learning produced by the team may not be enough to give the team a successful product. But other teams might be able to apply the learning in other areas. The learning team A produced might lead to three profitable new products produced by teams B, C and D. So even if team A did not produce a single dollar of revenue, they made a significant contribution to the company. This should be taken into account in their evaluation.

Companies have very different attitudes towards learning. MGE sometimes laid off people who had participated in 'failed' projects. By doing so, it reduced its chance of ever being able to exploit the learning produced by the project teams. Eastman Chemical, by contrast, carefully catalogs the 'learnings' produced by terminated (not 'failed') teams. Team members are congratulated for producing new knowledge, even if they have not produced any revenue.

Recognition A positive evaluation is a form of recognition. But there are others as well. Teams and individuals may be congratulated or recognized publicly for their accomplishments at any time during the course of a project. General managers can use recognition as a key way to motivate and reward teams. But recognition has a negative side as well. Managers who use recognition carefully can obtain its positive benefits without incurring the negative costs.

The positive side of recognition is that it gives teams moral support. Team members receive appreciation for work that the company needs. They may even be recognized as heroes. The negative side of recognition is that can bring resentment from others and higher, perhaps unreasonably high expectations for future performance. In some cases it may bring increased interference in the project from top management. 'You've gained recognition, so now you'd better succeed, and the best way to succeed is to do it our way', was the message the Safety Materials team got from MGE management.

Eastman Chemical manages to avoid most of the negatives of recognition through two techniques. First, it is widely spread. Innovation project teams regularly receive messages of support and appreciation from the CEO and other senior managers. Second, there are no strings attached to the recognition. It does not imply any additional performance expectations. Nor is there any obligation to follow suggestions from management on how the work should be done.

Eastman and other companies avoid arousing resentment by stating clear reasons why recognition is given. When management explains that success of the project is clearly in the long-term interests of the company, and will benefit everyone, then giving recognition to the project team is less likely to arouse resentment. This is particularly true when a wide range of projects get at least some recognition.

Protection There is a flip-side to recognition. When senior management takes too much interest in a project, mid-level managers may have to protect the project team from senior management interference. This is what happened after the MGE executive committee discovered the Safety Materials project.

First the executive committee asked the team to increase its revenue and profit projections. Then they asked the team to raise price. Then they insisted that a European team be set up. Then they asked for a more aggressive marketing program. After all these requests, the business unit head Frank Kelly began to protect the team from corporate interference. He took the team's side and argued that the team knew better than did the executive committee what the market needed.

Kelly's intervention gave the team breathing space, but it was not enough to stop the executive committee. The latter soon asked Kelly to replace the project manager. For a year, Kelly refused. But then it became obvious that the project manager no longer had enough time to run the project. So Kelly hired a replacement. He then successfully protected the replacement from corporate interference.

Protection is often not needed. It is needed only when senior managers take an overly strong interest in the details of the project's operations. Normally lack of senior management attention is the greater problem. But the mid-level manager should also be prepared to respond to the opposite problem, too much senior management attention.

Correcting problems

Detecting mistakes Part of supervision is detecting and reacting to problems. Virtually all supervisors will detect bad results when they occur. They will appear in the accounting system. More challenging is the problem of detecting mistakes before they affect the results, when it is still possible to correct them.

The cost of not doing this is clear. Projects will be delayed or fail unnecessarily. I have recounted how the Chemical Residues project leader made two serious mistakes. First, he failed to recognize the leading position of the US market. Thus, there was no effort to develop a viable product early enough to dominate this market. Second, he failed to document his technical tests adequately enough for anyone else (for example, regulators) to use the results.

Senior Industrial Chemicals managers might have caught these two errors if, first, they had been following the project closely and, second, they had been knowledgeable about the business the project was in. Unfortunately neither of these conditions held. The project was a minor project that was more or less lost in the MGE bureaucracy. No one was supervising it closely. And no one in the company knew enough about the anti-pollution business to effectively monitor the team's activity.

The lessons for managers are the following:

1. Whenever possible, a senior manager should follow a project team's decisions and activities closely enough to catch serious errors
2. Whenever possible, the project's supervisor should be knowledgeable about the technology and market the project is involved in.

Changing personnel When several things go wrong, and there is reason to believe that the project team could have avoided some of the problems, then there may be reason to change project personnel. This is the last important part of routine supervision that I will discuss. But it is quite important. My discussing it last does not make it any less important than the other activities I have discussed.

The key issue the supervisor has to consider is, 'Is the project leader doing his job effectively?' If the problem is at a lower level, it is the project leader's responsibility to take care of it. But if it is the project leader who is not doing his job effectively, the supervisor should step in.

A company should have a profile of what constitutes an effective project leader. Industrial Chemicals didn't, and its management failed to realize that George Marsh, the first head of Chemical Residues, did not have some of the key skills needed. To their credit, once this was recognized, Industrial Chemicals' management developed such a profile and applied it to all future project leader appointments. But, in the meantime, much damage was done to the Chemical Residues project.

Core skills of a project manager include:

1. Some familiarity with the technology
2. Some familiarity with marketing
3. Considerable skill with management and organization
4. In the case of regulated industries, familiarity with the regulatory process.

Depending on the industry and the specific needs of the project, other things may be added to this list. Examples are the ability to deal with suppliers or industrial partners, and ability to deal with internal politics and roadblocks. In addition, personality matters. Aggressiveness, alertness, a taste for cross-disciplinary work, and a willingness to deal with risk are all positive traits in a potential project manager.

When a project leader makes a mistake, it may be due to inattention, bad luck, bad judgement, or lack of skill. If mistakes are repeated, some action should be taken. The action may involve training or coaching the project manager, adding someone to the team to support him in a weak area, or, in the worst case, replacing him. If he is replaced, the supervisor should construct a profile of the skills needed and make sure that the new project manager has the needed skills. (See Table 7.4 for a summary of key issues in the area of routine supervision.)

This ends my discussion of the twelve tasks involved in routine supervision. In the next section I will discuss how general managers can contribute to projects by participating in them much as any project team member would.

Participation

Ad hoc participation of senior managers in innovation projects may happen more often than we think. If a senior manager joins a project team meeting and contributes an idea, she is, in effect, participating in the project team's work. If she contributes an insight from his own experience, she is contributing to the team much as any other member would. If she has an idea that germinates into a project, she is an idea generator, just like any person on the front line or in the laboratory. In

Table 7.4   Routine supervision and its impacts

Aspect of routine supervision	Tool or variable	Impact
Project mainenance	■ Facilitate routine vertical communication (top-down, bottom-up, horizontal)	■ Helps signal top-management interest in innovation, helps keep top mgmt informed
	■ Help identify critical issues, or ensure that they are identified	■ Helps focus teams on critical work
	■ Ensure project has necessary funds, but not an excess	■ Project will progress quickly, without wasting money
Managing the team's contacts with others	■ Facilitate contacts inside company, break roadblocks	■ Speeds project's progress
	■ Manage goal conflicts	■ Speeds project's progress
	■ Help team manage contacts with key outsiders	■ Speeds project's progress
Performance management	■ Set performance expectations	■ Gives projects goals to strive for
	■ Evaluate performance, learning as well as financial results	■ Gives company information on what team has produced, its value
	■ Give recognition when appropriate	■ Reminds team members that company values their efforts
	■ Protect team from interference	■ Helps team do its job
Correcting problems	■ Stay close enough to detect mistakes	■ Helps avoid costly losses of time and resources
	■ Stay close enough to identify key personnel problems, change people	■ Helps avoid wastage of time and resources

some projects, this type of participation may occur often. Two of the four projects we documented in detail benefited from it.

Participation is distinct from supervision in that it involves contributing to the work of the project. Supervision involves, by definition, monitoring or controlling the work of others. In participation, it is the general manager himself who is doing some of the project team's work. Participation is also distinct from consulting, coaching and mentoring, which will be discussed next. The latter involve advising and training. Participation, once again, involves doing some of the work.

There are two key issues for the general manager. One is to know when he has something to contribute. If he is familiar with the technology or market environment of the project, he may well have something to contribute. If he sits in on team meetings now and then, he will soon see if he does, indeed, have something to contribute.

The other key issue is to know how far to go. He is not a team member, nor is he the team leader. It is very likely that the team members and team leader will know more than he does about the project. He should present his ideas without insisting that they be adopted. The team leader and others, being much closer to the project and its problems, are in a much better position to decide what should be done. (See Table 7.5 for a summary of this section.)

Consulting, mentoring and coaching

I have put three words into the title of this section. These three words reflect similar concepts but they are not the same. In the context of an innovation project leader's relationship with his or her supervisor, we would define them as follows.

- *Consulting* occurs when a team leader asks his supervisor for advice or information on a specific decision or problem; or in some cases he may simply be asking the supervisor to review a decision for any unseen problems

- *Mentoring* occurs when the team leader is asking for more general advice on how to manage, not a specific problem, but the project in general. Like consulting, it occurs at the initiative of the project leader

Figure 7.5   Other types of intervention in individual projects

Type of intervention	Tool or variable . . . . Impact	
Participation in projects	■ Senior managers contribute knowledge, experience to projects as participants in team meetings	■ May help solve technical, marketing and other problems
Consulting	■ Senior managers give advice to team, when asked, on operational problems	■ May help solve technical, marketing and other problems
Mentoring	■ Senior managers give advice on how to manage project overall	■ Training for new project managers, improved project management
Coaching	■ Senior managers take initiative to give advice on specific issues	■ Training for project managers, improved project management
Direct management or control	■ Senior managers take over operational management of project	■ Generally worse results than project team would achieve

■ *Coaching* occurs at the initiative of the supervisor and involves making suggestions on how to deal with a specific issue, or on the spot training on general project management topics.

In all of these cases, the project manager benefits from the supervisor's greater (or at least different) experience. The supervisor does not take control. The project manager remains in control of the project and continues to make the decisions. But the supervisor gives him something, such as advice, information, knowledge, or consent.

Coaching is institutionalized at ConsumerCo. There are regular reviews of each project, and a new product is subject to review by the CEO before launch. Senior managers are still immersed in the business (they visit customers at least one day each month), and their advice is respected and sought out. There is a cost to these coaching sessions. In some cases, project teams have to wait for reviews. In others they have to spend time investigating things the senior managers brought up. In either case, the teams lose time and launches are delayed. Most team members interviewed wished that the delays could be reduced. Nonetheless, they found the coaching sessions valuable.

Consulting works best when senior managers remain in close contact with the businesses the project teams are in. This is the case at ConsumerCo. Mentoring and coaching, since they often deal with much broader issues of project management, do not require so much contact with the business. In fact, since much mentoring and coaching may involve issues of how to deal with internal barriers, the nature of the business may not matter much at all. (See Table 7.5 for a summary of this section.)

Direct management or control

Direct management differs from any of the other things I have discussed in that it involves taking control of a project. When a general manager makes decisions about how a project team should develop the product, in effect usurping the project manager's role, he is going well beyond his role as a supervisor. A consultant, mentor, or coach does not take over, he offers advice to be taken or rejected by the team. A participant, similarly, offers ideas or information that may be used or not used by the team at its option. But, in some cases, general managers do not just make suggestions, they impose their will on project teams, in effect taking over control of the project. (See Table 7.5 for a summary of this section.)

This happened a number of times to the LC49 project at Lawn & Garden. The division head and the division's senior managers decided what price the team would set, how the product would be distributed, and how it would be publicized. They made other, less important decisions as well. The results were little short of disaster. The product was mispriced, ineffectively distributed, and over-promoted. The division head told me later, 'I overestimated my understanding of the market'.

In tracking the histories of four innovation projects, I found twenty-six instances of general managers making decisions for a project team. In twenty-two of these cases, the general managers involved, or the project team leader, later said that the decision had been mistakes. When possible, the decisions were reversed.

Of the twenty-two decisions later identified as mistakes, all involved decisions that ran counter to the team's wishes. Of the four that were not regretted, two involved decisions general managers took very early in a project's life, before a project manager was even appointed. The other two involved decisions the project team didn't care about.

The lesson is that general managers can step in to run a project when there is no one in place to run it. But they should step aside and let the project manager make decisions for the project once one is in place.

The reason why general managers created so much trouble when they tried to run projects is revealed by the comment quoted above. The Lawn & Garden division head said that he had 'overestimated' his understanding of the market. In fact, he had once been immersed in that market. He had been a manager and a business unit manager in the area before being promoted to his position as divisional head. But, during his tenure as division head, he had spent far less time in contact with the market in question.

The project leader and project team members, by contrast, were in contact with the market daily. Most of them had been in contact with the market on a daily basis for ten years. At the time the project was being run, they knew much more about how the market worked than the division head did. But no one in Lawn & Garden recognized this, or at least they weren't willing to say it aloud. In a paternalistic system, no one could openly question the boss.

One lesson from this experience is that senior managers should pay attention to who knows what about the project's technology and market. Normally the project team will know a lot more than senior managers do. The second lesson is that senior managers should leave the running of the project to those who know the most about the relevant markets and technologies. Almost always, it is the project team that will know the most. So decisions about how to develop the project should be left in the hands of the project team and the project manager.

Blocking communication is a special case of direct management. In some cases general managers ignored negative signals around a project. This happened several times in the case of LC49. But at times they went further and absolutely suppressed the dissemination of negative information. Not surprisingly, this had a negative effect. The negative signals could have warned the team and senior management that the project was not going to meet expectations. Had management paid attention to the signals, they could have saved considerable money. They could also have prevented the damage that occurred to the company's reputation when the product failed in the eyes of its customers.

This ends my discussion of interventions by general managers in individual projects. I have already discussed interventions in the project management system and in the business as a whole. So there is only one class of interventions left to discuss, those that don't lead directly to action, but rather to reflection on the state of the company's innovation management system.

Asking People to Help Improve Your Innovation Management System

Sometimes general managers ask people to look at how their company's innovation system works. Sometimes they ask outsiders to do a formal study. At other times they ask insiders to do the same. Doing a study doesn't immediately change the way the company innovates. But such reflection can lead to substantial changes later.

In some companies, managers ask people to reflect on their own contribution to the company's innovation system. They may ask them to look at how they help innovation and how they get in its way. Or they may simply ask them to be humble, to be open to new information and new ideas, and to not assume they have all the answers.

The results of this kind of reflection can be quite positive. Lawn & Garden implemented a successful reform of many of its management practices after such a period of reflection. At the end of this chapter, we give several other examples of how companies in the sample benefited from periods of reflection. (See Table 8.1 for an outline of this chapter.)

Asking outsiders to help you improve your innovation system

The consulting study is the classic and most easily identifiable form of outside help. Management invites outsiders in and asks them to make recommendations on how to improve the company's innovation process. Northern Pharmaceuticals brought in consultants to help them sort out how to fund projects and which projects to fund. They later brought other consultants in to help them speed up their development process.

Consultants are not the only outsiders companies bring in. MGE brought in a group of academics to look at the company's innovation

Table 8.1   Methods of stimulating reflection and their impact

Method	Tool or variable	Impact
Reflection by outsiders	■ Invite consultants, other outsiders, to look at how innovation system works, how it could be improved	■ Gives company access to much broader experience than is available on the inside
Reflection by insiders	■ Invite the company's own managers to look at how the innovation system works, how it could be improved	■ Can mobilize the company's management team to recommend and implement improvements
Reflection on one's own role	■ Ask managers to look at how they help and hurt the company's innovation performance (may involve behavior analysis with help of facilitators)	■ Helps open individuals in the company to learning and change
Encouraging humility	■ Encourage managers at all levels to learn from others, look at what they can do better	■ Helps open the company to learning from its mistakes, learning from each other, from the outside

system. The academics' primary task was to develop an internal training program on innovation. But they were also asked to make recommendations about how the company's innovation system could be improved.

Companies sometimes hire new people for the purpose of getting an original perspective on how to innovate. Northern Pharmaceuticals made such hires. When it began its effort to improve innovation performance, it hired people from other pharmaceutical companies, companies that had more effective innovation systems. At other times, they got perspectives on how other companies operate through benchmarking processes.

General managers may have a variety of different attitudes when they invite outsiders in. They may truly not know what to do to improve their innovation system. Or they may have ideas about what should be done, without knowing how to do it. Or they may know in general how to do it, but need help with the details. A more interesting situation arises when they don't feel that they have the power to impose changes. In this case, they may be looking for the outsider to bring them increased leverage or credibility with subordinates. Or they may simply be looking to the outsider to help them mobilize subordinates.

Reflection by outsiders is a useful way to bring in perspectives and information from the outside. It is most useful, obviously, when the outsider has greater experience with the issue than anyone on the inside. In any case, it serves as a check on management's understanding of how to manage innovation. Companies, like Northern Pharmaceuticals, that use outsiders extensively are able to change faster. They change faster since they don't have to rely only on home-grown insights (often slow in coming) about what needs to be changed.

Asking your own people to help you improve your innovation system

Reflection by insiders works differently from reflection by outsiders. Insiders may resist looking at how they do things. It may force them to confront difficult, even painful issues that they are personally involved in. They may have personal interests in preserving the status quo, even though this is not in the company's best interests.

Nonetheless, there are advantages to asking insiders to reflect on how the company's innovation system works and how it can be improved. Not only do insiders know more about the system, but also they can implement changes very quickly once they have decided how the system should be improved. In addition, when senior management gives insiders the chance to have an influence on how their innovation system is run, they may find this very empowering. Such an exercise can lead to a dramatic mobilization of the management team, or even of the entire workforce.

There are several ways to manage reflection by insiders. After the failure of the LC49 launch, Lawn & Garden's division head proposed a series of substantial reforms in the way the division managed itself. The reforms involved a decentralization that would greatly increase the power of lower levels of management, as well as streamlining a large number of time-consuming procedures. The division head then asked his management team to divide itself into committees to consider the details of the reforms. The committees met over a period of eight months. They approved the overall shape of the reforms and worked out in detail how they would be applied in day-to-day operations.

Working out the details was a substantial task. The division head had deliberately proposed an overall framework without detailing how it would be implemented. The management team had the chance to critique the framework. They also had the chance to work out how all the division's procedures would be reformed to implement the decentralization.

Lawn & Garden's internal reflection was a one-shot affair. At the opposite extreme, Eastman Chemical has set up a system of permanent internal reflection. Around 1990, Eastman's senior management set up a team, called the innovation team, to permanently monitor the functioning of the company's innovation system. The team has since developed a number of means of measuring and monitoring the system. Several useful reforms have resulted, including methods of capturing ideas as soon as they are generated.

3M also practices regular internal reflection. But the process is not as formalized as at Eastman. Managers regularly discuss how well innovation projects are going. And they try to identify any systematic problems that appear. Much reflection has occurred on the issue of technology transitions. 3M has lost several markets because of changes in technology, although in some cases it could have developed the new, replacement technology as easily as the new entrants in the market did. 3M managers have reflected on how an established company can manage the transition between two technologies. I will present some of the fruits of their thinking later.

The 3M example underlines one key advantage of internal reflection. People in the company will retain whatever is learned. With a consulting report, there is a risk that the learning contained in the report will be filed away and forgotten. This cannot happen if internal people have done the analysis themselves. The learning will stay in the heads of the people who did the work, and they will have the chance to bring it up again and again, as appropriate.

In the 3M case, the loss of the coated copy paper market (see the story at the end of this chapter) was a difficult lesson. Although this happened several decades before my first visit to 3M, some managers were still talking about it as one of the most difficult lessons the company had ever learned. Since they had thought long and hard about the implications of this experience, some lessons about how to deal with technological transitions would stick with them forever.

ConsumerCo has sometimes used an interesting variation of internal reflection. ConsumerCo has many established, successful business units. Often these business units develop formulas for producing and marketing their products that are successful for many years. But ConsumerCo management is concerned that such business units not fall into ruts. Corporate management wants them to remain open to new ideas and change.

One exercise the management teams of such business units sometimes go through is an intense off-site seminar, facilitated by a psychologist. During a three day seminar, the psychologist will lead the management team through a series of exercises designed to achieve two things. First, the exercises will reveal the team's conscious and unconscious assumptions about their business. Second, they will help identify alternative ways of thinking about the business. These seminars do not bring any new information to the table. They simply help management find new ways to look at their market, their management methods and their products. Such reflection periods have often resulted in the design of successful new market positionings and marketing strategies.

The lesson for general managers is that reflection by insiders is a useful tool. When people are willing to look at their own ways of doing things, asking them to do so can set off a very constructive period of reflection. It can also serve to mobilize people to take an interest in the company's management practices and to design and take ownership of new management techniques. When it goes well, it can lead to permanent learning and to permanent improvement in the company's management practices.

Asking your people to think about how they, as individuals, impact innovation performance

When Eastman Chemical managers reach a certain stage in their career (usually in their late thirties), the company sends them to a one-week, off-site program run by the Center for Creative Learning. During this week, psychologists and others observe their management style and their ways of dealing with others. They also analyze questionnaire data provided by the manager's superiors, subordinates and colleagues.

The goal of the off-site program is to help the manager become familiar with his or her own management style, the strengths and weaknesses of that style, and what he or she can do to function more effectively. In addition, the psychologists help individuals to become more conscious of their values and of what they want to do in the long term with their life.

For the manager, it is quite an intense experience. Most people who go through it find that they learn much about themselves that they didn't know. In nearly all cases, managers come back with a better understanding of how they function as managers, of how they can improve their management style, of how their careers could best evolve within Eastman, and of what they want to do, in the long term, with their lives.

Every senior manager at Eastman has gone through this program. Every manager moving up the ladder is obliged to go through it. As a result, every senior manager at Eastman has been obliged, for at least one week, to examine in detail his or her own management style and how it affects other people. Further reflection, after the one week off-site program, is encouraged.

One possible result of requiring managers to go through this is that they will be more able, afterwards, to consider alternative ways of doing things. After reflecting intensely for one week on their own behavior, later discussions about changing the company's behavior (that is, its management practices) will be easier to handle. They will be more sensitized to how the company's management practices affect them and other people. They will also be better able to look at and implement alternatives.

ConsumerCo also expects its managers to think about their own management style, its strengths and weaknesses, and how it affects other people. While ConsumerCo does not have a formal off-site program like Eastman's, all managers are expected to be able to examine and change their own management practices. At least half a dozen ConsumerCo managers have told me that someone who is not able to do this will not be promoted.

The exact impact of the kind of seminar Eastman puts its managers through is hard to measure. But it is likely that it leads to more open discussions of what works and what doesn't, both in their personal style and in the company's management practices. The lesson to managers elsewhere is that such reflection can help break down rigidity and resistance to change.

Encouraging humility

The other thing Eastman's off-site seminar encourages is humility. After a week of careful examination of his behavior, the manager is likely to discover that he is good at some aspects of management, but not all. All people have flaws, and a close exposure to one's own flaws makes one more humble.

The advantage of humility in a manager is that it makes him more open to learning from others. He will presumably be more open to learning from people both inside and outside his company. In addition, he will be more open to change. Once he no longer believes that he 'does everything in the best possible way,' he will be more willing to look at the practices of others and to adapt them when he finds that they are better.

Some other companies value humility, although they didn't talk to me about it explicitly. ConsumerCo's demand that managers be willing to examine and change their own practices, for instance, is a demand for humility. The habit of regularly discussing, 'How we do things,' at 3M is also a sign of a kind of humility.

It may be that managers in companies that take a lot of risks automatically become humble. When you take risks and try to innovate, you don't always win. Every manager I ever talked to at 3M mentioned that they, and the company, had lost a few. They did not really have room to be arrogant, or to imagine that they would never lose. The evidence of having lost was there before their eyes. The experience of having seen the down side of the innovation experience, of having had a few failures, helps managers at risk-taking companies become more humble.

Examples of the results of reflection

In this chapter, I have talked about various methods of stimulating reflection. The reader may wonder what the fruits of reflection were for the companies involved. I will give several examples here. I have already talked about Lawn & Garden, where internal reflection led to major reforms in the division's management practices. Other MGE divisions similarly benefited from reflection. Industrial Chemicals invited consultants in to help determine how the division could innovate more effectively. The consultants helped design and implement a new organization structure for the division.

Northern Pharmaceuticals used consultants more extensively than any other organization I visited. Reflection facilitated by consultants led to major improvements in the company's project funding systems. Later analyses by other consultants led to a dramatic shortening of the time needed to perform clinical trials. Eastman Chemical used academic consultants to help design its competency management system. EurAuto used consultants to develop a quality program.

Reflection is often stimulated by disasters or other major problems companies experience. Lawn & Garden's reflection was stimulated in part by poor financial results and in part by the failure of the LC49 project to meet expectations. Industrial Chemicals and Northern Pharmaceuticals both brought in consultants to help them fix perceived low performance in these companies' innovation systems.

Another interesting story of a disaster stimulating reflection occurred at 3M. Here, the loss of the coated paper for copying business stimulated reflection on how the company could better navigate technological transitions. The result of that reflection was a set of techniques that the company has applied in later transitions. I will describe them here, before discussing benefits other companies have drawn from reflection.

Methods of managing technological transitions 3M was once the master of an important niche in the office products business. It provided a large share of the paper used for making copies. The business provided one-third of 3M's revenues. It was, obviously, a keystone of the company's revenues and profits.

However, this was in the 1940s and 50s, before xerography took over the office copying market. When Xerox's plain paper copiers took over the copying market, 3M's coated copy paper business disappeared. With it went one-third of the company's revenues.

The irony of the situation is that Chester Carlson, the inventor of xerography, approached 3M with his technology. He was an independent inventor. He could not fund development of xerography himself. He needed the help of a large company. He offered the technology to 3M. The company refused, not because it didn't see any value in the new technology, but because it saw that the new technology would kill its existing business. After refusing, it saw the Haloid corporation, which later renamed itself Xerox, become one of the most successful and fastest growing companies in the world for twenty years (from the mid-1950s to the mid-1970s). Xerox built a large and highly profitable business from xerography. 3M could have done it, but it declined the opportunity.

The 3M managers who told me this story fully saw its irony. Here, a company widely recognized as an excellent innovator, had refused a new technology to protect a soon-to-die business. 3M managers had long since recognized the mistake and resolved never to let it happen again. The question was, how could they ensure this?

Several 3M managers I interviewed spoke clearly and convincingly about how the company could navigate such technological turning points. They had developed a number of guidelines for handling technology transitions. The first was that the new technology would have to be separated from the old technology within the organization. No one could expect a single team to run an existing business while trying to destroy it at the same time. So anytime the company recognized that a new technology was threatening one of its existing businesses, a new unit would be set up to investigate and exploit the new technology.

The second guideline was that the new unit should include both new people and people from the unit exploiting the old technology. The new people would be needed because they would be better able to create a new conceptualization of the business. They would not be married to the current technology or to the current way of thinking about the business. But old people would also be needed because they would bring much knowledge about the customers and the market environment. But the old people could not be too numerous, or they might suppress the new concepts.

The task the new organization would be given would be to create a new business, to displace 3M's existing (old technology) operations if necessary. To do this, it would have sufficient resources to develop and exploit the new technology, and to apply it to the new business.

We do not know how often 3M has tested this new system for managing technology transitions. The business unit we were visiting was managing one such transition at the time we talked to them, and the appropriate structure had been set up. An independent unit within 3M was developing a new technology, which the business unit would adopt if it proved superior to the existing technology. Organizationally the company was ready to make the transition. So the issue would be whether the company would master the new technology quickly enough, not whether it's people and organization were ready to change.

Identifying key results 3M's method of managing technological transitions was an important result of reflection by 3M managers. It related to a specific type of situation, technological transition, that large organizations have particular difficulty dealing with.

Reflection is not limited to finding solutions for such specific, narrow situations. Sometimes reflection relates to ways of managing the entire innovation process. Such is the case at Eastman Chemical, where ongoing reflection has resulted in new approaches to overall management of the process. One thing Eastman's innovation team has done is to break the innovation process down into phases and to devise ways of measuring interim results at various points on the innovation pipeline. Some of the results they measure, on a company-wide basis, are:

1. The number of ideas generated
2. The value of ideas generated
3. The number of projects in the pipeline
4. The value of projects in the pipeline
5. Sales coming from new products and processes.

The last item, sales from new products and processes, is a common measure. 3M quite famously measures this and has set up an innovation quota for each unit in the company based on the measure. The third measure, number of projects in a pipeline, is equally common. Some companies also try to value projects. But it is rare for companies to try to measure the number of ideas generated, or to value them. By identifying these as a key result of the earliest phase of the innovation process, Eastman has given itself the means to monitor and manage a part of the process that many companies simply leave to chance.

Methods of results measurement Eastman's reflection process has also led to new ways of measuring results. The company went beyond simply identifying ideas as a key early result of the innovation process. They devised a way to monitor idea generation so that they could measure, in detail, how many ideas were being produced. This allowed them to measure the effects of other practices on idea generation. It also allowed them to measure how many ideas were not being used of those generated. In addition, by capturing all (or nearly all) ideas generated, the company could assure that no ideas were lost.

The reader may be wondering, 'How does Eastman monitor idea generation?'People can have ideas at any time. How can a company capture them all?

Eastman's solution to this problem was innovative in itself. They ask anyone who thinks of an idea to enter it into a databank. The process of entering the idea is simple and takes little time. The advantage to the person who enters the idea is that his or her idea immediately comes to the attention of a several other people. If viewed as a valuable idea, it may enter into development very quickly. If not, it will still be recorded as a possible avenue for the company to explore in the future.

Such a system will work only if people want it to work. Eastman has set up incentives for managers to encourage their people to use the system. Senior managers regularly ask business unit heads how many ideas they have in their systems. If the answer is, 'We haven't been using the tracking system', the manager in question will be instructed to begin using it. In addition, she will be reminded that part of her bonus will be based on the number and value of ideas currently entered into the tracking system from his unit. Ideas not entered into the system don't count. So managers systematically ask their people to enter ideas into the system.

Entering and counting ideas is not all Eastman does. It also values them. When a person enters an idea into the system, the system automatically asks him several questions. One is the likely size of the market the idea could aspire to, assuming it is a new product idea. Another is the likely cost savings to be achieved, if it is a process improvement idea. Someone then audits these estimates for realism. The auditor will be someone else in the business unit who is familiar with the markets or technologies in question.

Given these estimates of market size (or cost savings), other key factors are estimated based on past experience. Eastman has analyzed its own past experience to determine what typical market penetration rates are in its businesses. It also knows what market shares are realistically achievable, and when. It also has standard estimates of investment and start-up costs in different businesses, as well as fixed and variable costs. It can judge likelihood of success based on past experience as well. It plugs these estimates into a model. The model constructs a prospective cash flow and estimates the value of each idea. The standard estimates of penetration, cost, and so on are modified as new information comes to light.

Eastman managers can, at any time, tap into the idea monitoring system to determine what ideas have been generated, what potential value they have, and which are being worked on. This system gives them an easy method to identify and screen ideas. They can use the valuations to determine which ideas should be worked on next, as well as to estimate the value of opportunities being missed.

This ends my discussion of the many different methods general managers can use to improve the performance of their companies' innovation systems. In the next chapter I will conclude the book.

9

Conclusion

My purpose in writing this book was twofold. First, I wanted to demonstrate to the reader that many, many different aspects of corporate management practices influenced innovation performance. Second, I wanted to show how the most effective innovators used these corporate management practices to encourage innovation. Chapters 3 through 8 covered both these things. In those chapters, I showed that twenty different types of management tools can be used to impact innovation performance. (See Figure 9.1 for a summary of the twenty types of tools.) I also discussed how the most effective innovators use these tools.

It remains for managers to look at how their companies manage innovation and to determine how they can alter their management systems to encourage more innovation. Managers can use the discussions in this book to make a diagnosis of what works and what doesn't work in their management systems. With this diagnosis in hand, they can then turn to my discussion of how to organize a change program. This discussion appeared in my earlier book, *Competitive Innovation Management*. I will present a short summary of that discussion here.

The biggest difficulty in maximizing the innovation performance of a company is that so many things impact innovation performance. Through six chapters and more than two hundred pages of this book, I have discussed aspects of different management systems that impact innovation performance. After reading this, the average reader may find that there are dozens of things he would like to change, or have changed, in his company. The question is where to start.

	Changing the way business systems are managed		Changing the way projects are managed	Intervening in single projects
Strategy/goals	Structure/process	People		
Strategy	Organization structure	Incentives	Management of idea generation	Set-up
Competences and M&A	Communication and information management	Other personnel management systems	Management of laboratories	Supervision
Goals	Decision-making methods	Culture	Funding system	Participation
			Project structure	Mentoring, consulting
			Project management methods	Operational control

Other: Stimulating reflection

Figure 9.1 Management tools classified by scope

In my previous book I recommended a simple sequence of steps to follow to address this complex problem. The steps were as follows:

1. Diagnose what's not working well within the company, using the process outlined in Chapter 4 of *Competitive Innovation Management*, and repeated in Chapter 2 of this book
2. Decide which two or three of the problems identified should be corrected first
3. Do the work, make the changes, and then repeat the steps
4. Repeat step 1. Assess progress, reassess what's not working
5. Repeat step 2. Decide what to work on next
6. Repeat step 3. Do the work, make the changes.

The main decision to be made, presuming that your company has problems in more than two or three areas, is the following: which area to work on first. Normally, it is best to work on no more than two, three or four aspects of management at a time. If a company tries to change more of its management systems than that, all at once, it risks overloading the system. In the exceptional case of a completely frozen system, it may be necessary to make a large number of changes quickly in order to get any change moving at all. Equally, if the management team is highly mobilized and eager to proceed with the changes, it may be possible to proceed faster. But, under normal circumstances, it usually works better to proceed step-by-step, assuring that the management team understands what is being changed, why, and how they need to participate in the change.

In my previous book, I looked at the logic of the change process: which changes could most appropriately be made first, which next, and which should be delayed until late in the change process. I looked particularly at the case of a company that had not put much emphasis on innovation performance in the past. In the case of this type of company, many simple changes can often be made, changes which do not disturb the ongoing operations of the company to any great extent. A summary of the impact, ease of change, and riskiness of various tools is presented in Figure 9.2.

Some management systems and practices, those on the left of Figure 9.2, are relatively easy to change. Often these simple changes present little risk. It is logical for a management team that is just learning to manage innovation to try these types of changes first. Changes in project budgets, project personnel, and project reporting

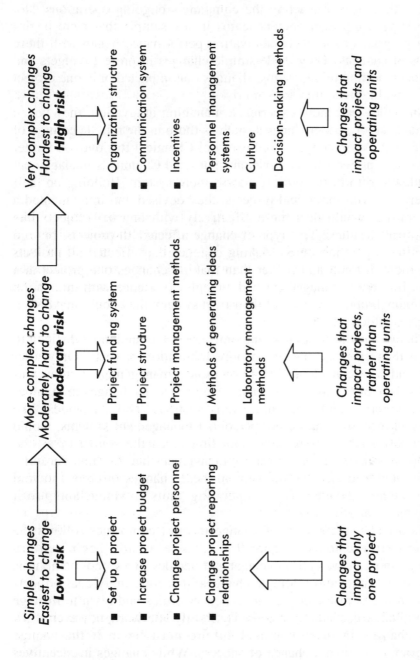

Figure 9.2 Impact, ease of change, and riskiness of various tools

Simple changes
Easiest to change
Low risk

- Set up a project
- Increase project budget
- Change project personnel
- Change project reporting relationships

Changes that impact only one project

More complex changes
Moderately hard to change
Moderate risk

- Project funding system
- Project structure
- Project management methods
- Methods of generating ideas
- Laboratory management methods

Changes that impact projects, rather than operating units

Very complex changes
Hardest to change
High risk

- Organization structure
- Communication system
- Incentives
- Personnel management systems
- Culture
- Decision-making methods

Changes that impact projects and operating units

relationships can often be made very quickly, very simply, and with very little risk of impacting the company's ongoing operations. Not surprisingly, top management teams in my sample that were beginning programs to improve innovation performance began with these kinds of changes. They made simple changes in project budgets and project reporting relationships, changes that impacted only one project at a time. In effect, they took no risks.

Once they had more experience managing innovation, they began to make larger, riskier changes, such as those in the middle column of Figure 9.2. After studying the history of Chemical Residues and other innovation projects in the division, Industrial Chemicals management decided to reform the project management system. Building on their experience with individual projects, they devised and implemented a system that would deal more effectively with unusual projects like Chemical Residues. This type of change affected all projects, but did not affect operating units. Making changes that affected all projects was more difficult and riskier than making changes one project at a time. But, once management had enough experience with innovation and enough understanding of their own system, they could make such changes effectively.

Changes that impact operating units are riskier and more difficult to make than changes that affect only innovation projects. Only after they had done considerable work on project management systems was Industrial Chemicals management ready to tackle changes in organization structure and communications systems. These changes, like those in incentives and other personnel management systems, would inevitably have an impact on operating units, the source of all the company's revenues and profits. Management had to think carefully about how to design and implement these changes in order to avoid causing any damage to the operating units' revenue and profit producing capacity.

As a result, the pattern of change in most companies follows the pattern represented in Figure 9.3. Change usually begins with a change in strategy, as top management decides to put more emphasis on product innovation. Simple changes impacting individual projects then ensue, as managers reassess their priorities and learn to manage individual projects more effectively. Shortly afterward, however, difficult changes in incentives and culture must begin if the change program is to have a chance of success. While changes in incentives and culture are difficult to make, if these are not done early the whole

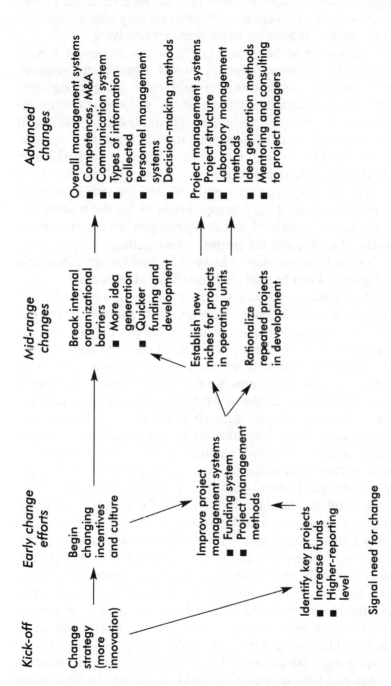

Figure 9.3 General sequence of change efforts

change program may collapse because of resistance from the people who are supposed to implement it. Such changes may take a long time to implement, another reason for beginning them early.

Once top management has fixed key projects as best it can, it should then turn its attention to overall project management systems. The project funding system and project management methods normally receive considerable attention at this point. Then, management should turn its attention to broader changes, changes that will improve the innovativeness of operating units. Changes in organization structure and in company wide communications networks may be particularly important at this stage.

Finally, there are many further details of the company's management systems that may need to be changed in order for the company to innovate optimally. Methods of managing competences, communications networks, decision-making methods, and methods of generating ideas may all need to be changed. The systems listed in the right-hand column of Figure 9.3 can be analyzed and changed as needed.

Figure 9.4 summarizes another aspect of planning and implementing change. Some changes are very simple to implement and can be imposed from the top. Changes in individual project budgets and reporting relationships are good examples. Other changes require more thinking, more preparation, and the cooperation of a small group of people. Project funding systems are a good example. Changing an organization structure or methods of decision-making require the cooperation of far more people. Such changes are neither simple nor quick to implement. They may have to be proceeded by extensive planning and training. Finally, changes in incentives, personnel management systems and culture can only be effective if they are made in a coordinated fashion, and if the change involves long-term persistence and follow-through. These needs for training, planning, cooperation and coordinated follow-through should be taken into account when management plans and implements the change process.

To summarize, managers wanting to improve innovation performance should carefully analyze their management practices to determine which encourage innovation and which don't. Of those that don't, they should pick between two and five to change right away. Generally the first changes should be simplest and lowest risk ones. Changes in individual project budgets and reporting relationships are examples. More high-risk changes should not occur until the management team has had time to weigh the risks, to design an appropriate

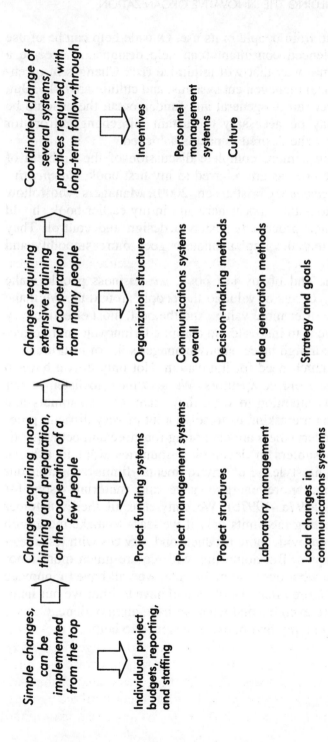

Figure 9.4 Knowledge, complexity and the change process

Simple changes, can be implemented from the top

Changes requiring more thinking and preparation, or the cooperation of a few people

Changes requiring extensive training and cooperation from many people

Coordinated change of several systems/ practices required, with long-term follow-through

Individual project budgets, reporting, and staffing

Project funding systems

Organization structure

Incentives

Project management systems

Communications systems overall

Personnel management systems

Project structures

Decision-making methods

Culture

Laboratory management

Idea generation methods

Local changes in communications systems

Strategy and goals

new system, and to train people in its use. Outside help can be of use here, since experienced consultants can help design and execute a change program in a way that will minimize risk. Changes in incentives, other personnel management systems, and culture are risky. But, because their effects are so general and fundamental, they should be made early. It may be necessary to sustain this change effort for several years before the desired impact is achieved.

Readers desiring a more complete discussion of the problem of planning a change process are referred to my first book, *Competitive Innovation Management* (Christiansen, 2000). Managers who follow the recommendations that appear here and in my earlier book should find that the change process is easier to design and control. They should also find that the implementation goes more smoothly and more effectively.

As I said at the end of my last book, we business people make money by offering things of value to the people around us. We make more money if we offer more value. And the best, most effective way to offer more value is to innovate. So learning to innovate more effectively should have a high place on any manager's list of priorities.

Today there is much need for innovation. Not only do we have to deal with pressure from competitors. We also have to listen to our customers and pay attention to what they want. Our customers and potential customers are asking us to solve a lot of very difficult problems. Customers everywhere are clamoring for more and better goods and services. Consumers in developing countries want to achieve developed world lifestyles. But environmental limits constrain our ability to consume more energy, space and materials (see, for example, OECD, 1997a, 1997b). We can serve all these customer needs while respecting the limits only if we learn to make more with less, if we learn to provide more products and services with less material and energy inputs. But doing this will require much more innovation. To achieve what our customers want, we will have to innovate more quickly and more often. All of us will have to improve our innovation performance even beyond what we have already done. Can we do it? This book, like my first book, is designed to help.

Bibliography

Ackoff, R.L. 1978. *The art of problem solving: accompanied by Ackoff's fables*. New York: John Wiley & Sons.

Adams, J.L. 1986. *Conceptual blockbusting: a guide to better ideas*, 3rd edn. Reading, MA: Addison-Wesley.

Adler, P.S. 1990. Shared learning. *Management Science*, **36**: 938–57.

Allen, T.J. 1977. *Managing the flow of technology: technology transfer and the dissemination of technological information within the R&D organization*. Halliday.

Anderson, P. and Tushman, M.L. 1990. Technological discontinuities and dominant designs: A cyclical model of technological change. *Administrative Science Quarterly*, **35**: 604–33.

Angle, H.J. 1989. Psychology and organizational innovation. In Van de Ven, A., Angle, H. and Poole, M.S. (eds) *Research on the management of innovation*. New York: Harper & Row, pp. 135–70.

Angle, H.J. and Van de Ven, A.H. 1989. Suggestions for managing the innovation journey. In Van de Ven, A., Angle, H. and Poole, M.S. (eds) *Research on the management of innovation*. New York: Harper & Row, pp. 663–97.

Archibald, R.D. 1992. *Managing high-technology programs and projects*, 2nd edn. New York: John Wiley & Sons.

Ardrey, R. 1970. *The social contract: a personal inquiry into the evolutionary sources of order and disorder*. New York: Atheneum.

Argyris, C. 1985. *Strategy, change, and defensive routines*. Boston: Pitman.

Argyris, C. and Schon, D.A. 1974. *Theory in practice: increasing professional effectiveness*. San Francisco: Jossey-Bass.

Argyris, C. and Schon, D.A. 1978. *Organizational learning: a theory of action perspective*. Reading, MA: Addison-Wesley.

Arnold, J.D. 1992. *The complete problem solver: a total system for competitive decision making*. New York: John Wiley & Sons.

Ashkenas, R., Ulrich, D., Jick, T. and Kerr, S. 1995. *The boundaryless organization: breaking the chains of organization structure*. San Francisco: Jossey-Bass.

Barr, P.S., Stimpert, J.L. and Huff, A.S. 1992. Cognitive change, strategic action, and organizational renewal. *Strategic Management Journal*, **13**: 15–36.

Bartlett, C.A. and Ghoshal, S. 1989. *Managing across borders: the transnational solution. Boston*: Harvard Business School Press.

Bartlett, C.A. and Ghoshal, S. 1994. Changing the role of top management: Beyond strategy to purpose. *Harvard Business Review*, (November–December): 79–88.

Bartlett, C.A. and Ghoshal, S. 1995. Changing the role of top management: Beyond systems to people. *Harvard Business Review*, (May–June): 132–42.

Bartlett, C.A. and Mohammed, A. 1994. *3M optical systems: managing corporate entrepreneurship*. Harvard Business School case 9-395-017.

Bartlett, C.A. and Mohammed, A. 1995. *3M: profile of an innovating company*. Harvard Business School case N9-395-016.

Bower, J. 1970. *Managing the resource allocation process*. Homewood, IL: Irwin.

343

Brown, S.L. and Eisenhardt, K.M. 1995. Product development. Past research, present findings, and future directions. *Academy of Management Review*, **20**: 343–78.

Brown, S.L. and Eisenhardt, K.M. 1998. *Competing on the edge: strategy as structured chaos*. Boston: Harvard Business School Press.

Burgelman, R.A. 1983. A process model of internal corporate venturing in the diversified major firm. *Administrative Science Quarterly*, **28**: 223–44.

Chandler, A.D. Jr 1962. *Strategy and Structure*. Cambridge, MA: MIT Press.

Child, J. 1978. The myth at Lordstown. *Management Today* (October): 80–3, 177, 183.

Christensen, C.M. 1997. *The innovator's dilemma: when new technologies cause great firms to fail*. Boston: HBS Press.

Christiansen, J.A. 1997. *Learning to improve innovation performance: the role of the general manager*. Doctoral dissertation, INSEAD.

Christiansen, J.A. 2000. *Competitive innovation management: techniques to improve innovation performance*. London, Macmillan.

Clark, K.B. and Fujimoto, T. 1991. *Product development performance: strategy, organization, and management in the world auto industry*. Boston: Harvard Business School Press.

Cohen, W.M. and Levinthal, D.A. 1990. Absorptive capacity: A new perspective on learning and innovation. *Administrative Science Quarterly*, **35**: 128–52.

Czikszentmihalyi, M. 1996. *Creativity: flow and the psychology of discovery and invention*. New York: HarperCollins.

Daft, R.L. 1989. *Organization theory and design*, 3rd edn. St. Paul: West.

Dougherty, D. 1992. Interpretive barriers to successful product innovation in large firms. *Organization Science*, **3**: 179–202.

Dougherty, D. and Heller, T. 1994. The illegitimacy of successful product innovation in established firms. *Organization Science*, **5**: 200–18.

Doz, Y.L. and Hamel, G. 1998. *Alliance advantage: the art of creating value through partnering*. Boston: Harvard Business School Press.

Dunn, D.T. Jr 1977. The rise and fall of ten venture groups. *Business Horizons*.

Eisenhardt, K.M. 1989. Building theories from case study research. *Academy of Management Review*, **14**: 532–50.

Eisenhardt, K.M. and Tabrizi, B.N. 1995. Accelerating adaptive processes: Product innovation in the global computer industry. *Administrative Science Quarterly*, **40**: 84–110.

Garud, R. and Van de Ven, A.H. 1992. An empirical evaluation of the internal corporate venturing process. *Strategic Management Journal*, **13**: 93–109.

Ghoshal, S. and Bartlett, C.A. 1995. Changing the role of top management: Beyond structure to process. *Harvard Business Review*, (January–February): 86–96.

Ghoshal S. and Bartlett, C.A. 1998. *The individualized corporation: a fundamentally new approach to management*. London: Heinemann.

Ghoshal, S. and Nohria, N. 1992. Explaining innovation in multinational corporations: Reconceptualizing the structure of M-form organizations. In Nohria, N. and Eccles, R.G. (eds) *Networks and organizations: structure, form and action*. Boston, Harvard Business School Press.

Glaser, B.G. and Strauss, A.L. 1967. *The discovery of grounded theory: strategies for qualitative research*. Chicago: Aldine.

Goldratt, E.M. and Cox, J. 1992. *The goal: a process of ongoing improvement*, 2nd rev. edn. Great Barrington, MA: North River Press.

Goold, M. and Campbell, A. 1987. *Strategies and styles: the role of the centre in managing diversified corporations*. London: Basil Blackwell.

Grove, A.S. 1996. *Only the paranoid survive*. New York: Currency Doubleday.

Hall, R.H. 1996. *Organizations: structures, processes, and outcomes.* Englewood Cliffs, NJ: Prentice Hall International.

Hamel, G. and Prahalad, C.K. 1994. *Competing for the future.* Boston: Harvard Business School Press.

Haspeslagh, P. 1985. *Toward a concept of corporate strategy for the diversified firm.* Stanford Business School Research Paper Number 816.

Haspeslagh, P. 1986. *Conceptualizing the strategic process in diversified firms: the role and nature of the corporate influence process.* INSEAD working paper number 86/09.

Haspeslagh, P.C. and Jemison, D.B. 1991. *Managing acquisitions: creating value through corporate renewal.* New York: Free Press.

Hatch, M.J. 1997. *Organization theory: modern, symbolic, and postmodern perspectives.* Oxford: Oxford University Press.

Hayes, J.R. 1989. *The complete problem solver,* 2nd edn. Hillsdale, NJ: Lawrence Erlbaum.

Hedlund, G. and Rolander, D. 1990. Action in heterarchies: new approaches to managing the multi-national corporation. In Bartlett, C.A., Doz, Y. and Hedlund, G. (eds) *Managing the global firm.* London: Routledge.

Henderson, R. and Clark, K.B. 1990. Architectural innovation: the reconfiguration of existing product technologies and the failure of established firms. *Administrative Science Quarterly,* **35**: 9–30.

Henry, J. 1963. *Culture against man.* New York: Random House.

Imai, M. 1986. *Kaizen: the key to Japan's competitive success.* New York: McGraw-Hill.

Itani, J. 1963. Paternal care in wild Japanese monkeys. In Southwick, C.H. (ed.) *Primate social behavior,* New York: Van Nostrand.

Jaikumar, R. and Bohn, R.E. 1992. A dynamic approach to OM: an alternative to static optimization. *International Journal of Production Economics,* **27**: 265–82.

Kao, J. 1996. *Jamming: The art and discipline of business creativity.* London: Harper-Collins.

Kaplan, R.S. and Norton, D.P. 1996. *Translating strategy into action: the balanced scorecard.* Boston: Harvard Business School Press.

Katz, R. and Allen, T.J. 1982. Investigating the NIH syndrome: a look at the performance, tenure and communication patterns of 50 R&D projects. *R&D Management,* **12**(1): 7–19.

Kawamura, S. 1963. Process of sub-culture propagation among Japanese monkeys. In Southwick, C.H. (ed.) *Primate social behavior,* New York: Van Nostrand.

Kearns, D.T. and Nadler, D.A. 1992. *Prophets in the dark: how Xerox reinvented itself and beat back the Japanese.* New York: HarperCollins.

Kim, W.C. and Mauborgne, R. 1997a. Value innovation: the strategic logic of high growth. *Harvard Business Review,* (January–February): 103–12.

Kim, W.C. and Mauborgne, R. 1997b. Fair process: Managing in the knowledge economy. *Harvard Business Review,* (July–August): 65–75.

Kotler, P. 1997. *Marketing management: analysis, planning, implementation and control,* 9th edn. Upper Saddle River, NJ: Prentice Hall.

Kotler, P. and Armstrong, G. 1999. *Principles of Marketing,* 8th edn. Upper Saddle River, NJ: Prentice Hall.

Laing, R.D. 1967. *The politics of experience.* New York: Ballantine.

Lawrence, P.B. and Lorsch, J. 1969. *Organization and environment: managing differentiation and integration.* Homewood, IL: Richard D. Irwin.

Leonard-Barton, D. 1992. Core capabilities and core rigidities in new product development. *Strategic Management Journal* **13**: 111–25.

Leonard-Barton, D. 1995. *Wellsprings of knowledge.* Boston: HBS Press.

Leonard-Barton, D. 1988. Implementation as mutual adaptation of technology and organization. *Research Policy* **17**.

Lock, D. 1977. *Project Management*, 2nd edn. Westmead: Gower.

Maidique, M. and Hayes, R.H. 1984. The art of high technology management. *Sloan Management Review*, (Winter): 17–31.

Meredith, J.R. and Mantel, S.J. Jr 1995. *Project management: a managerial approach*, 3rd edn. New York: John Wiley & Sons.

Meyer, C. 1998. *Relentless growth: how Silicon Valley innovation strategies can work in your business*. New York: Free Press.

Miles, M.B. and Huberman, A.M. 1994. *Qualitative data analysis: an expanded source book*, 2nd edn. Thousand Oaks, CA: Sage.

Morison, E.E. 1966. Gunfire at sea: a case study of innovation. In *Men, machines and modern times*. Cambridge, MA: MIT Press.

Muzyka, D. 1989. Management practice in large complex projects: lessons from nuclear power plant construction and NASA's shuttle program. Unpublished doctoral dissertation, Harvard Graduate School of Business Administration.

Nadler, G. and Hibino, S. 1998. *Breakthrough thinking: the seven principles of creative problem solving*. Rocklin, CA: Prima.

Neill, A.S. 1960. *Summerhill: a radical approach to child rearing*. New York: Hart.

Nohria, N. and Ghoshal, S. 1997. *The differentiated network: organizating multinational corporations for value creation*. San Francisco: Jossey-Bass.

O'Keeffe, J. 1998. *Business beyond the box: applying your mind for breakthrough results*. London: Nicholas Brealey.

Organization for Economic Cooperation and Development. 1997a. *Towards sustainable transportation: Conference organized by the OECD and by the government of Canada, Vancouver, BC, 24–27 March, 1996*. Paris: OECD.

Organization for Economic Cooperation and Development. 1997b. *The world in 2020: towards a new global age*. Paris: OECD.

Pearce, J.L. and Page, R.A. 1990. Palace politics: resource allocation in radically innovative firms. *Journal of High Technology Management Research*, **1**: 193–205.

Porter, M.E. 1980. *Competitive strategy: techniques for analyzing industries and competitors*. New York: Free Press.

Prahalad, C.K. and Bettis, R.J. 1986. The dominant logic: a new linkage between diversity and process. *Strategic Management Journal*, **7**: 485–501.

Prahalad, C.K. and Hamel, G. 1990. The core competence of the corporation. *Harvard Business Review*, (May–June): 79–93.

Proctor, T. 1995. *The essence of management creativity*. London: Prentice Hall.

Randolph, W.A. and Posner, B.Z. 1992. *Getting the job done! Managing project teams and task forces for success*, rev. edn. Englewood Cliffs, NJ: Prentice Hall.

Ray, M. and Myers, R. 1986. *Creativity in business*. Garden City, NY: Doubleday.

Roberts, E.B. and Fusfeld, A.R. 1981. Staffing the innovative, technology-based organization. *Sloan Management Review*, (Spring): 19–34.

Rumelt, R.P. 1991. How much does industry matter? *Strategic Management Journal*, **12**: 167–85.

Schmalensee, R. 1985. Do markets differ much? *American Economic Review*, **75**: 341–51.

Schmidt, R.L. and Freeland, J.R. 1992. Recent progress in modeling R&D project-selection processes. *IEEE Transactions in Engineering Management*, **39**: 189–201.

Schroeder, R.G., Van de Ven, A.H., Scudder, G.D. and Polley, D. 1989. The development of innovation ideas. In Van de Ven, A., Angle, H., and Poole, M.S. (eds) *Research on the management of innovation*. New York: Harper & Row, pp. 107–34.

Sharpe, P. and Keelin, T. 1998. How Smithkline Beecham makes better resource-allocation decisions. *Harvard Business Review*, (March–April): 45–57.

Simon, H.A. 1985. What we know about the creative process. In Kuhn, R.L. (ed.) *Frontiers in creative and innovative management*. Cambridge, MA: Ballinger, pp. 3–20.

Smith, D.K. and Alexander, R.C. 1988. *Fumbling the future: how Xerox invented, then ignored, the personal computer*. New York: W. Morrow.

Spilker, B. 1989. *Multinational drug companies: issues in drug discovery and development*. New York: Raven Press.

Stalk, G. Jr. and Hout, T.M. 1990. *Competing against time: how time-based competition is reshaping global markets*. New York: Free Press.

Strauss, A.L. and Corbin, J. 1990. *Basics of qualitative research: grounded theory procedures and techniques*. Newbury Park, CA: Sage.

Thompson, J.D. 1967. *Organizations in action: social science bases of administrative theory*. New York: McGraw-Hill.

Tushman, M.L. and Anderson, P. 1986. Technological discontinuities and organizational environments. *Administrative Science Quarterly*, **31**: 439–65.

Utterback, J.M. 1971. The process of technological innovation within the firm. *Academy of Management Journal*, **12**: 75–88.

Van de Ven, A. 1986. Central problems in the management of innovation. *Management Science*, **32**: 590–607.

Van de Ven, A., Angle, H. and Poole, M.S. (eds) 1989. *Research on the management of innovation*. New York: Harper & Row.

Von Hippel, E. 1986. Lead users: a source of novel product concepts. *Management Science*, **32**: 791–805.

Von Hippel, E. 1987. Cooperation between rivals: informal know-how trading. *Research Policy*, **16**: 291–302.

Wheelwright, S.C. and Clark, K.B. 1992. *Revolutionizing product development*. New York: Free Press.

Whyte, W.H. Jr 1956. *The organization man*. New York: Simon & Schuster.

Womack, J.P., Jones, D.T. and Roos, D. 1990. *The machine that changed the world*. New York: Macmillan.

Yin, R.K. 1984. *Case study research: design and methods*. Beverly Hills, CA: Sage.

Zuboff, S. 1988. *In the age of the smart machine*. New York: Basic Books.

Index